HOLLYWOOD AND THE CULTURE ELITE

FILM AND CULTURE John Belton, General Editor

FILM AND CULTURE A SERIES OF COLUMBIA UNIVERSITY PRESS Edited by John Belton

Peter Decherney

HOLLYWOOD

AND THE CULTURE ELITE

HOW THE MOVIES BECAME AMERICAN

COLUMBIA UNIVERSITY PRESS
NEW YORK

COLUMBIA UNIVERSITY PRESS
Publishers Since 1893
New York   Chichester, West Sussex
Copyright © 2005 Columbia University Press
All rights reserved

Library of Congress Cataloging-in-Publication Data
Decherney, Peter.
    Hollywood and the culture elite : How the movies became american /
Peter Decherney
        p. cm. — (Film and culture)
    Includes bibliographical references and index.
    ISBN 0–231–13376–6 (alk. paper)
    1. Motion picture industry—United States—History.
2. Motion pictures—United States—History.   3. Motion pictures—Social aspects—
United States.   4. United States—Social life and customs—20th century.
I. Title.   II. Series.
    PN1993.5.U6D36   2004
    384' .8'0973—dc22   2004061786

Printed in the United States of America
c 10 9 8 7 6 5 4 3 2 1

Designed by Lisa Hamm

In memory of my brother Nicholas, 1978–2001

CONTENTS

ACKNOWLEDGMENTS

W HEN DOING RESEARCH, you quickly learn to identify good writers. It isn't until you begin writing that you start to identify and appreciate good readers. It's probably no coincidence that they are frequently the same people. While working on this book, I have had help from many gifted readers. First among them are John Belton and Robert Sklar. John Belton spent hours listening to my thoughts on the material in this book when there was little chance that any of those thoughts would find their way to paper. Later, his reading of the complete manuscript helped transform it into a book. Robert Sklar's careful reading and questioning gave me volumes to think about, and he set as high a standard as a reader as he does as a scholar and writer.

This is a book about the Hollywood–Washington–New York connection. It is probably not an accident that I wrote it in New York and Washington. Scholars, friends, and teachers in both cities read parts or all of the manuscript at various stages and offered invaluable suggestions for research and revision. They include Thomas Bender, Thomas Cripps (in

Baltimore), Douglas Gomery, Antonia Lant, Annette Michelson, and Toby Miller. A few of the chapters even made trips out to Los Angeles, where Jan-Christopher Horak and David James read with the passion they share for avant-garde film.

This book would never have been finished without the support of three colleagues at Johns Hopkins. Frances Ferguson gave me the purpose and time to write it—even though life intervened. Ben Ginsberg and Robert Kargon infused me with excitement for building institutions, which, it turns out, is central to this book.

Jennifer Crewe, Juree Sondker, and Roy Thomas at Columbia University Press set records for speed and attentiveness. Surely, no first-time book author has ever felt so appreciated.

My greatest debt is to my wife Emily Steiner, who is always my first and best reader. I am also grateful to my daughter Sophia for setting the manuscript "due" date and to my parents and my brother Alec for all their support. The book is dedicated to the memory of my brother Nicholas. I can only imagine what he would have said after reading it.

HOLLYWOOD AND THE CULTURE ELITE

INTRODUCTION
HOW FILM BECAME ART

O DISCUSS HOLLYWOOD film as art is already to fall into a trap. Not because film isn't art, whatever that may be. The trap is, rather, to think that if film is art it somehow exceeds or is opposed to commerce and politics. On the contrary, what has been seen as the gradual acceptance of film as art since the 1910s is in fact the product of political and commercial brokering between Hollywood producers, on the one hand, and museum curators, university professors, and government officials on the other. Film didn't become art until Hollywood moguls decided it was good business for film to become art *and* the leaders of American cultural institutions found it useful—politically useful—to embrace and promote Hollywood film.

At pivotal moments in Hollywood's development, defining film as art has served some very different and often surprising management goals for movie moguls, including postponing the unionization of filmmaking talent and transforming Hollywood films into effective war propaganda. But Hollywood producers and their marketing departments were in no position to declare film to be art on their own. They were able to seize various opportunities presented by cultural institutions—universities, museums, and government art and information agencies—whose leaders had their own designs on turning popular film into an American art form and transforming the everyday act of going to the movies into a civic ritual. These cultural institutions included Harvard University, the Museum of Modern Art, and the National Endowment for the Arts, among others. Often working at cross-purposes, Hollywood and its unlikely partners used film to preserve a coherent, though obviously shifting, American identity in the face of ethnic diversity, class tensions, and the global spread of American culture. In the process, elite universities and museums maintained their position as quintessential American institutions, and Hollywood claimed a place alongside them.

We are so used to viewing Hollywood as a representative American art and industry that it might seem impossible to question how it got that way. But Hollywood is neither inherently representative of American culture nor has it had a smooth ascent to that position. Many studies have chronicled American film's rise, between roughly 1907—1908 and 1915, from a suspect working-class entertainment and repository of vice to a mainstream, middle-class industry.[1] By the end of World War I, Hollywood had established itself as a major American industry, and it was on its way to being viewed internationally as the wellspring of a new art form. This book is about what happened next: entrenched American institutions worked with Hollywood to adapt to both the transformations of American life and America's changing role as a leader of world art, entertainment, and ideology.

More specifically, this book makes two overarching arguments, one about the institutions that guide American culture and one about American film. I argue, first, that museums, universities, and government agencies embraced film and the film industry to maintain their hold on American art, education, and the idea of American identity itself. They formed partnerships with Hollywood in order to expand their reach to the swelling and increasingly diverse mass audience for art and entertainment—the audience, that is, that had already been captured by Hollywood. This expansion entailed neither a one-directional reassertion of traditional values nor a wholesale adoption of popular culture. Instead, high and low culture, ethic minorities and WASPs, and movie producers and university professors mixed in unpredictable patterns. Second, I argue that the leaders of the film industry welcomed the opportunity to join forces with established institutions, because they saw it as a means of stabilizing their industry and retaining their new and tenuous hold on

American popular culture. Together, these two arguments reconnect intertwined histories that have previously been considered parallel.

I do not claim, nor do I believe, that Hollywood's relationship with museums, universities, and the government had a significant impact on the political or artistic content of films. Film narrative and style are not the only measure of Hollywood's politics and influence.[2] The collaborations discussed in this book did, however, have a considerable impact on the reception and interpretation of American film and on the image of Hollywood as an American culture industry. I am much more interested, in this book at least, in how Columbia University taught Jewish immigrants to interpret the moral messages of films and how London film critic Iris Barry trained British citizens to decode the Americanizing politics of Hollywood films than I am in trying to develop my own readings of films. Moreover, the overwhelming identification of film with Hollywood and American culture is the result of commercial tactics and government intervention as much as it emanates from something in the films themselves. Understanding the institutional filters that guide the reception of film, I would argue, is essential to any understanding of the politics of film texts or the many ways viewers understand them.

The history of Hollywood's collaboration with cultural institutions is an integral yet virtually unexamined aspect of the golden era of the Hollywood studio system, from around 1915 through the mid-1960s. And this history complements the more familiar commercial, cultural, regulatory, and aesthetic histories of the studio system. Filmmaking is an inherently unstable business, always at the whim of public taste. No amount of research and development has ever resulted in the production of more financially successful films. The star system and the genre system are perhaps the only two (relatively) consistent methods producers have adopted to give Hollywood's product some stability in the marketplace. Marilyn Monroe, for example, drew audiences even when she was in a mediocre film. And science fiction fans usually turn out to see any new contribution to the genre. Several recent studies have shown that, for similar reasons, Hollywood's management has actually embraced many of the regulations imposed by religious groups or the government. With their eyes always on the bottom line, Hollywood's leaders welcomed the Production Code, which regulated moral and political content, and they even welcomed the blacklist in part because its limitations promised yet another form of stability. The Production Code amounted to a contract between Hollywood and its audience, and it successfully helped keep out competition until the late 1960s. The blacklist allowed studio management to both take power back from the unions and stave off further government antitrust regulation at the worst economic period in Hollywood's history.[3] Clearly, the Production Code and the blacklist were morally and ideologically driven, but they would have been much less successful if they hadn't also been profitable. Indeed, many earlier attempts to regulate the film industry in exactly the same way failed. As Hollywood conformed to moral and political regulation for financial reasons, films and the film industry were brought in line with the dominant institutions of mainstream American ideology: the church and the state. The star system and the genre system provided a similar function, making Hollywood characters and narratives into illustrations of American mythology. These elements of the Americanization of Hollywood have already been examined in many previous studies.

Hollywood and the Culture Elite shows that, largely for financial reasons, Hollywood management also responded to overtures from the institutions that guard elite and national culture in the United States. If stars, genres, and internal regulations shaped Hollywood's product and industrial structure, the collaborations with museums, universities, and government agencies redefined Hollywood as an ideal American industry, the perfect marriage of art and commerce. When we look at these collaborative efforts in more detail, each exposes the individual ways studio heads used other institutions to seize control of their industry during critical transformations: the initial establishment of the oligopoly we call Hollywood, the restructuring of studio labor relations, and the enlistment of Hollywood in World War II and the cold war, among others. The tendency to reach out to cultural institutions in moments of crisis produced a history of starts and stops. But each affiliation with a museum, university, or government agency successfully wove Hollywood further into the fabric of American culture.

If Hollywood benefited financially from its affiliations, it is more difficult to see what the leaders of universities, museums, and government agencies thought they could achieve by establishing ties to Hollywood. There is no overarching answer to this question. In many different ways, cultural institutions used Hollywood to maintain or claim their positions as guardians of American culture, especially as popular culture and a growing middle class challenged their dominance and relevance. The reasons for individual collaborations between, say, Columbia University and Hollywood producers or the Museum of Modern Art's film department and government intelligence agencies lie at the intersection of institutional crises and a changing American national culture. Individual chapters delve into the details of specific projects, experiments, and contracts, and I excavate the collaborations by closely examining the internal politics of both Hollywood and the various institutions involved as well as the points at which institutional changes intersected with a larger sphere of national politics.

These collaborations are rooted in crises of Hollywood and individual institutions, but they are not isolated instances or case studies. The same people, ambitions, and institutions, we will see, recur throughout this history. Each new project reveals itself as part of the larger, seamless story of how a few central figures, the culture elite, enlisted Hollywood in the process of redefining American identity. The group of individuals who tied Hollywood to the institutions of American culture included intellectuals, bureaucrats, philanthropists, and—the apples among oranges—movie moguls. The list of power players includes Hollywood lobbyist Will Hays, museum curator Iris Barry, film producer Adolph Zukor, philanthropist turned politician Nelson Rockefeller, and a generation of art world leaders trained by Paul Sachs at Harvard University's Fogg Art Museum. Many members of the group had their own reasons for claiming film as art and incorporating it into the purview of the institutions they led. Iris Barry, for example, began her career by looking for films to serve as both a feminist canon and the roots of a British national film style. But personal ambitions were soon subsumed by larger commercial and political tides. In the 1930s, Barry found herself as curator of film at the Museum of Modern Art and adviser to American government agencies and powerful private foundations. Charged with developing a method of using film to combat communist and fascist politics, she ended up as one of the most important individual forces in the campaign to Americanize Hollywood and use the film industry to promote American values abroad, precisely the opposite of her initial intention.

The story of this group's collaborations is largely a New York—or at least an East Coast—story. It isn't surprising to find many of the art and educational institutions that embraced film located in New York. The institution that proved to be the fulcrum of this history, the Museum of Modern Art, has become an essential element of New York's identity. But the segments of the film industry most closely tied to art and educational institutions were based in New York as well. By the 1920s, Hollywood had been transformed from an entrepreneurial field into a full-blown commercial industry, financially beholden to Wall Street.[4] Not only the money but also much of Hollywood's power was in New York. Will Hays ran Hollywood's public relations arm, the Motion Picture Producers and Distributors of America, from New York, although the MPPDA had offices in Los Angeles as well. Throughout the reign of the studio system, many of the filmmakers and producers were themselves transplants from New York's vaudeville circuit, the Broadway theater, or New York newspapers. So even the Los Angeles-based film community had direct personal ties to New York. When producer Jesse Lasky decided to help start America's first film school at Columbia University in 1915, for example, the affiliation came in part from one of his top writer-directors, William C. de Mille (Cecil's brother), who was an alumnus of the university. Both Lasky and de Mille continued to work with friends and colleagues to conjoin Hollywood and American universities, and together, all the members of this group created the network that united American film, politics, and art.

The leaders of cultural institutions wanted to use Hollywood without competing with it. As a result, they sought to create noncommercial forms of film distribution, exhibition, and spectatorship. The campaign to unite Hollywood and the institutions of American culture frequently led to the establishment of film collections in the mold of libraries and museums and the formulation of methods for the proper viewing and evaluation of films, or what might now be called film literacy. The earliest musings about film collecting and film literacy began almost with film's invention and grew out of the widespread conviction that the invention of film held revolutionary potential. Many theorists and filmmakers believed that film's visual codes added up to a universally intelligible language, that its uncanny reproductions presented objective historical records, and that its venues might become all-inclusive, equalizing spaces. Public film collections and standards of film literacy were conceived as tools for harnessing and directing—rather than celebrating and assisting—the potential populism of these revolutions.

Popular poet Vachel Lindsay's seminal book of film theory, *The Art of the Moving Picture* (1915, revised 1922),[5] didn't propose the first models of the film collection or film literacy. But Lindsay's ability to connect film with a wide rage of political and artistic traditions made *The Art of the Moving Picture* the richest and most influential theoretical text on the use of film in institutions of national culture, including museums, libraries, and universities. In his book, Lindsay extended nineteenth-century ideas about the civic function of museums and libraries to imagine an all-purpose film institution that would replace the Hollywood film industry, overtake the tavern as a social meeting place, and displace the existing technologies of American democracy (the politician's stump, the press, and the voting booth). Chapter 1 examines Lindsay's vision for a film library or film museum that would have recaptured an ideal public sphere of democratic debate and representation. His plan included the projection of films side by side for comparison and the elimination of musical accompaniment so that patrons could engage in polite and sober debate. Lindsay even envisioned the translation of this public debate into direct political representation as spectators actually voted by ballot for the films to be projected. As you might expect from these grandiose and curious ideas, Lindsay's book is often dismissed as idiosyncratic and naively poetic. Yet his book spoke to Progressive reformers in the 1910s, proponents and critics of the globalization of American culture in the 1920s, and modernists in the 1930s. As a result, *The Art of the Moving Picture* spurred and shaped the next half-century's attempts to create film schools and film museums and to transform Hollywood into a civic industry.

For a few faculty members at Columbia University, Lindsay's book proved that film had become a new art form with the potential to shape American democracy, and they adopted it as a textbook in some of the earliest film courses taught in the United States. For British film critic Iris Barry, Lindsay's book served as proof that Hollywood was Americanizing the world, and it led her to consider alternatives to Hollywood film. Later, Barry invoked Lindsay's book when, wearing a new hat, she designed the Museum of Modern Art Film Library as a center for spreading American democracy through film.

At Columbia in the 1910s, at Harvard University in the 1920s, and in the ranks of Marxist cultural critics in the 1930s, however, Lindsay's emphasis on film as a universally comprehensible medium was replaced by efforts to set standards for film literacy and to build communities of properly trained film "readers." All three of these interventions involved attempts to grapple with changing class and ethnic constituencies of universities and movie theaters, which began to overlap for the first time.

Chapter 2 investigates the creation and development of Columbia University's little-known film education programs, which began in 1915. The Columbia program is a perfect example of how Hollywood producers and university professors could embark on a mutually beneficial endeavor with the hope of achieving very different results. Columbia's foray into film education arose at the intersection of three histories: the history of Columbia's influential Great Books program, the history of Jewish immigrants in America, and the history of the invention of Hollywood. From the perspective of Columbia's faculty and administrators, the film program, housed in the extension school, was intended for Jews who had been displaced from the university proper through selective admissions policies. Film appreciation courses taught in the Great Books mode served to inculcate American identity in ethnic minorities. And screen-writing courses became a training ground for Jews to enter what was seen as the Jewish film industry.

The two film producers who funded the project, Jesse Lasky and Adolph Zukor, had their own motives. They hoped the screenwriting courses would professionalize the craft of screenwriting as it emerged as one of the most important elements of film production. They also hoped their affiliation with Columbia could help blunt the working-class conno-tations of movie attendance and bring more middle-class viewers into the-aters. One immediate tactic to attract middle-class patrons involved pub-licizing the story that Columbia would start a film collection in order to help dispel the fear that film, made on highly flammable stock, could ig-nite at any moment.

The Columbia film program continued to function as a training ground for both screenwriters and Americans through the 1930s, when it was taken over by Iris Barry and the Museum of Modern Art's new Film Library. By the time MoMA took over the program, however, the move-ment to use film courses as a moral training ground had been conjoined with another goal: to create a class of film experts who would guide the re-ception of film in the United States and abroad. Chapter 3 looks at the ed-ucation of the generation of Harvard graduates who went on to found MoMA's Film Library and define the class of film experts who moved flu-idly between film production, government work, and arts administration. Two projects in particular attempted to bring film evaluation into the realm of skilled experts. The first project was a 1927 collaboration between the directors of Harvard's Fogg Art Museum and a number of Hollywood producers, including Lasky and Zukor. Together they planned what, I argue, became a direct precursor to the Academy of Motion Picture Arts and Sciences and its Oscar awards.[6] Two years before the first Oscar cere-mony, Hollywood producers negotiated with Harvard art historians to de-velop a film library and a professionalized system of film connoisseurship that would have culminated in an annual awards ceremony and a perma-nent film collection. Examining this history, we can see how the Academy Awards grew out of producers' efforts both to stabilize film as a commod-ity and to redefine filmmaking as artistry rather than labor in response to the growing threat of unionization. The producers realized that the value of art, when packaged properly, increases with time. They knew also that portraying screenwriters, directors, and actors as artists challenged at-tempts to protect writing, directing, and acting as contract labor.

Like the Columbia film courses, the Harvard film project grew out of

American universities' struggle with the incorporation of minorities and the children of immigrants. But at Harvard film was used to address the makeup of the faculty rather than the student body. The Harvard art historians had their own motives, and they planned to use the film library to extend a new discipline of connoisseurship to film by preserving a small body of films based on selective criteria. Chapter 3 argues that the emphasis on skilled evaluation and the extension of connoisseurship to popular culture were part of a larger move within the field of art history to replace the paternalism of cultural stewardship based on lineage with a new model of art appreciation defined by professional skills and credentials. The new professional standards allowed Jews in particular and anyone not born to the genteel class more generally to enter the ranks of art historians and curators.

In the end, however, the Hollywood producers decided to bring their proposal closer to home. They dropped Harvard for the University of Southern California, and they founded their own film institution, the Academy of Motion Picture Arts and Sciences in Los Angeles, which hosted the Academy Awards and negotiated labor contracts.

Hollywood's influence, however, continued to be felt by Harvard's art history and museology students. The Fogg's students moved en masse to New York in the 1930s, flirted with Marxist theories of art, and went on to make film a central element of the New York art world and American museum work. During World War II, many of the Fogg graduates worked in the intelligence community, bringing film, art, and museums into the service of American propaganda.

During their leftist period in the 1930s, members of the Fogg group published the work of the Marxist film critic Harry Alan Potamkin in their journal *Hound and Horn*. In the culmination of Potamkin's writing for the periodical, he reworked the Harvard-Hollywood plan of 1927 to conform to Bertolt Brecht's call for "a theater full of experts, just as one has sporting arenas full of experts."[7] Potamkin employed a historical-materialist vision of art and collecting to draft a detailed plan for a film school and a taxonomy for a film library. His school and library were intended to lay bare for every viewer the hidden class and national foundations of the film industries. These institutions would have encouraged proletarian and middle-class audiences to escape the spoon-fed advertising of Hollywood and the alienating elitism of the growing film intelligentsia. Potamkin's reworking of the Harvard plan brought the movement to found a noncommercial film institution into dialogue with the international spread of mass politics. But Potamkin died in 1933, while still in his early thirties. And the powerful use of film by fascist and communist governments over the next few years led to a search for an American film institution capable of spreading democracy and responding to its critics.

At MoMA, the Fogg-trained cinephiles continued the movement to build a film institution, replacing Potamkin as their resident film expert with Ezra Pound's protégé Iris Barry. Chapter 4 explores Barry's various political transformations, and her influence on the reception and international definition of American film. Barry was an important British film critic of the 1920s, and in that role she articulated one of the strongest positions against the global spread of Hollywood films and American culture. Her writing and activism influenced quota bills in the House of Lords, the anti-American film policy of the League of Nations, and the programming of London's important Film Society. Like her contemporaries, Virginia Woolf and H. D. (poet-novelist Hilda Doolittle), Barry theorized film in gendered terms. She diagnosed Britain's emasculation by U.S. cultural imperialism on the one hand, and, on the other, she speculated about film's ability to transport women out of their culturally prescribed gender roles. Barry's experience as a film critic in London convinced her that film had emerged as a central force in world politics. When she moved to America in the 1930s, however, personal and institutional affiliations caused Barry to rethink her anti-American politics. In America, she used her post at MoMA to become perhaps the most important player in the development of cultural institutions dedicated to promoting American democracy through film.

Largely under Barry's direction, MoMA's Film Library moved to the center of efforts by the government, foundations, and the film industry to mobilize film for World War II and the cold war. Chapter 5 intervenes in the still heated debates over MoMA's and Hollywood's association with government intelligence organizations. The chapter charts the points of contact between commercial public relations and war propaganda since World War I, controversies over the presentation of Nazi and Soviet films in the United States during the 1930s, and the long arm of the Rockefeller Foundation in the brokering of Hollywood–government–cultural organization interaction from the 1930s to the 1950s. During World War II, MoMA's Film Library was contractually employed by almost every government intelligence agency to put theories of visual propaganda into action. Barry and the rest of the Film Library's staff followed criteria set by the Rockefeller Foundation's communication theorists and Frankfurt School fellow-traveler Siegfried Kracauer to control the circulation, production, and preservation of film in the United States, Latin America, and

Europe. After the war, in conjunction with cold war policy, MoMA's film staff helped to secure Hollywood's place as the quintessential American art form; they presented Hollywood as an ideal environment where the creative individual and the commercial free market came together.

By the end of World War II, Hollywood had assumed its role as a national art form and a propagator of Americanism. When the National Endowment for the Arts was established in 1965, the new organization funded avant-garde art in every other medium, and it supported *Hollywood* film. Yet, as chapter 6 shows, MoMA, and later the NEA, inadvertently created a movement of avant-garde film in America while supporting Hollywood and attempting to eliminate every alternative. The organizations of the avant-garde were designed to gain government and foundation support, as painters, sculptors, and performers had done. When avant-garde filmmakers failed to find government and institutional patronage, they were not supported by a growing audience for countercultural art and politics, as has been argued. They were supported by a single, previously anonymous, patron: Jerome Hill, scion of the family descended from railroad magnate James J. Hill. With Hill's support, the avant-garde established an alternative system of film institutions that briefly challenged Hollywood and the art establishment. But in the end, the NEA, the museums, and the film festivals effectively warehoused avant-garde film in order to continue bolstering Hollywood as a weapon of the cultural cold war.

Hollywood's collaboration with cultural institutions faded with the transformation of the studio system in the 1950s, 1960s, and 1970s. Hollywood's need for the Americanizing effect of cultural institutions ended when the studio system gave way to what has been called the New Hollywood. Hollywood became a blockbuster-driven, global industry that no longer benefited from being identified as the font of American art and ideology. Hollywood studios continue to work with museums, universities, and the government but on a smaller scale and on more contained projects. Universities, for example, have largely taken over the training of filmmakers. But on the whole, cultural institutions served their purpose too well. The leaders of the New Hollywood no longer needed museums to create a market for their film libraries; they no longer needed universities to teach Americans how to watch films; and for the most part they no longer needed the aid of government agencies to sell films around the world.

VACHEL LINDSAY AND THE UNIVERSAL FILM MUSEUM

We must realize that the halls and art objects are but the container, whose content is formed by the visitors. It is the content that distinguishes a museum from a private collection. A museum is like the lung of a great city; each Sunday the crowd flows like blood into the museum and exits purified and fresh.

—Georges Bataille, "The Museum" (1930)

But it will take a heap of reviewing [i.e., revising] to make [*The Art of the Moving Picture*] the same oracular Moses in the Mountain deliverance of two tablets of stone I want to make it.

—Vachel Lindsay to Harriet Moody (1915)

ONE OF THE first ways anyone imagined cultural institutions embracing film was in the form of a collection, often described as a film library or film museum. Indeed, all the collaborations discussed in this book entailed some form of film collection. The first theorists of film collecting responded to the suggestion that film was a new universal medium: a purveyor of universal truths and an envoy for universally intelligible images, or, more commonly, a new universal language. Advisers to presidents and monarchs viewed the universal dimension of film as a threat to state or institutionally authorized history. They quickly saw the need to contain the production and circulation of film documents, and calls for public film collections—either state-owned or open to the public—emerged out of a desire to control film's power to present realistic and indisputable evidence of important events. The scattered discussions of public film collections before World War I were, almost without exception, tied to attempts to control visual documentation of national narratives.

Within this one-note doctrine of containment, the poet Vachel Lindsay stands out as the prescient de Tocqueville of film collecting. The consolidation of the American film industry in Hollywood in the mid-1910s stirred Lindsay to imagine the cinema as a singular national institution on an unprecedented scale. When speculating about an ideal film collection, Lindsay focused less on films themselves and more on the technologies of cataloging and display. Like other theorists, he began with the premise that film was a new universal language, but, more importantly, he thought film theaters could be made into all-inclusive venues for yielding universal consensus. Lindsay looked to nineteenth-century public libraries and museums to find models for a new film institution that would forge, for the first time, a truly democratic American national identity.

Lindsay's vision was first published in *The Art of the Moving Picture* in 1915 and revised in 1922. As we will see in later chapters, Lindsay's vision ignited early university and museum projects, which sought to take film out of the commercial sphere, and his book was read in Europe, by Iris Barry and others, as a harbinger of the Americanization of the world. This chapter recovers the context of Lindsay's musings and clarifies what often reads like a conglomeration of personal interests marshaled in an attempt to claim film as art. His case for the art of film, however, served another goal: to claim cinema as a civic institution that might implement American democracy on a universal scale.

NATIONALISM AND FILM COLLECTING FROM EDISON TO LINDSAY

As early as 1895 Thomas Edison's assistant, W. K. L. Dickson, envisioned a national film collection in a book cowritten with his sister Antonia. The authors concluded their self-serving commemoration of Edison's innovations by speculating about the educational uses of cinema. They foresaw a film collection that preserved history free of the historian's cant and with greater precision than written texts: "Instead of dry and misleading accounts, tinged with the exaggerations of the chroniclers' minds our activities will be enriched by the vitalized pictures of great national scenes, instinct with all the glowing personalities that characterized them."[1] All at once, this sentence presents film as inherently truthful; it demonstrates film's usefulness as a national tool; and it *represses* the commercial system of film production that was increasingly controlled by Edison. The Dicksons' image of an unbiased historical collection restricted to bringing into one place "great national scenes" is perhaps evidence of little more than a corporate attempt to place a patriotic face on its monopolization of the emerging film industry. It is apt, in this context, that W. K. L. Dickson's other important contribution to the history of film collecting was also both incidental and commercially motivated; Dickson inaugurated the largest extant collection of pre-Hollywood film when in 1893 he started to deposit "paper prints" of Edison films at the Library of Congress for copyright purposes.[2] The Dicksons' inclination to imagine a historical film collection of national importance, however, is emblematic of early visions of film collecting. As we will see, that vision gained momentum because it appealed, for different reasons, to civic reformers, government officials, and filmmakers who, like the Dicksons, were attempting to replace the impression that films and the film industry were harmful to society with an image of cinema as a civic institution. To be sure, some proponents of film collecting sincerely hoped to transform the cinema itself and not just its public image.

Just a few years after the publication of the Dicksons' book, a Polish cinematographer in Paris, Boleslas Matuszewski, submitted an editorial to *Le Figaro* (March 25, 1898) in an attempt to create a new career for himself. Matuszewski's editorial made the case for a French national film collection, and one can't help notice how his powerful description of a film collection both resembled and amplified the nationalistic image of the Dicksons' projected collection. Matuszewski repeated the familiar invocation of film as a historical recorder superior to the "useless torrents of ink" as well as celebrating film's direct, evidential access to empirical facts:

> Animated photography . . . will give a direct view of the past. . . . How many lines of vague description in books intended for young people will be rendered unnecessary, the day we unroll in front of a classroom in a precise, moving picture the more or less agitated aspect of a deliberative assembly; the meeting of Heads of State about to ratify an alliance; a departure of troops or squadrons; or even the changing, mobile physiognomy of the city![3]

If this seems typical of the celebrations of what Annette Michelson has called film's "epistemological implications,"[4] its ability to yield knowledge of the world, it is important to remember that public film collections were born out of a desire to control rather than facilitate this power.

Matuszewski, for instance, did not limit himself to a positivist stance toward visual documentation. He qualified his vision of a film collection, suggesting that film prints contained momentary, skewed views of events rather than straightforward, objective historical records. For Matuszewski, a film was a "piece of history" as well as a "historic document." As a result, he insisted on the use of partisan documentary filmmakers, "aiming [their] lens[es] the same way a soldier does his gun." Moreover, he insisted on a "competent committee" to determine the veracity of film documents. In the end, Matuszewski, like the Dicksons, called for a film collection limited to national interests. Such a collection, he continued, would "of necessity be restricted in the beginning" until filmmakers turned, properly, to capturing "*slices of public and national life.*"[5] This was the dilemma shared by many early theorists of the film collection: how to preserve film's power to represent history while keeping its interpretation within a national— really a nationalist—framework.

Matuszewski, like many of his successors, argued that the national film collection necessitated two new jobs: a trained cinematographer like himself and a curator. The changing job description of the film curator, we will see, is the battleground on which the design of the national film collection was fought. Matuszewski, for his part, left the description of the curator to the reader's imagination. He was much more interested in the job of cinematographer, for which he was preemptively applying. To highlight his qualifications for the job, Matuszewski carefully timed his appeal to the Parisian reading public to follow an incident in which one of his own short films helped France avoid international embarrassment. His article reminded readers that in his previous post as official cinematographer for Russia's Tsar Nicholas II, Matuszewski made a film of French president François Faure's visit to St. Petersburg. Simply recording a state visit, the film inadvertently absolved Faure of accusations that he had not tipped his hat at an appropriate official moment.[6] In addition to boosting his candidacy, this story further corroborated Matuszewski's picture of the film collection as a necessary tool of national security able to contain and control film's potent ability to represent historic events.

In contrast to the national collections invoked by the Dicksons or Matuszewski, individual private collectors found a variety of uses for film collections, including experiments in visual historiography, scientific study, and personal enjoyment. A Swiss Jesuit priest, Abbé Joye, acquired a collection of over two thousand films by 1910, which he used, most likely, for teaching in the school he started in Basel. One of the largest early private collections belonged to a wealthy French intellectual, Albert Kahn. Kahn created a utopian documentary archive of everyday life that he hoped would be used to promote international peace and understanding, although it was viewed only by a small circle of friends. Of course, there is no telling how many other archives have been lost to history.[7]

In discussions of public film collections, however, state leaders and their advisers persistently echoed Matuszewski's call for officially sanctioned film collections. Early examples include Franz Goerke lobbying Kaiser Wilhelm II in 1912 (and possibly as early as 1897) to begin a German national film collection; French undersecretary of education and the arts Léon Bérard's 1913 call for a French national cinémathèque; and U.S. president Warren Harding's 1923 plan to store film records of nationally significant events in the White House basement.[8] Not surprisingly, discussions of national film collections have typically proliferated and intensified during periods of military conflict. The most significant film collection to appear during World War I, the collection of the British Imperial War Museum, was explicitly nationalist in purpose. The museum's first film archivist, E. Foxon Cooper, had pretensions to universal representation that included gathering and preserving every scrap of footage from newsreels to reenactments (or "faked scenes"). But despite Cooper's ambitions, the museum's staff selectively organized its film collection from the outset, and four years after the end of the war a committee of museum trustees and naval officers convened to reevaluate the collection and discard infelicitous material.[9] Shortly after that, the Imperial War Museum's selective collection was mined for a series of documentaries celebrating Britain's triumphs during the war, including *Ypres* (1925), *Mons* (1926), and *The Battles of the Coronel and Falkland Islands* (1927).[10] By the time of World War II, Germany, France, Italy, Great Britain, Belgium, Sweden, Russia, and the United States were all engaged in a struggle to design or redesign archives in the service of national ideologies (a period discussed in chapter 5).

All these plans and collections, despite the common rhetoric of objective or universal documentation that surrounded them, barely concealed their nationalistic ambitions. As repositories of facts, the calls for state collections generally emphasized preservation of evidence and elided questions of access and use. But not all collections with nationalistic objectives have sought to imbue their objects with the inert quality of historicity. In 1915, for example, we find two instances in which national film collections were imagined in liberal-democratic terms, and appeals to nationalist historiography were replaced by—or at least mixed with—the desire to provide universal access to collections, making their venues into civic training grounds. One example is D. W. Griffith's brief but vivid account of a future public library and the other is Vachel Lindsay's extended and more complex prognostications in *The Art of the Moving Picture*. In these models, built on the examples of public libraries and museums, the viewing space became more important than the objects themselves. Films were valued for their ability to represent history to a mass public rather than as uncanny historical documents. As a result, containment of evidence became less of a problem than the proper method of display and consumption. The new placement of the collection in the hands of the people rather than the state, however, couldn't entirely conceal the still strong nationalist program of the film collection, now imagined as a library or museum.

Griffith began his sketch for a film library by reiterating the image of a historical collection superior to written histories in both accuracy and completeness:

> Imagine a public library of the near future, for instance, there will be long rows of boxes or pillars, properly classified and indexed, of course. At each box a push button and before each box a seat. Suppose you wish to "read up" on a certain episode in Napoleon's life. Instead of consulting all the authorities, wading laboriously through a host of books, and ending bewildered, without a clear idea of exactly what did happen and confused at every point by conflicting opinions about what did happen, you will merely seat yourself at a properly adjusted window, in a scientifically prepared room, press the button, and actually see what happened.
>
> There will be no opinions expressed. You will merely be present at the making of history.

But then he took it all back:

> All the work writing, revising, collating, and reproducing will have been carefully attended to by a corps of recognized experts, and you will have received a vivid and complete expression.[11]

Griffith, like the other early advocates of film collecting, concluded that film's exceptional ability to represent the past presented a problem of containment. He proposed a solution to the problem that entailed replacing one set of experts—the historians, who guarded information and confused the general reader—with another set of experts who would present history clearly to all.

Many calls for state film collections explained the need for containment as a necessity of national security and assumed that state-authorized experts would supervise collections. But the experts-curators in Griffith's sketch were not state employees, and their role was not to eliminate unwanted footage. In Griffith's account, the promise of unlimited access was to be expedited by generic experts who were there merely to sift through the overwhelming number of documents. Griffith's experts provided the assurance that viewers' access to the past wouldn't be hampered by the burden of making choices themselves. Griffith's film library, in short, appears to put the experts directly—if condescendingly—at the service of the people rather than the state.

But when put in context, Griffith's vision appears to be another attempt to transform the film collection into a national technology. As a film producer-director, Griffith made claims for film's educational potential that were clearly the result of a combination of commercial and nationalist motivations, as were Matuszewski's and the Dicksons' in different ways. Written in direct defense of Griffith's controversial racist epic, *The Birth of a Nation* (1915), this palpable image of film's historiographical usefulness was intended, as Miriam Hansen has shown, to bolster the claims of objectivity made by his revisionist account of the Civil War and Reconstruction.[12] Ironically, where Griffith's claims for a film library rest on the assertion that images are more objective than words, his film corroborates the accuracy of its images by quoting from the text of Woodrow Wilson's *A History of the American People*. In both cases, Griffith appealed to the authority of experts over any essential qualities of either medium, film or writing. For all the weight Griffith placed on the readability and objectivity of film, his image of a film library, in the end, highlights the role of the experts, who would organize and validate the versions of history offered by film.

Rather than reinforcing convictions of film's ontological objectivity, Griffith's picture of a public film library is a plea for the public to trust the institutionalization of historical representation on film. Griffith's imagined film library worked to validate not only his own historical film but also the consolidation of film studios, which, at the time, were emerging into the oligopoly we have come to call Hollywood. Griffith's film library was just one more call for the top-down control of all movies.

Griffith's image of a film library may have been another front for corporate rapaciousness and a controversial vision of American history, but it also tapped into cultural discourses of universal representation that exceed both his reactionary political motivations and the Hollywoodization of the film industry. Matuszewski, in theory, and the British Imperial War Museum, in practice, also emphasized the role of experts in their visions of the film collection. But unlike those examples, Griffith's collection, it is implied, would have been international not national in scope; the only example he offers of the library's contents is the life of Napoleon. Indeed, if we ascribe a national function to Griffith's description of a collection at all, it is not because of the proposed content (which we assume would have been encyclopedic) or because of the politics of its collecting authorities (who are described simply as generic experts). Griffith's collection has a nationalist function because it cloaks the emerging Hollywood oligopoly in the democratizing claims of universal education.

As such, Griffith's image of the universal film library helped to push the film industry further into the hands of Progressive reformers. Griffith shared many Progressive reformers' desire to turn the movie theater into a civilizing space. But as a film producer himself, he refused to do this by resorting to censorship. To be sure, Griffith's vision of a public film library is an expression of his ambivalent relationship to Progressive reform and, more specifically, to the temperance movement.[13] Throughout his career Griffith mocked the figure of the holier-than-thou temperance reformer, but many of Griffith's films were themselves temperance-friendly morality plays. Several scholars have noted that between 1907 and 1915 Griffith yoked stories of sobering transformations with a melodramatic narrative form that often revolved around the containment of drunkenness and other transgressions.[14] For Griffith, his temperance narratives were developed with an eye toward converting the movie theater into a civic venue.

Griffith explicitly likened the reform potential of the movie theater to the temperance movement. "I believe in the motion picture," he wrote, "not only as a means of amusement, but as a moral and educational force. Did you know that there has been less drinking in the past five years and that it is because of motion pictures? It is absolutely true."[15] Griffith's use of the public library as a trope to explain one social function of the film theater contributed to reform efforts to redefine the movie theater as a noncommercial, educational space — objectives that continually subtended both real and imagined early film collections. But Griffith's brief description of a film library only paved the way for a fuller theorization of the film libraries and museums as technologies of citizenship. Vachel Lindsay accepted that challenge.

About two-thirds of the way through *The Art of the Moving Picture*, Lindsay paused to apologize because, "the chapters thus far might be entitled: 'an open letter to Griffith.' "[16] Lindsay's book of film theory is sympathetic to Griffith's political and aesthetic ambitions, but Lindsay's discussion of film libraries and museums is also indebted to a wide and often contradictory range of American poetic, political, and social traditions. Griffith invoked the image of the film library to aid in the validation of a racist national narrative and to justify the Americanness of a growing culture industry. Lindsay picked up on this nationalist motivation when writing his own evocation of a universal film collection, but Lindsay far surpassed Griffith. As we will see, by imagining the film theater as the inheritor of the nineteenth-century museum and library, Lindsay produced the seminal text in the invention of film collecting, and he defined the dream of the civic film institution.

In one of the first books of film theory published anywhere, Lindsay theorized the film museum and library out of nostalgia for a preindustrial, rural democracy. Cinema appeared to Lindsay, as it would for his unlikely successors Siegfried Kracauer and Stan Brakhage, to be an instrument capable of counteracting the capitalist and industrialized society that produced it. Lindsay characterized his millennialist prescriptions for the uses of film as the organic counterpart to the technophilic futurism of Karl Marx, H. G. Wells, and Edward Bellamy (his examples). In contrast to Bellamy's "press-the-button complacency," for example, Lindsay implored filmmakers to, "Make a picture of a world where machinery is so highly developed it utterly disappeared long ago" (312). Drawing comparisons between the apparatus of cinema and the writing and oratory of Ralph Waldo Emerson, Walt Whitman, Andrew Jackson, and William Jennings Bryan, Lindsay celebrated the realism of film's indexicality as a means of circulating pastoral images and, ultimately, restoring a bond between American national identity and the landscape of its frontier. In *The Art of the Moving Picture*, Lindsay combined these literary and political examples with examples from late-nineteenth-century public museums and libraries to weave a theory of film as an inherently democratic art with a vision for a new "circuit" of institutions to carry this art to and transform "the people."

According to Lindsay's Mosaic pronouncements, this new film institution was to have been a site for the replacement of both ecclesiastical and recreational pursuits with civic rituals. Lindsay's book was written at the tail end of a period of unprecedented activity in the creation of rituals of national heritage and identity. As historian Eric Hobsbawm has observed, "'Traditions' which appear or claim to be old are often quite recent in origin and sometimes invented." The period from 1870 to World War I saw an unusual frenzy of tradition-inventing as many nation-states and social movements adapted to the mass politics of universal (white manhood) suffrage by introducing new rituals of belonging. The United States, for example, assimilated a wave of European immigrants, institutionalizing celebrations of Americanness on the one hand (e.g., schoolchildren's daily pledge of allegiance to the flag and Thanksgiving) and absorbing immigrants' own ethnic—previously national—rituals on the other (St. Patrick's Day, for instance).[17] Lindsay intended moviegoing to take its place among the most central American civic rituals. "Particularly as the sons and daughters of a new country," Lindsay wrote toward the end of the book, "it is a spiritual necessity for us to look forward to tradition, because we have so few from the past identified with the six feet of black earth beneath us" (305–306).

Lindsay's prescriptions and prophecies for the transformation of cinema into a civic institution were based on the widespread idea that film was a new medium of universal democracy. His concept of universality included a version of the popular discussion of film as a universal language—a new "hieroglyphics" in Lindsay's formulation—rapidly displacing print in the increasingly visual world of the marketplace.[18] More directly relevant to his embrace of libraries and museums as models for film exhibition, however, is Lindsay's theorization of the movie theater as an all-inclusive space for reclaiming Enlightenment ideals of polite debate and universal consensus. A sober alternative to the saloon, film libraries and museums, Lindsay argued, had the potential to meld the politician's stump, the coffee house, and the voting booth into a singular national technology.

These are not idiosyncratic metaphors. Lindsay's discussion of film libraries and museums tapped into a larger politicization of culture, and his use of these tropes of universality were, in many ways, typical of the idealizing Populist and Progressive reformers who rhapsodized about nickelodeons as instruments of democracy. Yet Lindsay was one of the first theorists to mobilize the example of libraries and museums, central institutions of reform, in discussions of cinema as a universal communicator. This new admixture, couched in immodest, utopian prose, catalyzed discussions of and plans for new film institutions in both Britain and the United States. *The Art of the Moving Picture* became a central text for later theorists of film collecting and education, including Victor Oscar Freeburg and Iris Barry, both of whom will be discussed in subsequent chapters. If the seeming idiosyncrasies of Lindsay's writing on cinema have led to their neglect by contemporary film theorists and historians— Lindsay's work is still mentioned but rarely engaged—his book of film theory spoke to immediate concerns of the 1910s, 1920s, and 1930s.[19] By unraveling Lindsay's convoluted text and its complicated web of associations, we can uncover how *The Art of the Moving Picture* acted as a conduit between mythic notions of a democratic state and the real and continuing function of film collections, whether those collections sit on the shelves of the Library of Congress or a Blockbuster video store.

TECHNOLOGIES OF THE CITIZEN I: A SHORT HISTORY OF THE PUBLIC LIBRARY

In *The Art of the Moving Picture*, Vachel Lindsay drew inspiration from the public library system and, more specifically, from two of the first public museums in America: the Metropolitan Museum of Art in New York and the Chicago Art Institute (both founded in the 1870s). Lindsay had spent time in both museums as an art student, and his reveries about cinema's future were closely tied to his reminiscences of walking through museum corridors as a student. In a chapter that compared movies to sculpture, for example, Lindsay digressed to offer a note on his method: "I have gone through my old territories as an art student, in the Chicago Art Institute and the Metropolitan Museum, of late, in special excursions, looking for sculpture, painting, and architecture that might be the basis for the photoplay of the future" (114–15). Perhaps the clearest indication of Lindsay's parallax vision (in the nineteenth and twentieth centuries, in the museum and the movie theater) can be found on the dedication page, where we read: "Dedicated to George Mather Richards in memory of the art student days we spent together when the Metropolitan Museum was our picture-drama." These analogies—of the museumized film and the filmic museum—are more than just the fanciful musings of an aesthete contemplating a popular medium. In his firsthand experience of public libraries and museums, Lindsay found both points of aesthetic comparison for his film analysis and models of civilizing institutions. Before delving into Lindsay's extension of these reforms to film, then, it is both necessary and rewarding to step back and look at the redefinition of libraries and museums that took place in the late nineteenth century. More specifically, this relatively long historical detour will illuminate the way in which civic utility and mechanically reproduced art became part and parcel of public collections of art and literature, a combination that eventually made the public film library and museum seem inevitable.

Lindsay's primary examples, the Metropolitan Museum of Art and the Chicago Art Institute, were among the institutions that followed the British example and led a transformation of American collections in the 1870s. As Tony Bennett has shown, between the 1830s and 1880s British libraries and museums fell under government jurisdiction and, at least at the level of policy development, were reconceived as public utilities analogous to prisons and waterworks. With the aim of turning recently enfranchised working-class men (and later women)[20] into levelheaded citizens, a new breed of professional museum administrators tested

Benthamite and Ruskinian theories of social control. "Taking culture to the workingman," Bennett continues,

> was only one of the many means by which he was to be led to be both sober and prudent. This tactic was to be complemented by the distribution of puri- fied water to houses, and via public drinking fountains, to provide an alter- native to beer, just as public lavatories were envisaged as an alternative to the facilities that public houses offered as an inducement to their customers.[21]

As purifying alternatives to the saloon, libraries and museums became civ- ilizing spaces in which the "rough and raucous" learned to police them- selves, watching the deportment of others while, at the same time, feeling their own behavior under scrutiny in the panopticon of gallery halls and reading rooms. Thus through the performance of attendance, visitors re- hearsed a public-oriented mode of behavior and identity that could be taken beyond the library and museum walls. Libraries and museums be- came, in Ruskin's phrase, "panorama[s] in a pillbox."[22]

American museums and libraries with comparable civilizing missions began to appear in the 1870s, along with public parks, zoos, and sympho- ny halls.[23] These nineteenth-century public spaces were not created through government regulation, as they were in Britain, but by moneyed elites who sought to provide homogenizing sites of acculturation. If British cultural policy was overt in its civic and civilizing aspirations, American reform measures were couched in the often veiled language of Gilded Age uplift and cultural stewardship. Nevertheless, a reorganization of collec- tions of art and literature followed the ambition to fashion rational, moral citizens. In turn, utility and enlightenment became the touchstones of public library and museum reform. The curators at the Metropolitan Museum of Art in New York, for example, adopted the slogan "Make the Galleries Work,"[24] and in a classic pamphlet on museum administration, the Smithsonian's George Brown Goode defined the museum as

> an institution for the preservation of those objects which best illustrate the phenomenon of nature and the works of man, and *utilization* of these for the increase of knowledge and for the culture and *enlightenment of the people.*[25]

The image of the "pillbox" in Ruskin's neologism captured the new sense of utility with which museums and libraries were imbued, but the "panorama" was an equally important part of the equation. The defining characteristic of the transformation of museums and libraries into useful governmental tools was the creation of panoramic collections that claimed to represent *all knowledge* for *all visitors*. Roger Chartier suggests that, "The dream of a library (in a variety of configurations) that would bring together all the accumulated knowledge and all the books ever written can be found throughout the history of Western civilization."[26] There is much to be learned, however, from the historical transformation of that dream. In the second half of the nineteenth century, for instance, the ideal of a universal collection took on a new meaning. Renaissance collections like those of the Medici family represented microcosms equal to the Royal domain. Natural history museums designed in the eighteenth century were ordered to conform to rational categorizations of the world. But nineteenth-century public museums in Europe and America followed their educative mandates by turning these all-encompassing cognitive structures over to new classes of patrons.[27] As even a brief description can demonstrate, the adoption of meticulously prepared panoramic organizational systems dominated library and museum reform in the late nineteenth and early twentieth centuries. As a result, mass-reproduced copies that could facilitate complete collections became more important and often more valuable than the unique or original objects within collections.

The revolution of American library classification began at the inaugural meeting of the American Library Association in 1876, where Melvil Dewey introduced the Dewey decimal book cataloging system. Dewey's system effectively replaced the practice of organizing books in the order in which they were acquired with a subject classification system that merged the Baconian tree of knowledge with emergent theories of efficiency and economy. To be sure, in Dewey's scheme utility always superseded philosophy. His original plan, for instance, included ten ideal categories of books and knowledge, but that number was swiftly reduced to nine when Dewey realized that the numeral ten introduced an extra, untidy digit into the labels. Dewey proposed his pseudoscientific classification scheme as just one step in an epochal rationalization of American society that would have included the widespread adoption of the metric system and fully standardized American spelling. If Dewey didn't initiate the mass rationalization he hoped for, his classification system effectively reorganized almost every public library in the United States. Facilitated by the professionalization of librarianship and the proliferation of Andrew Carnegie–endowed public libraries, libraries rapidly implemented Dewey's system. By 1927, 96 percent of public libraries in America used the Dewey decimal system.[28]

Janice Radway has argued that this reordering marked a large-scale shift in the perception of books as material objects. The new classifications replaced an author-driven system that valued books as unique specimens of artistic production with a reader-driven system that remade the library into an easily navigable research station. The perpetually shifting order of books on the shelves to accommodate new volumes further placed the books "in dialogue with one another," a process ultimately "oriented toward increasing the circulation of books."[29]

This revaluing of books can be located in, among other places, the influential public library handbook, *The Library Primer*. The *Primer* was a compendium of American public library policy assembled by the influential director of both the Newark Museum and the Newark Public Library, John Cotton Dana. First published in 1896, the *Primer* remained a constantly changing indicator of public librarianship in its six revisions before 1920. Throughout its development, the *Primer* consistently promoted the virtues of access and use. The 1900 edition, for example, implored librarians to discard out-of-print volumes: "If you get [one], sell it and buy a live book."[30] And the test of a public library's success became the ease with which visitors could navigate the shelves. The seeming innateness of the order of books was intended to give visitors the impression of a great command of knowledge. As the *Primer* put it:

> The public likes . . . the arrangements in the library to be simple; they object to red tape and rules. They like to have their institutions seem to assume — through, for example, the absence of signs — that they know how to conduct themselves courteously without being told. . . . They like to feel at home in their library.[31]

In other words, the public library was effective as an institution to the extent to which it receded for the visitor and expedited universal and immediate access to knowledge and literature, an objective Griffith extended to his film library. Following this prescription, libraries were consciously turned into new technologies of the subject that encouraged visitors in the stacks to internalize the guiding signs and rules.

More specifically, libraries functioned as technologies of the citizen. "The public library," the *Primer* stated, "helps in social and political education — in the training of citizens."[32] This training took two forms, both of which tended toward comparisons to cinema. First, the ease of library use was intended to break down impediments to moral and political education; public libraries were frequently referred to as institutions of adult education or "people's universities."[33] Progressive reformers with a variety of motivations also claimed nickelodeons as "people's universities," and reforms often put forward the idea of combining these two popular venues by employing films in public libraries. Children's divisions in libraries occasionally screened films in the early 1910s, but technical demands and fire hazards generally kept film out of public libraries until the late 1930s.[34]

Second, by aiming to make reading a universal activity, libraries attempted to lure citizens away from taverns and create a space for sober, rational reflection. "The free reading room," the *Primer* remarked, " . . . is a powerful agent for counteracting the attractions of saloons and low resorts."[35] Librarians rarely addressed the problem of exactly how to lure saloon patrons from bar stools to library stacks, but the vision of public libraries as educational substitutes for saloons motivated the rhetoric of universal access from very early on. In 1912, Dana identified his roots by reprinting one of the first tracts connecting public libraries with temperance: Jesse Torrey's *The Intellectual Torch; Developing an Original, Economical and Expeditious Plan for the Universal Dissemination of Knowledge and Virtue; By Means of Free Public Libraries. Including Essays on the Use of Distilled Spirits* (1817). In one of the documents contained in *The Intellectual Torch*, Torrey announced his intention to lobby Congress to fund public libraries with a tax on liquor.[36]

Like the public library, the nickelodeon was often considered a potential substitute for the saloon, and it is largely as a "saloon surrogate" that Vachel Lindsay, like D. W. Griffith, conceived the public film library. By the 1910s several sociological studies corroborated the observation that the rise of nickelodeons in urban areas did in fact lead to a decline in alcohol consumption.[37] These data, however, were used for a variety of different ends. For opponents of censorship, like Griffith, the nickelodeon's record of alcohol prevention was evidence of its already present social good.[38] For proponents of censorship like Charles Sprague Smith—who founded the People's Institute in Brooklyn and helped launch the most successful film censoring body of the 1910s, the National Board of Censorship—the fact that nickelodeons drew customers from saloons indicated film's potential to become a counterattraction to the saloon if used properly.[39] Still another faction worried that film viewing was a vice worse than the drinking. One survey of *Substitutes for the Saloon* (1901, revised 1919), which strongly endorsed the civic and temperance value of public libraries, concluded: "Close inspection has discovered that a large percentage of motion pictures are as harmful to the mind as alcohol is to the body."[40] Saloon owners too were aware of the threat posed by nickelodeons and many of them

chose to join the enemy, blurring the lines between the saloon and its sur-
rogates. Saloon owners in major cities often opened nickelodeons themselves, sometimes in adjacent buildings. A 1910 Chicago survey found that
"saloonkeeping constituted the largest occupational group of those enter-
ing the [movie] theater business."[41] Both libraries and nickelodeons were
thus brought into the fold of Populist and Progressive social reform and
paved the way for grafting the civic value of one public collection of mass
culture, the library, onto another, the film library.

TECHNOLOGIES OF THE CITIZEN II: A SHORT HISTORY OF THE PUBLIC MUSEUM

The museum, like the public library, became an influential model for
transforming film collections in civic institutions. In museums, as in libraries, collections were reorganized as civic and civilizing spaces.
Throughout the second half of the nineteenth century, American museum collections strove to fulfill their educative mission by procuring representative sets of great artworks. This organizing dictate subordinated the
aesthetic value of individual works to their place in the evolution of art history. As a result, the organizational series was on display as much as the
works of art. The art museum became, in Philip Fisher's phrase, a "technology of the series."[42] Seeking to fill out their series, major museums in
New York, Chicago, Boston, Philadelphia, and Washington, D.C., built
regal classical structures and filled their galleries with *copies* of masterpieces in European collections. As even André Malraux was forced to
admit—when in the 1950s he predicted the crumbling of museum walls as
a result of the invention of color photographic reproduction—public museums of *original* artworks were themselves a recent invention.
Preeminent art critics of the late nineteenth century, Malraux acknowl-
edges, "had visited two or three galleries, and seen reproductions (photographs, prints, or copies) of a handful of masterpieces of European art;
most of their readers had seen even less."[43] The Boston Museum of Fine
Arts, which opened in 1876, boasted the largest American collection of
plaster replicas; its trustees had agreed from the outset that the museum
should be "a comprehensive gallery of reproductions, through plaster casts
of the many treasures of Antique and Medieval Art, or photographs of original drawings by the most renowned artists of all periods."[44] Cast collecting gained considerable momentum in the 1890s, and New York's
Metropolitan Museum of Art launched a massive campaign to increase its
cast collections.[45]

If the majority of reform-minded educators embraced the democratizing capability of reproductions, genteel arbiters of taste often opposed the popularizing effect of casts and chromolithographs. During the first few decades of the twentieth century, J. P. Morgan and other robber barons began to bequeath important original works, which permitted a regime of connoisseurship and a cult of authenticity that reconfigured museum display and educational policies. Photographs began to enter the museum as unique artworks, and the casts and other reproductions quickly lost both prestige and pecuniary value and were quickly shuttled off to basements or temporarily placed in unfilled wings.[46] (This shift is taken up again in chapter 3.)

Educational collections, however, continued to utilize reproductions for decades. And the museums that pioneered film collecting—Harvard's Fogg Art Museum in the 1920s and the Museum of Modern Art in the 1930s—continued to use reproductions of paintings and sculpture selectively as popularizing tools. The preference for copies over originals in late-nineteenth-century American museums took up, often directly, Ruskin's proposal for the creation of dual collections: a "great gallery" for enlightened appreciation of masterpieces and a "popular gallery" comprised of works "of sufficient value to interest the public, and of merit enough to form the basis of early education, and to give examples of all art."[47]

In the same way that the well-organized library put the reader in a position to intuitively command great resources of knowledge, panoramic museums organized by period and school gave the visitor the impression of mastering the evolution of art and of civilization. "The supposition was," as Carol Duncan puts it, "that by walking through this history of art, visitors would live the spiritual development of civilization."[48]

It is in this vein that Vachel Lindsay looked to the universal collections of the late nineteenth century as models for film museums that would serve as institutions of mass education. His advice to filmmakers, for example, included prescribed museum trips, not to the Metropolitan Museum of Art or the Chicago Art Institute, but to the generic, universal ur-museum. Lindsay took for granted that, "There are two bronze replicas in all museums. They are generally on either side of the main hall, towering above the second-story balustrade" (116). "Go to any museum," he instructed filmmakers, "Find the Parthenon room. High on the wall is a copy of the famous marble frieze of the young citizens who are in the procession in praise of Athena. . . . Let it be studied by the author-producer" (117). As an avatar of sculpture on which to base future action films, Lindsay submitted, "the great Victory of Samothrace, that spreads her wings at the head of the steps of the Louvre, and in many an art gallery beside" (124). Museums were, for Lindsay, who began to study in them in the 1870s, identical buildings that housed mass-reproduced copies of masterpieces, and as such they were an obvious precursor of the movie theater. Museums' pretensions to universal representation and appeal found their natural extension in movie theaters, which promised to be sites for the mass dissemination of information to an undifferentiated public.

Of course neither the user-friendly Dewey decimal system nor the representative models of art history changed the forces minding the gates of the institutions. The volumes that were welcomed into the dialogue of books continued to come from genteel canons (dime novels and popular fiction, for example, were almost categorically excluded),[49] and museums continued to tell the story of Western art forged by European collectors and art historians. When Walter Benjamin observed the Social Democrats' comparable attempts to "popularize knowledge" through the creation of "universal collections" in German museums, he concluded that they ignored class difference by appealing to a general, homogeneous public rather than recognizing the separate needs of different classes.[50] And Andrew Ross neatly summarizes "the contradiction between the use of the museum as a vehicle for universal education and its use as a means of reforming the manners and conduct of its new audiences; one goal addressed the audience as an undifferentiated group, the other actively differentiated its audience according to their level of social and cultural refinement."[51]

Libraries and museums did more than just passively embody these contradictions. The scientifically ordered, universal collections actively sought to homogenize their publics by placing visitors in a position to assume and enact the identity of the ideal spectator to whom the collections were targeted. In Carol Duncan's penetrating analysis of the ritual function of museums, she concludes that the organizing model adopted by the Chicago Art Institute and the Boston Museum of Fine Arts,

> conceives the public art museum as a ritual that makes visible the ideas for a republican state, frames the "public" it claims to serve, and dramatizes the unity of the nation. To be an effective civic symbol of this kind, the museum had to construct the visitor as an ideal bourgeois citizen, an individual with interests and needs very different from those of the courtier or aristocratic visitor implicit in older displays of art. As implied by the museum, this visitor was, as its most ideal, a self-improving, autonomous, politically empowered

(and therefore male) individual who enters the museum in search of moral and spiritual enlightenment. As a dramatic field, the public art museum prompts visitors to enact—and thereby ritually assume—this identity.[52]

This picture of the moral and political, identity-forming function of public libraries and museums does not, of course, exclude the potential for museum visitors to resist the top-down designs of museum policymakers. Nor does it exclude the potential for disingenuous motives of patrons and reformers.[53] Yet it does capture both the rhetoric of museum (and library) policy and, as sociological studies have continually borne out, it also captures the reasons museums appear intimidating to the uninitiated.[54] You can't walk through the careful design of a museum without telling others whether or not you belong.

Significantly, Lindsay's book—and American film theory generally— accompanied the vertical integration of the film industry and the standardization of the filmgoing experience. It is with the increased homogenization of film style that Lindsay saw the seeds of a universal language and the potential for a museumized film industry, rededicated to universal education and democratic training. Miriam Hansen argues that, when applied to film, the metaphor of film as a universal language facilitated the film industry's transformation into a pervasive middle-class art form (without losing its working-class patrons). Citing Lindsay as a representative example, Hansen demonstrates that the use of the universal language metaphor intensified in the mid-1910s during the consolidation of what has become known as the classical Hollywood style. The classical Hollywood style refers to the replacement of the heterogeneous modes of address found in pre-Hollywood film with an institutionally codified system of representation directed toward a singular, ideal spectator.[55] Moreover, for Hansen, the universal language metaphor ultimately served the economic ambitions of Hollywood big business. "The universal-language metaphor," she concludes, "in effect became a code word for broadening the mass cultural base of motion pictures in accordance with middle-class values and sensibilities."[56]

The universal language metaphor may have facilitated Hollywood's embourgeoisement and, as a result, increased the size of the film audience. But the notion that Hollywood film spoke clearly to everyone also gave rise to new attempts to bring film production and filmgoing under the control of noncommercial authorities. More clearly than anyone else, Vachel Lindsay saw an opportunity to borrow from the lessons of the public library and museum and turn the newly captive public of the movie theater into a national public that, for the first time, embodied the purest ideals of a democratic state.

VACHEL LINDSAY, 1915: THE FILM LIBRARY AS THE NEW HOLLYWOOD

In 1915 and again in 1922 when revising The Art of the Moving Picture, Vachel Lindsay was convinced that because of its potential to speak to and include a universal public, cinema sat on the cusp of a new period in its development. It was evolving into an educational instrument. Lindsay saw the film library and film museum fulfilling the promise of the public library and public museum. By tracing his different uses of the library and the museum as models for a new film institution, we can see how Lindsay built a bridge between Populist/Progressive reform and the image of the film library and the film museum as tools for controlling American identities.

In the first edition of Lindsay's book, the example of the public library system outweighed the museum as a model for an ideal film collection. Lindsay predicted that at least "one-quarter" of the "dead printed matter" produced by the government and the press would soon be made into films and, he speculated further, textbooks illustrated by films were just around the corner. But even as Lindsay described the many ways moving images would displace print, he could not abandon the analogy of books and newspapers. "Photoplay libraries are inevitable," he stated prosaically, "as active if not as multitudinous as the book-circulating libraries" (254). Not unlike Griffith's vision of a future film library, Lindsay described urban centers that would house the film equivalent of textbooks, encyclopedias, and dictionaries:

> The motion pictures will be in the public schools to stay. Text-books in geography, history, zoölogy, botany, physiology, and other sciences will be illustrated by standard films. Along with these changes, there will be available at certain centres collections of films equivalent to the Standard Dictionary and the Encyclopedia Britannica. (The Art of the Moving Picture, 253)

This paragraph exhibits the already familiar tenets of early predictions for film collections: the replacement of dramatic films with educational films and the implication of sanctioned arbiters to standardize the meaning of films. But if other early images of film collections supported state or corporate authority, Lindsay saw the film library and museum as utopian spaces, the foundation of a new national identity forged wholly by the au-thority of the people.

Lindsay's discussion of exhibiting and collecting were directly inter-twined with his general theories of cinematic representation and American politics. The print analogy was essential both to Lindsay's un-derstanding of cinema's ontology and to his geopolitical interpretation of American society. In a move characteristic of writings on film as a new universal language, Lindsay explained the potential of cinema by com-paring it to the introduction of the printing press. "Edison," Lindsay de-clared, "is the new Gutenberg. He has invented a new printing. The state that realizes this may lead the soul of America, day after to-morrow" (252). Lindsay hoped that a rural state might take control of film production and forge a new national identity ("the soul of America") as the printing press had created imagined communities in the sixteenth and seventeenth cen-turies. Lindsay's strange addition to this common equation—that a state rather than an industry might control the medium—arose from his pecu-liar interpretation of the American agrarian tradition.[57] Lindsay saw the United States divided into ideologically distinct sections based on a com-bination of landscape, industry, and culture. As a result, he attributed the natural qualities of a place to its industry and inhabitants.

The starting point for Lindsay's vision for a new geopolitical cinema was the relocation of the film industry from New York and New Jersey to California in the early 1910s. In this relocation, the birth of Hollywood, Lindsay recognized that the backdrop of American cinema had changed, and a new landscape was being projected across America. He became more entranced by the Pacific Ocean and the Hollywood Hills in the background than by film narratives. Lindsay explained: "When the Californian relegates the dramatic to secondary scenes, both in his life and his photoplay, and turns to the genuinely epic and lyric, he and his in-strument may find their immortality together as New England found its soul in the essays of Emerson" (250). Although Lindsay superimposed an idiosyncratic nomenclature onto his map (he called the West Coast "New Italy" and the Southwest "New Arabia"),[58] he was simply applying the en-trenched Emersonian idealization of the machine as mediator between the American landscape and U.S. national identity. Leo Marx classically summarized the Emersonian position in *The Machine in the Garden*: "Machine power . . . is an instrument of national unity. . . . Like a divin-ing rod, the machine will unearth the hidden graces of the landscape."[59]

Not only Lindsay's suggestions for film as a new machine in the garden came from an Emersonian tradition. His descriptions of the universal dimension of film libraries, film encyclopedias, and film museums also has precursors in Emerson's early journals—with titles like "Wide World," "Universe," "Encyclopedia"—as well as in Emerson's adulation for the universal natural history collection at the Jardin des plantes, which he visited in 1833.[60] To be sure, Lindsay's vision of a new film institution fell somewhere between an art museum and the natural history museum. The overlapping vocabulary that merged art and nature is evident, for example, in Lindsay's primitivist writings on American Indians. He suggested that the producers of western films use Edward Curtis's "Ethnological collection of photographs of our American Indians" (114) as a model of representation. With a tone of inevitability, Lindsay predicted that filmmakers would abandon storytelling for a poetic synthesis of life, environment, and art.

Lindsay may have traced the genealogy of his new film institution back through Emerson's writings to ancient Egyptian hieroglyphics, but his vision of a new American cinema was firmly rooted in the idealism of the Age of Reform. With the replacement of the movie theater by film libraries and film museums, Lindsay saw an opportunity to take hold of cinema as a technology of national identity.

Like the Dicksons, Matuszewski, and Griffith, Lindsay held film's realism to be the key to its national function. In the film library and film museum, Lindsay predicted two transformations of the mass audience as a result of their encounter with the realistic film image. The mimetic quality of films, Lindsay argued, first had the capacity to bring spectators into contact with a virtual window onto nature. In the 1915 edition of *The Art of the Moving Picture*, Lindsay saw the film industry growing into a new Emersonian voice, speaking for the pastoral tradition and circulating images of the natural splendor of California's landscape as an antidote to the industrialization of East Coast cities: "Our mechanical East is reproved, our tension is relaxed, our ugliness is challenged every time we look upon those garden paths and forests [of the West Coast]" (251).

In addition to cinema's ability to circulate pastoral images, Lindsay celebrated a related genre of films he designated "The Picture of Crowd Splendor." This genre provided a second function, offering spectators a mirror of society. Films in this category used realism to depict and critique crowd behavior for the cinema's mass audience. In an exemplary instance—*The Birth of a Nation*'s representation of the frantic audience at the Booth Theatre after Abraham Lincoln's assassination—Lindsay noted, "the real crowd [of film spectators] touched with terror beholds its natural face in the glass" (77). Through realistic representations of America's landscape and society, Lindsay expected the cinema to become a crucible of

Americanness in which the movie screen replaced the unself-conscious behavior of the crowd and reconnected spectators with a preindustrial mode of subjectivity.

But film's ability to represent nature and reflect the crowd to a mass audience wasn't enough to transform national identity. Lindsay wanted the conditions of film's dissemination controlled as well. He considered a chapter on cinema as "The Substitute for the Saloon" a "special commentary on chapter five, 'The Picture of Crowd Splendor' " (235). As we have seen, by 1910 more than one study suggested that nickelodeons drew business away from saloons, and Lindsay, like Griffith, speculated that film was replacing alcohol as a safer intoxicant, a placebo—even a cure. Lindsay commented ambiguously that spectators now had "fire pouring into their eyes instead of into their bellies," but he continued the physiological metaphor to suggest a useful function: "Blood is drawn from the guts to the brain" (236). Lindsay condemned the saloon as the antithesis of educational institutions: "[The bartender's] cynical and hardened soul wipes out a portion of the influence of the public school, the library, the self-respecting newspaper" (243). In response, he campaigned for film to be used as an educational force, a nationwide "university extension," that would form a moral, public training ground to challenge the appeal of the saloon (261).

Written the same year as Griffith's description of a film library, Lindsay's book invoked a similar expert-run model. He foresaw universities endowing motion picture programs. There, removed from commercial demands, films could be made and used as instruments of public education in which academic knowledge, translated to visual form, would serve a useful social function. When that was achieved, he concluded, even ivory tower "professors may become citizens" (262). Almost a copy of Hollywood's industrial structure, Lindsay's expert-run cinema would have been held to an equally institutionally sanctioned criteria: "The relentless fire of criticism which the heads of departments would pour on the production before they allowed it to pass would result in a standardization of the sense of scientific fact over the land" (261). Like Griffith, Lindsay saw this moment as a battle for the institutional control of American cinema. However, where Griffith wanted to consolidate power in the commercial film industry, Lindsay wanted universities and libraries to take control. It is a testament to the timeliness and power of his argument that within a year of publication, Columbia University adopted *The Art of the Moving Picture* as a textbook (as will be discussed in chapter 2).

In the 1922 revision of *The Art of the Moving Picture*, however, Lindsay adopted the model of the museum that had been overshadowed by the library, the encyclopedia, and the university in the first edition. In the museum, he saw new hope for a film institution that could finally be guided by the people.

VACHEL LINDSAY, 1922: THE FILM MUSEUM AS A NEW PUBLIC SPHERE

In the revised edition, Lindsay's ideal American landscape had shifted too: from California to the Southwest, which Lindsay referred to as "the New Arabia" where "individualism, Andrew Jacksonism, will forever prevail, and American standardization can never prevail" (27). His image of the absorbed crowd taking in the American landscape and confronting its own reflection was replaced by an image of a more active crowd of individuals. Lindsay created a picture of a film museum that would replace taverns as community centers and reclaim a deteriorating public sphere rooted in the free exchange of rational, sober individuals. In this new edition, Lindsay compared films to the writings of Joseph Addison and Benjamin Franklin—the foundation of the eighteenth-century public sphere—and he pleaded that the films discussed in his volume be collected and studied as "the first newspapers, and the first imprints of Addison's *Spectator*, and the first Almanacs of Benjamin Franklin, and the broadside ballads and the like, are ever collected and remembered" (1–2). Claiming these new antecedents for motion pictures, Lindsay prescribed a model for a film museum that would function as an engine for the production of rational discourse and universal consensus in the negotiation of national identity.

Lindsay's design for a film museum entailed showing films side by side on screens for comparison in "Art Museum study rooms" (8). As an example, Lindsay suggested screening *The Cabinet of Dr. Caligari* (1920) next to Griffith's *Avenging Conscience* (1914). Comparing set design in such a study room, Lindsay claimed, audiences would see the films in relation to the entire history of art, and they might find that

> There is nothing experimental about any of the setting, nothing unconsidered or strained or over-considered. It seems experimental because it is thrown into contrast with extreme commercial formulas in the regular line of the "movie trade." But compare *The Cabinet of Dr. Caligari* with a book of [Arthur] Rackham or [Edmund] Du Lac or [Albrecht] Dürer, or Rembrandt's etchings, and *Dr. Caligari* is more realistic. (*The Art of the Moving Picture*, 10)

Unlike Griffith's or Lindsay's own image of the "properly classified and in-dexed" film library, spectators in Lindsay's film museum would have ques-tioned and, in this case, overturned the experts.[61]

To promote direct engagement with both films and other spectators, Lindsay prescribed the then revolutionary suggestion of eliminating musi-cal accompaniment to films.[62] In silence, he argued, spectators could freely discuss the films they saw projected before them. But the demo-cratic space of Lindsay's film museum was not entirely free of circum-scribed norms. As the nineteenth-century public museum and the eighteenth-century coffee house enforced a basic level of deportment, Lindsay's "Conversational Theatre," as he called it, required a similar sys-tem of self-regulation in which spectators monitored their neighbors. "There will be some people who disturb the neighbors in front," he sug-gested, "but the average crowd has developed its manners in this particu-lar, and when the orchestra is silent, murmurs like a pleasant brook" (224). Reproducing the paradox of the universal museum, pointed out by Walter Benjamin and Andrew Ross above, Lindsay's film museum was at once all-inclusive and regulatory.

As Lindsay envisioned film libraries in every town center, so too would film museums be pervasive.

> In a democracy, the arts like the political parties, are not founded till they have touched the county chairman, the ward leader, the individual voter. The museums in a democracy should go as far as the public libraries. Every town has its library. There are not twenty art museums in the land. (*The Art of the Moving Picture*, 213)

Once everyone from the party boss down to the voter were corralled into film museums, Lindsay called on theater proprietors to introduce an in-strumentalized form of direct, participatory democracy:

> At the door let each person be handed the following card:
> "You are encouraged to discuss the picture with the friend who accom-panies you to this place. Conversation, of course, must be sufficiently sub-dued not to disturb the stranger who did not come with you to the theatre. If you are so disposed, consider your answers to these questions: What play or part of a play given in this theatre did you like most to-day? What the least? What is the best picture you have ever seen anywhere? What pictures, seen here this month, shall we bring back?" Here give a list of the recent productions, with squares to mark like the Australian ballot system: approved

or disapproved. The cards with their answers could be slipped into the ballot-box at the door as the crowd goes out. (*The Art of the Moving Picture*, 225–26)

At first, this description recalls Hollywood test screenings in which small segments of filmgoers are employed by industry representatives to aid in crafting more marketable products. Conceived of on a universal scale, however, this imagined institution begins to take on the form of a thoroughly representative technology of democracy, especially for Lindsay, who considered the images on movie screens conduits to the roots of American identity: its geography and its people.

Lindsay's rhetoric may have been even more utopian than that of earlier theorists of the film collection, but his vision was not free of institutional affiliation or the ambition to see his vision in action. Lindsay revised *The Art of the Moving Picture* in 1922 with the promise of a partnership with the Denver Art Museum. In a foreword to the new edition, the director of the Denver museum, William Eggers, reinforced many of the assertions about crowds, universal language, and cultural control that Lindsay explored in the first edition. "What is the type of institution," Eggers asked,

> that will ultimately take the position of leadership in culture though this new universal instrument?
>
> What possibilities lie in this art, once it is understood and developed, to plant new conceptions of civic and national idealism? How far may it go in cultivating concerted emotion in the ungoverned crowd?[63]

Eggers seems to have thought he was getting Lindsay's endorsement for an educational film institution, like the one discussed in the first edition of the book. Instead, Lindsay produced a radical plan for a new form of society in which every citizen was a film critic. By that time, Lindsay was moving away from the idea that film could control the ungoverned crowd, and the second edition put its faith in and encouraged the freedom of the crowd of individuals in the movie audience to govern the nation.

Based on his geopolitical map, Lindsay identified Denver as the capital of "New Arabia." Through the production and circulation of films, Lindsay expected the Denver Art Museum to do nothing less than spread an individuating model subjectivity and provide an example of a new civic film institution that would replace Hollywood. "Now it is the independence of Spirit of this New Arabia," Lindsay wrote, that I hope the Denver Art Museum can interpret in its photoplay films, and send them on circuits to the Art Museums springing up all over America, where sculpture, architecture, and painting are now constantly sent on circuit. Let that already established convention—the "circuit exhibition"—be applied to this new art. (*The Art of the Moving Picture*, 27)

The phrase "circuit exhibition" gives us a clear idea of what Lindsay had in mind. By "circuit exhibition" he referred to the circuits of traveling exhibition pioneered by nineteenth-century entertainment industries (circuses and vaudeville) and grassroots adult education movements (lyceums and Chautauquas). For Lindsay, this combination provided the perfect combination of education, entertainment, and political forum.

Throughout the nineteenth century, these two sides of commercial exhibition fed off each other. If vaudeville circulated performers primarily to entertain urban audiences, lyceums (from the 1820s to the 1840s) and circuit or tent Chautauquas (from the 1870s to the 1920s) sent many of the same acts to rural populations under the guise of education, family entertainment, and political stump. Begun as a Methodist educational retreat and correspondence school in upstate New York, Chautauqua soon sprouted many imitators and grew into a nationwide system of university extension. Thomas Schlereth describes Chautauqua as "simultaneously . . . a kind of moral vaudeville and an early institution of mass culture for the middle class."[64] In the public presentations of his poetry, Lindsay attempted to fuse the popularity of Chautauqua and vaudeville. He dubbed his traveling readings "the higher vaudeville," and he sought to emulate the political and moral oratory of popular Chautauqua lecturers as diverse as P. T. Barnum, Jane Addams, and—perhaps the most popular of all— William Jennings Bryan.[65] Lindsay had one of his books of poetry bound to resemble a Chautauqua publication and wrote to Carl Sandburg of his desire to reach a wider audience: "Bryan is really the American poet, till we can take the Chautauqua platform, and sing to as many."[66]

The Chautauqua circuit was at the peak of its popularity when Lindsay revised *The Art of the Moving Picture* in 1922. Its connections to the temperance movement and its large rural constituency made it the ideal model for Lindsay's circulating film museum. But in an outcome that we see repeated throughout the history of Hollywood's collaborations with cultural institutions, rather than Chautauqua diverting the film industry from Hollywood, the film industry lured Chautauqua's most popular performers away from the circuit and contributed to its rapid decline in popularity. In his attempt to look forward to tradition, Lindsay was just as often looking backward at soon-to-be-outmoded educational and directly political uses of mass culture. And even as *The Art of the Moving Picture* set the parameters for the debates about film libraries and film museums, it also signaled the end of a period of utopian reform. Denver never started its film department and Lindsay's agrarian populism did not find its way into the successful American film collections of the 1930s. Indeed, many of the films most important to Lindsay no longer survive. But *The Art of the Moving Picture* successfully drew from the examples of the public library and museum to create an ideal model of a film institution capable of creating a new national identity. Lindsay's book remained a springboard for many of the most important attempts to enlist Hollywood in the creation of an American national film institution.

2

OVERLAPPING PUBLICS

HOLLYWOOD AND COLUMBIA UNIVERSITY, 1915

> Moreover, students do need to be qualified for professions, and this
> entails some degree of specialisation, without which there can be no
> skills or knowledge or, save in exceptional cases, any intellectual discipline
> at all. None the less, wider knowledge is worth striving for. It is not
> necessary to believe that all knowledge always makes men happier or freer
> or morally better.
>
> —Isaiah Berlin, "General Education" (1969)

A FTER THE PUBLICATION of *The Art of the Moving Picture*, Vachel Lindsay enjoyed some success as a public film theorist. He lectured on film at the Chicago Art Institute; he wrote a few articles on film for the *New Republic*; and he began work on a second book of film theory.[1] *The Art of the Moving Picture* was even adopted, as Lindsay himself boasted, by the first college-level film courses in the United States at Columbia University. Following Lindsay's suggestions, Columbia's faculty immediately addressed the task of creating university-approved standards of filmmaking and film viewing, and their efforts found the support from the commercial film industry that Lindsay desired.

The publication of Lindsay's book helped to spur the creation of the Columbia film program, but Columbia's faculty quickly produced several of their own textbooks to replace *The Art of the Moving Picture*. They followed Lindsay in thinking of film as a new battleground in the definition of American national identity. But where Lindsay sought the erasure of all class, ethnic, and geographical difference through the resuscitation of a mythical age of natural consensus, Columbia's faculty and administrators employed film to define and disseminate a normative model of Americanness for its increasingly diverse student body. Columbia's film program was housed in the university's extension school, and it targeted Jewish students, who were simultaneously being excluded from Columbia through selective admissions policies. The film courses were designed to make film viewing into a form of training in American values for a new generation of New York Jews attending college and, at the same time, offer career instruction to students who might pursue the new profession of screenwriting. Although it was never stated explicitly, it seems more than a coincidence that Columbia's faculty and administrators chose to prepare Jewish students for what was seen as the Jewish film industry.

The Columbia film program reveals the many intersecting ambitions of educational institutions and the film industry in the mid-1910s. In a flash of insight predicted by Lindsay, professors and film producers realized that American universities' changing curricula and student bodies complemented Hollywood's changing structure and audience, however briefly. Columbia's emphasis on vocational training aided in Hollywood's move toward a professionalized division of labor, and the film script was the centerpiece of this transformation. Moreover, Columbia's adoption of film as an instrument for instruction in American values promised to complete Hollywood moguls' quest to link film with middle-class American theater and literature, which had themselves only recently been included in university education.

Columbia's film program was both mired in fleeting concerns and incredibly influential. As we will see in later chapters, Columbia established a model of film education that Hollywood producers reworked a decade later when designing a film program at Harvard. And in the 1930s, the Museum of Modern Art took over the by-then-diminished Columbia film program to disseminate a paradigm of film education on an international scale. This chapter re-creates the intersecting histories that allowed Columbia University to invent American film education. The first section describes how the promise of a professional field of screenwriting enticed Columbia's faculty and two Hollywood production companies to join forces and support screenwriting courses and a film script collection. The next two sections step back to uncover larger cultural and institutional discourses that framed the project. These include a panic over film as a dangerous flammable object and the nativist ideology of adult education at Columbia. Both were cast in terms of the changing class and ethnic makeup of university students and movie audiences, which began to overlap for the first time.

SCREENWRITING AND THE COMMERCE OF EDUCATION

The arrival of "Photoplay Composition," as the screenwriting courses at Columbia were called, coincided with the consolidation of the Hollywood studio system and the film industry's most intense efforts to reach a middle-class audience, around 1914–15. The influx of personnel from the Broadway theater, the dominance of feature-length films, and the codification of a narrative grammar all signaled the success of the industry's struggle to align itself with middle-class American theater and literature. The press even adopted a new term for the medium, the *photoplay*, to signal a new stage in its development.[2] Significantly, Adolph Zukor and Jesse Lasky, the two producers most prominently associated with American cinema's transformation into a middle-class form, both publicized schemes for collecting films and both independently forged relationships with Columbia University. But if, in retrospect, Hollywood's turn toward literary and dramatic storytelling forms and courting Broadway stars seems a natural part of this transformation, the accompanying models of the film collection and film school look as incidental to us as the passing term *photoplay*.

The Columbia film program is so closely tied to the specifics of the changes in Hollywood in 1914–15 that it seems unlikely the program could have existed even a year earlier or that it would have looked at all similar if it had been started just a few years later. Columbia established screenwriting courses and a script collection, in part, as an offshoot of the film industry's adoption of the script as a precise blueprint for the final film. Several factors converged to make the script a central element of the production process by 1914. First, methodically detailed scripts became increasingly important tools for scientifically managed, vertically integrated studios coping with the unwieldy process of making longer and more complex films. Instruction manuals and professional script technicians standardized a script style—the continuity script—complete with descriptions of camera placement, mise-en-scène, and performance. This innovation, often associated with the producer Thomas Ince but used widely, had become standard practice by 1914. A second motivation for Hollywood's increased emphasis on the script was the 1911 Supreme Court ruling on a film adaptation of Lew Wallace's *Ben-Hur*, which, for the first time, made filmmakers liable for copyright infringement. To avoid paying the high fees required to adapt popular literary and stage works, studios began a frenzied search for original stories. The ensuing "scenario fever" produced dozens of how-to books, contests, and privately run screenwriting schools. (The legacy of this culture in which everyone has a screenplay is still with us.) In the rush to find original stories and professional screenwriters, Thomas Ince and Thomas Edison, among other producers, approached college students for scenarios, and the Jesse L. Lasky Feature Play Company began an association with Columbia University that helped launch its film courses.[3]

The alliance between Columbia and the Lasky Company was premised, in part, on a mutual investment in screenwriting. As Sumiko Higashi has shown, Lasky promoted screenwriting over other elements of production in order to advertise his employment of the successful Broadway playwright-brothers William de Mille and Cecil B. DeMille. For a brief time before becoming directors, William and Cecil also endorsed screenwriting as a means of asserting authorship;[4] they aspired to something akin to the contemporaneously successful German *Autorenfilm* (or "author's film") in which famous literary figures allowed their names to be advertised in conjunction with films they had written or that were adapted from their work.

The celebration of the screenwriter as auteur was short-lived, but the relationship between the Lasky Company and Columbia that grew out of the vogue lasted for over a decade. In 1915, William, himself an alumnus of Columbia, helped launch the photoplay courses by offering a scholarship (a trip to the Lasky studios and $350) to the Columbia student who wrote the best scenario. When the Lasky Company produced the winning scenario, *Witchcraft*, written by R. Ralson Reed in October 1916, it proved that Columbia's screenwriting courses could generate original stories in addition to training professional continuity scriptwriters. After the Lasky Company merged with Adolph Zukor's Famous Players to create Famous Players–Lasky (later Paramount) in 1916, the company's screenwriters regularly visited Columbia classes, and, if the writings of Columbia's instructor Frances Taylor Patterson are an accurate indication, the Columbia courses were, in turn, designed to celebrate the films of its benefactor. The textbook Patterson wrote for the course, *Cinema Craftsmanship* (1920), is filled with examples from Famous Players–Lasky films, and in an anthology of exemplary continuity scripts edited by Patterson, two of the three selections are from Famous Players–Lasky films.[5]

Patterson's textbooks strengthened the corporate sponsorship that had been initially established in 1915 by her former teacher and predecessor Victor Oscar Freeburg. After completing his doctoral dissertation at Columbia on Elizabethan drama, Freeburg taught an experimental course in film art using *The Art of the Moving Picture* as his textbook. Freeburg developed a friendship with Vachel Lindsay and the two exchanged letters and ideas.[6] But Freeburg soon redesigned the course to conform to his own interest in dramatic writing. He recognized the opportunity to offer a screenwriting course at a moment when the art of film appeared to be turning into a genre of dramatic writing. As he witnessed the increased importance of the screenplay, Freeburg began to theorize cinema as a temporal art analogous to music. He saw the script functioning like a musical score, containing every visual and narrative element. This image of the script-as-score perfectly matched the emerging vision of the continuity script as blueprint for the feature film. With the Hollywood connections of his dissertation adviser, Brander Matthews, Freeburg quickly attracted industry support from Lasky and William de Mille.

In order to study screenwriting as a part of Columbia's author-centered curriculum, Freeburg and later Patterson developed an early version of auteurism. By the 1920s, both Columbia instructors had yielded auteur status to the director, but in writings of the late 1910s they entertained the possibility that the screenwriter would prevail as the dominant film artist. Patterson taught that, "In art there should always be a single controlling mind and the finished creation must be stamped indelibly with the personality of the maker."[7] Freeburg adapted the Ruskinian model of rereading that was soon to become the basis of Columbia's "Great Books" courses, and he suggested that the recognition of the script's importance lay in repeated viewing. He speculated that the popular celebration of movie stars stemmed from their recurrent appearances on screens while the films themselves vanished after their title left the marquee. Freeburg foresaw a future in which films would be run habitually in homes (like phonographs), and through repetition the structure and art of the writing behind the films could eventually be gleaned.[8]

In support of his own theories and the Lasky/Zukor patronage, Freeburg undertook three initiatives that placed the script at the center of Columbia's film curriculum: he taught courses devoted to the craft of screenwriting, he started a film society for "cinema composers" to see films not available in commercial theaters, and he developed a "photoplay museum" that collected scripts rather than films. But the emphasis on professional training in screenwriting was only the most concrete element of the collaboration between Hollywood and higher education. All of the courses also contained both moral and aesthetic dimensions. And both the professors and the moguls invested the act of collaboration itself with the potential to redefine their respective institutions and industries. The next two sections of this chapter turn to the larger cultural and institutional background from which the Columbia film program emerged, tracing the

FIGURE 2.1 Jack Cohn, vice president of Columbia Pictures, contributes the original script of Robert Riskin and Frank Capra's *Lady for a Day* (1933) to Frances Taylor Patterson for Columbia University's Photoplay Museum.   *(Courtesy of Richard Koszarski)*

circuitous route that allowed Lasky, Zukor, Freeburg, and Patterson to discover the points at which their ambitions intersected.

TRIAL BY FIRE: FILM COLLECTING AS UPWARD MOBILITY

As it would in most collaborations between Hollywood and cultural institutions, the promise of a film collection that could confer new value on old, unprofitable, or even unsafe films was one of the first ideas to be proposed and tested. In the 1910s, every production company and distributor needed some sort of vault for holding negatives and film prints, but the industry as a whole had little beyond a commercial interest in preserving films.[9] Even if companies considered the possibility of saving films, the physical danger posed by storing them—what Noël Burch calls the "bioideological" factor[10]—presented a critical barrier. Not much was known about the proper maintenance of the highly flammable nitrate film stock in use before 1951 (when the Eastman Kodak Company permanently replaced nitrate stock with a safer acetate-based stock). In the absence of solid data about film storage, a panic over film's flammability gave rise to various myths about the dangers of nitrate stock. As part of their quest to bring middle- and even upper-class patrons into movie theaters, Zukor and Lasky took part in this struggle to affix meaning to the precarious act of storing film. Their publicized discussions of film collecting and the courting of Columbia seem motivated by calculated attempts at self-definition and self-promotion more than by a real desire to save films. Or to put it another way, they invoked and manipulated the promise of a film collection as a trope in order to reclassify the film industry—through the tangible example of the film print—as safe, enduring, and respectable.

Zukor and Lasky's purpose was to redirect the public image of film's volatile materiality that, from the beginning, had been exploited by the media. Newspapers frequently printed alarming reports of film fires, and the fear that a nickelodeon could burst into flames was made to reflect badly on that class of patrons who would so willingly enter the crucible. We may never know the exact class makeup of nickelodeon audiences,[11] but the image of nickelodeons as unsafe spaces because they posed a risk of fire, theft, mashing of women, and eyestrain from the flickering images on the screen clearly contributed to the impression that primarily working-class men and women frequented nickelodeons. Noël Burch suggests that the danger and discomfort of the nickelodeon paralleled conditions in factories. Manual laborers were thus more likely to attend films because, compared with the extremity of the factory, "the cinema, with its smoke, its poor ventilation, its uncomfortable seats and the poorly policed atmosphere that was long the norm at every projection point, still seemed a haven of relaxation." The same incommodious conditions that failed to deter the working class, Burch adds, "helped put off a more squeamish middle-class audience."[12]

The picture of the nickelodeon as an unsafe space of social differentiation also contributed to the impression that the film print itself was a dangerous object. A fire at an 1897 Charity Bazaar screening in Paris served as the ur-story of film's precariousness. That screening ended when a projector lamp caused a fire that killed over 125 people, including many wealthy patrons and children, and the disaster proved to be a major setback for the acceptance of the burgeoning film exhibition business in Paris. It ensured that, at least in France, films would remain the province of fairs and amusement parks,[13] and the moral tale of the fire lingered in the cultural memory of Europe and the United States. In Russia, Yuri Tsivian has shown, the Charity Bazaar fire fueled the imagination of audiences who created a romantic folklore around the figure of the brave projectionist hidden behind fire-resistant walls.[14] Even twenty-nine years after the Charity Bazaar fire, the incident continued to loom so heavily that the film historian–industry apologist Terry Ramsaye devoted a chapter of his *A Million and One Nights* (1926) to proving human negligence not film had caused the disaster.

Ramsaye's excursus on the Charity Bazaar fire was intended to dispel the "public and official opinion . . . that motion picture film is a deadly explosive,"[15] and earlier attempts to improve cinema's reputation often made similar gestures toward quelling the fear of fire. The Motion Picture Patents Company, for instance, threatened to enforce fire ordinances in theaters as part of its 1909 campaign to make theaters appear more suitable for middle-class crowds.[16] As the Hollywood studio system began to take hold in the mid-1910s, a series of fires, including one at the Edison studios in West Orange, New Jersey, exacerbated both the public's concern for safety and the film industry's need to allay public anxiety. In 1914 the semitechnical American journal *Motography* started to report regularly on film fires and the related issue of film storage. *Motography*'s writers were unusually attuned to the dangers of film storage because the journal was published out of Chicago, a central hub for film distributors and a common location for the temporary storage of prints. The *Motography* articles, however, demonstrate little real knowledge of the chemistry of film preservation, and a brief detour into the journal's pages reveals how the idea of film storage and the more active process of collecting could function as cultural tropes at the service of class and, during World War I, nationalist assertions. In this context, we can see why Jesse Lasky decided to publicize the creation of his film vault in *Motography* shortly before joining forces with Columbia.

In a front-page story in 1915, "The Alleged Relation Between Films and Fires," *Motography*'s reporter indignantly disputed the suggestion that nitrate film stock had caused a train car to explode in Chicago. According to the article's analysis, the exaggerated accounts of this accident had little factual basis and were, instead, indicative of the press's general antifilm bias. The reporter tried to shift the terms of the antifilm bias and suggested that the true cause of most film fires was not the improper storage conditions of nitrate film stock but the accumulation of rubbish in the vaults of "lower-class" companies. These allegations were supported with the melodramatic (and false) statement that nitrate film is no more dangerous than "a woman's comb or a celluloid paper knife." And to really make the claims of film's dangerousness seem ridiculous, the article added: "We are expecting the editorial suggestion now in some enterprising newspaper that reels of film be used as bombs in the European War."[17]

Ironically, the signification of film fires and film prints would change so dramatically during World War I that *Motography* itself was led to make exactly this claim. From the war's inception, *Motography* drew strong connections between film collecting and nationalism. A few months after the publication of the article discussed above, another front-page story in *Motography* called for a British film collection to document the war and thus preserve usable fragments of history. The author of this article worried about rumors that a German collection had already been formed and insisted that the flammability of film was a negligible concern when weighed against the potential nationalist uses of the collection, or, as the reporter put it, "the opportunity to imbue future sons of England with a proper patriotism."[18] Spurred on by the threat of German competition and influenced by the knowledge of film's impermanence, this article replaced the popular vision of a complete, historical collection, such as the one D. W. Griffith envisioned, with one based on selective uses of the past.

After the United States entered World War I, *Motography* became concerned with containing the circulation of film stock in addition to the images printed on it. The turning point here was the U.S. government's Bureau of Explosives imposing specifications on the containers used to ship film prints.[19] Once film stock entered the purview of the government—and the Bureau of Explosives no less—a minor panic ensued. *Motography* quickly ran an article warning exhibitors not to sell damaged film lest it fall into enemy hands and be used to make explosives. The journal offered this dubious proof:

[A film industry official announced that] information had come to him which tended to prove that Germany and her allies had secret agents in this country who were attempting to corner the market of disused and mutilated films which they were using for the manufacture of high explosives.[20]

Motography deployed the collection-trope, as Vachel Lindsay had, to draw class and national distinctions. In comparison to *Motography*'s discussions of collecting, D. W. Griffith's or Vachel Lindsay's musings seem all but disconnected from a concern for the materiality of film. Zukor's and Lasky's discussions of film collecting, however, and their collaboration with Columbia University were constructed in dialogue with the discourse of film as a material object. Their imagined collections must be seen as in-

BUREAU OF EXPLOSIVES

OFFICE OF THE CHIEF INSPECTOR
UNDERWOOD BUILDING
30 VESEY STREET

New York City, December 21, 1914.

B. E. SPECIAL BULLETIN NO. 1.

MOVING PICTURE FILMS IN SMOKING CAR.

On the evening of November 24th, 1914, a passenger on a suburban train running out of Chicago, carried into the combination smoking and baggage car a paper wrapped package containing four reels of moving picture films which he had secured from a film company in Chicago for use in an exhibition at a suburban club. This film company did not prevent this highly inflammable product, in criminally careless packing, leaving its premises, although its representative must have had intimate knowledge of the danger and must have been familiar with the safe packing prescribed by the Federal regulations. The film company saved a few cents; the public paid with valuable lives.

The package was placed on the floor of the car between two seats near the center of the car, and about four minutes after the train had left its Chicago terminal a puff of smoke arose from the package, which was instantly followed by a burst of flames. Passengers in front of the flames rushed for the door of the baggage compartment, and in opening it let in a draught that caused a rapid spread of the fire. The train was stopped, but before the passengers could get out of the car **38 persons were badly burned. Two have died as a result of the injuries and one is not expected to live.** The damage to railway equipment amounted to $2,465.00.

FIGURE 2.2 The Bureau of Explosives' special bulletin on the hazards of nitrate film.
(Courtesy of Richard Koszarski)

tertwined in the changing cultural mythology surrounding dangerous canisters of nitrate film stock.

When, for example, *Motography* reported that the Jesse L. Lasky Feature Play Company had announced plans for a new film vault, it drew sharp distinctions between the proposed Lasky vault and "lower-class" vaults filled with rubbish. In contrast to the "lower-class vaults," Lasky's studio had purportedly designed the perfect fireproof incarcerator for film negatives. The plan specified that each negative would have its own cell cooled to 50 degrees Fahrenheit (an exorbitantly expensive precaution in 1914), and each cell would be equipped with an individual ventilation system to prevent the spread of fire. It was advertised, moreover, that the Lasky plan had been partly prepared by the well-known cinematographer Oscar Apfel and had gained the approval of "the prominent insurance man" Morris Rose.[21] In the ongoing *Motography* discussion of film storage, the announcement of the Lasky vault is clearly framed to distinguish Lasky's company from "lower-class" studios by highlighting its concern for public safety. Of course all of these precautions also corroborated the fears that films were indeed dangerous objects that needed to be handled carefully.

The description of the Lasky vault also suggests an interest in preserving films for posterity, another concern directly related to the film industry's mid-1910s struggle for cultural legitimacy. Lasky's announcement might be seen as an attempt to surpass his competitor (and future partner) Adolph Zukor, who just one year earlier had announced his own plan to preserve his company's films. If Lasky's plan was impractical, the news story that a professor at Columbia University would collect every film produced by Adolph Zukor's company, Famous Players in Famous Plays, seems merely a public relations ploy. Yet the statement indicates the attraction a film collection held for both a film producer and a university at pivotal moments in their respective histories.

A 1913 article on Zukor's company in the *Moving Picture World* reported that Famous Players, well known as the first production unit devoted entirely to making feature films, was ready to embark on its mission "to impress educated people." The firm had assembled a stock company of popular stage actors, planned to increase its output, and aspired to a narrative clarity that would no longer depend on explanatory intertitles. These are the typical markers of a company trying to define itself as "high-class." But the reporter added an unusual detail:

> Brander Matthews, of Columbia College, has made an offer to the Famous Players Company to preserve in his private collection a copy of every film made by the company and to make suitable provision for the conveyance of these at his death to some organization which will guarantee their care. The offer has been accepted absolutely. That this fact will be the strongest inducement to all the players of the American stage to impel them to consent to portraying their work for the screen needs no saying.[22]

There is no evidence that the agreement progressed beyond this announcement or that Matthews or Zukor had any real intention of improving the storage conditions of Famous Players' films. Any precautions that

Zukor might have taken had little effect since one building of the Famous Players studio burned to the ground two years later in a nitrate fire.[23]

Why then would the promise of a collection have been so appealing? And how did Columbia, Lasky, and Zukor get from these short notices in trade papers to their collaborative screenwriting courses and script collection?

It is easy to imagine the attraction of Zukor and Broadway performers to the idea of a permanent film collection and the status conferred by the venerable names of Columbia University and the eminent scholar–drama critic Brander Matthews. According to Zukor's son Eugene, "In order to give himself validity, [Zukor] was always looking for [someone of stature] to put a stamp on it and say 'This man is on the right track. He's going to use the screen for a purpose beyond anyone's conception. He's going to take the library shelves and open them up visually.' "[24] But the suggestion of a collection interested Matthews and his Columbia colleagues as well. The introduction of film into the Columbia curriculum and the accompanying creation of the "photoplay museum" present a very different set of motivations from the industry's cultivation of the same ideas. If Zukor and Lasky welcomed the immediate boost in social status promised by their Ivy League affiliation, they were careful not to let it slip out in the trade papers that Columbia taught film through its adult education divisions or that the classes were comprised, in part, of immigrants, housewives, and, by correspondence, at least one prison inmate.[25] As these examples begin to suggest, Columbia taught film and collected scripts (rather than films) in part to reach out to the same public that Zukor and Lasky were trying to leave behind.

GREAT FILMS AND THE MAKING OF AMERICANS

Although Victor Oscar Freeburg emerged as an important film theorist in his own right, his initial film courses were, in many ways, the result of an educational project inherited from his dissertation adviser, Brander Matthews. And Matthews's dialogue with Zukor one year before Columbia started to teach film fits a pattern of intellectual and pedagogical ambition. At Columbia, Matthews lectured on a wide range of literature, history, and politics, which he used as springboards to discuss morality, national identity, and the human condition. As Gerald Graff characterizes him, Matthews was a second-generation American generalist academic — opposed to philological research and academic specialization — who served as a link between nineteenth-century generalists like Harvard's Charles Eliot Norton and the post–World War I Great Books curriculum at Columbia initiated by John Erskine (another of Matthews's students). With these other influential teachers, Matthews considered American culture inferior to British tradition and modern literature less important than its classical antecedents. But unlike Norton or Erskine, Matthews made use of the art of his own country and time, even if he considered it merely the seeds of a national literature. In his first year at Columbia, in 1891, Matthews offered groundbreaking courses on American literature, and in 1896 he published one of the first textbooks on the subject. Matthews's enthusiasm ran to drama as well as literature, and he persuaded Columbia's extension school to include drama classes in its offerings. The drama program eventually developed into the School of Dramatic Arts housed in Brander Matthews Hall.[26] Nothing may have come of Matthews's flirtation with the idea of starting a film collection, but his successful experiments expanding the scope of Columbia's curriculum paved the way for his advisee, Freeburg, to teach Columbia's first film course and start the "photoplay museum" in the extension school the following year. Moreover, Matthews's legacy insured that Columbia's photoplay courses would ultimately be taught in the generalist tradition of civic education in addition to offering the professional skills of screenwriting.

Matthews's enthusiasm for film was indicative of larger institutional changes that enabled Columbia to teach film courses in its extension school when the widespread incorporation of film into American universities was still decades away, if indeed it has ever been achieved. Columbia's film program, like Lindsay's book, placed film in the realm of adult education but to a different end. The Chautauqua model of the traveling lecturer that Lindsay employed was imported from the Oxbridge example of the university's civic responsibility. The British tradition of providing moral tutelage to the community outside the hallowed walls through public lectures on an Arnoldian canon dominated American adult education until the turn of the nineteenth century. Between the 1870s and around 1915, however, many American universities consciously refashioned themselves after the German model of the research institution oriented toward "the idea that knowledge has a social function."[27] One characteristic of this transitional period was that rural universities with government land-grants and urban universities situated in large ethnically diverse communities began to refocus their adult education curricula to better serve the practical as well as the moral needs of their surrounding populations. The University of Wisconsin—to use the benchmark land-grant university as an example—collaborated with state and local governments to develop a far-reaching extension program, offering scientific agricultural training courses.[28] The German model of the university found strong supporters at Columbia too. During Seth Low's presidency in the 1890s, Thomas Bender has shown, "the ideal of the German university was fused with the tradition of civic learning and responsibility."[29]

By the 1900s, however, the function of a Columbia University education was less certain than ever, and its adult education programs were riven by the intense factionalism that pulled the university as a whole between the poles of professional graduate training and liberal undergraduate instruction. These two roles of the university may seem entirely compatible today, but during the late nineteenth and early twentieth centuries the restive debates about the education system reached heated moments that, more than once, resulted in the resignation of prominent Columbia faculty members. Toward the end of this period, Thorstein Veblen concluded that the "holding together of these two disparate schools [graduate and undergraduate] is at best a freak of aimless survival."[30] At an extreme moment in the debate in 1905, Columbia's president Nicholas Murray Butler announced a plan, which was eventually rejected, to reduce undergraduate requirements at Columbia to two years before students could matriculate into a professional or academic graduate program. When in the thick of these debates Columbia began to offer screenwriting courses through its adult education school, that curriculum also evinced the friction of the university.[31]

Many of the schools that led the transformation of adult education—including Columbia and Wisconsin—also galvanized both the use of film in the classroom and noncommercial film collecting. By 1914, for example, sufficient demand for educational films existed for the University of Wisconsin to operate a circulating library that provided films to other institutions. The universities of Missouri and Minnesota, Yale, and the Naval Academy at Annapolis maintained smaller film collections, and three years later a report delivered at the third annual convention of the National University Extension Association noted that "seven universities owned a respectable number of films."[32] Many more state university film collections were fed with government-produced documentaries after World War I, and by 1923 at least twenty-two technical colleges and state universities operated film libraries, with Wisconsin remaining one of the largest.[33] These libraries consisted largely of films designed specifically for classroom use. The schools employed films as visual aids to popularize academic subjects, and the film libraries accumulated rather than actively collected film.[34]

When the University of Wisconsin was busy distributing film prints in 1914, Columbia's literature, economics, science, history, and psychology classes were just starting to show films on the screen in the journalism department.[35] The following year, however, the new film courses enlisted the same screen to teach film as art rather than as illustrations of other subjects. Columbia's faculty showed commercial, narrative films, and the new focus on film education included production skills, aesthetics, and film history. Columbia's faculty was the first to teach film as a unique medium and, as a result, Columbia's program is more directly relevant to the genealogy of university film education than the state universities that showed films as part of a Progressive education movement that promoted visual instruction.

Columbia's radical curricular invention grew out of the enthusiasm and vision of Brander Matthews and Victor Freeburg and the financial support of Jesse Lasky and Adolph Zukor. But in the 1920s, the film courses were brought under the umbrella of Columbia's Great Books program and were subsumed by the transformation of the institution. In addition to a philosophical debate among Columbia's leaders (couched in terms of the English/German dichotomy) about how to best serve their students and the larger New York base, Columbia's academic community struggled with other pertinent changes including increased applications from New York's immigrants, a relatively new location on the outskirts of the city, new commercial interests in universities that fed the growth of professional schools, competition from other private and public educational institutions in New York, and divisive political infighting over the United States' entrance into World War I. Shortly after the war, Columbia's faculty settled on a solution to these competing demands when they instituted what became known as general education. Columbia adopted the famous Great Books curriculum devoted to making undergraduates into "intelligent citizen[s] of the world"[36] through exposure to the canon of Western literature, and the university implemented selective admission policies implicitly designed to reduce the enrollment of (primarily Jewish) immigrants.[37]

This is not the place to rehearse the complex history of general education, and, in any case, film education at Columbia doesn't fit smoothly into that history. Film entered Columbia's curriculum as part of the changes that led to the dominance of general education, but it entered through the overlooked adult education schools, where many of the new curricular changes were tested.

As Columbia redefined its mission to accommodate its changing constituency, the university frequently used its adult education school as "an experiment station" for new programs. The extension divisions acted as a buffer for Columbia's bifurcated mission: to train both professionals and moral citizens. The burden of contradictions that the extension school was forced to bear were manifested as nominal divisions within its structure. The Extension School proper evolved into an exaggerated version of the German university and focused exclusively on inculcating specialized, professional skills in its students. A new division founded in 1913, the Institute of Arts and Sciences, took over the inheritance of the English model and offered "civilizing" public lectures on "the best that has been thought and said" (the Arnoldian dictum that appears in most literature put out by the institute). A third division, Home Study, consciously modeled itself on the Chautauqua programs and offered correspondence courses to as broad a public as possible (keeping that public at bay even as the university appeared to be reaching out to a wider community).[38] These divisions were always sharper in policy than in practice, however, and, as the film program demonstrates, there was significant overlap in course offerings and educational intentions.

At different times, film courses were offered as part of all three divisions and fulfilled several competing missions of the university. As the affiliation with Lasky's and Zukor's screenwriting departments demonstrated, one goal of the photoplay courses was to actively aid in the professionalization of screenwriting. This obviously helped move Columbia in the direction of providing vocational skills, and it encouraged the involvement of and funding from major corporations, and Columbia's administrators continually pushed for greater offerings in film production. During World War I, Columbia housed one of two motion picture training divisions of the Army Signal Corps,[39] and in the 1920s Columbia tried unsuccessfully to offer an expanded range of film production skills. In 1923 the extension school got as far as advertising a new course, "Motion Picture Production," which never met. President Butler tried once more to build a film production program in 1926 when he wrote to the head of the Motion Picture Producers and Distributors of America, Will Hays, asking for funds to start a technical film school. But, again, no course offerings resulted from this overture.[40]

Although the Columbia film courses continued to focus on screenwriting skills through the 1930s, they were increasingly influenced by the university's move toward general education in the 1920s. The film courses were quickly identified as part of the effort to "civilize" and "Americanize" the increasing number of immigrants and children of immigrants in the adult education classes. To be sure, this was the result of the Columbia administration's ambivalence toward its increasing number of Jewish applicants after new subway lines linked Brooklyn to Morningside Heights. The university actively and successfully reduced the number of Jewish students admitted to the college, but for economic reasons as well as out of civic duty they didn't want to lose those students either. The Institute of Arts and Sciences actively competed with other immigrant-targeted adult education programs in New York including the New School for Social Research, the People's Institute in Brooklyn, the Brooklyn Institute of Arts and Sciences, and the League for Political Education.[41] As William Uricchio and Roberta Pearson have shown, the People's Institute and other educational institutions screened selected films as "counterattractions" both to instill "common values" and "fill workers' leisure hours with less harmful pursuits."[42] Under the influence of general education, Columbia's film courses began to address and compete for the same working-class, immigrant populations. But Columbia sought to cultivate techniques of film spectatorship and standards of film literacy, as its Great Books courses cultivated reading skills, rather than exhibiting films to create alternative spaces for the working class to spend its new leisure time.[43]

Tellingly, the ill-fated 1923 "Motion Picture Production" course would have been offered through the Institute of Arts and Sciences, the non-credit, "civilizing" arm of the adult education program. The institute's director, James Egbert, promoted the film course because, as he put it, "motion pictures are destined to play an important part as a civilizing influence on the modern world."[44] Reinforcing Egbert's position, the course brochure took every opportunity to employ the rhetoric of general education. It advertised that in addition to teaching technical skills, the production course would have covered "pictorial values" (i.e., aesthetics) and "moving picture history." "It is also of value," the brochure added, "as part of a general education."[45] Starting in 1920, Frances Taylor Patterson began to describe the redefined film courses in similar terms. In her class textbook, Patterson acknowledged that the "dual purpose" of the photoplay courses was to provide a "shortcut" for prospective screenwriters and to cultivate the taste of film viewers. Both projects, she hoped, would improve the quality of film production. Twisting Matthew Arnold's famous phrase, Patterson announced that the photoplay courses were intended to "[bring] the public at large to a more real appreciation of the best in photoplays and by that appreciation to demand the best that can be attained by producers." In a promotional article, Patterson insisted that film education had become "a necessary part of liberal education." "One of the ideals of the University," she mimicked the general education party line, "is to bring general knowledge within the reach of the many rather than special knowledge to the few." [46] And in other articles and interviews, Patterson took advantage of every opportunity to list the range of nationalities, professions, and social classes represented in the photoplay courses. She described one class as comprising "as diverse a group of people, I venture to say, as ever gathered together in a common interest."[47]

If the photoplay courses were eventually enlisted as part of general education, they continually demonstrated the tensions of the divided university. The advertisement for Freeburg's classes in the 1916–17 extension catalog highlighted the professional training and industry involvement so important to Columbia's adult education school. The catalog stressed instruction in "technically correct scenarios" and visits to "first-class motion picture companies" (we can assume this included the recently formed Famous Players–Lasky).[48] Yet at the same time, Freeburg's articles and book, *The Art of Photoplay Making* (1918), showed that he thought of the photoplay courses as following in the generalist tradition of moral education. As Freeburg makes clear, his intention was to carve a new "public" out of the filmgoing "crowd," and the distinction here is important. Freeburg argued that in movie theaters the influence of the crowd, the sheer numbers of people, transformed individual psychology: "The close contact is spiritual as well as physical." Crowds, as Freeburg describes them, are fleeting and attracted to "spectacle." Publics, on the other hand, are comprised of individuals with cultivated responses to works of art: "the public is permanent in its existence. Its groups come into contact, though not simultaneously, views are exchanged, discussions are carried on, letters are written, until as a result of all this reflection a deliberate expression is arrived at. This deliberate expression is called public opinion."[49] Vachel Lindsay, by contrast, wanted public opinion returned to the collective and natural will of "the people." Freeburg wanted to preserve a timeless cultivated public opinion from the sway of the broadening crowd.

Freeburg's theory tapped into popular discussions of crowd psychology that included works by Gustave Le Bon, Sigmund Freud, and John Dewey, among others. At around the same time, several other theorists published evaluations of film through the lens of crowd psychology, and the interest in crowd psychology assumed increased importance as the middle class was drawn into the movie theater. One 1915 monograph on cinema by a screenwriter named William Morgan Hannon, for example, argued that in the movie theater even intellectuals exhibited the "primitive" demands of the crowd.[50]

Freeburg's theoretical speculations, however, are most closely connected to Columbia's version of the Great Book philosophy. John Erskine first articulated this philosophy in a course proposal in 1917, and Erskine's writing and institutional power had a great impact on Freeburg, Patterson, and the film courses. As literary historian Joan Shelly Rubin has observed, Erskine's Great Books program "encompassed self-transcendence as well as greater individualism." Synthesizing the pragmatism of William James and John Dewey with the Arnoldian bent of his mentor, George Woodberry, Erskine called on students to "get [themselves] a comfortable chair and a good light—and have confidence in [their] own mind," on the one hand, and to " 'free [them]selves from the prison of egotism' and take part 'in the complete citizenship of mankind,' " on the other.[51] These seemingly contradictory exhortations can be seen as a unified rejection of academic specialization and all the ideological weight that entailed.

The Great Books program guided students to cultivate reading skills and recognize the spiritual value of great literature that spanned history and nations. Its focus on the act of reading and direct engagement with primary texts reinforced the idea of a common and timeless human experience rooted in the literature of the Western canon. In an oft-cited criticism of Erskine's plan, Lionel Trilling considered its return to spiritual education and a fixed curriculum, "a fundamental criticism of American democratic education."[52] The Great Books curriculum sought to fix the canon just as the field of authors and readers/interpreters was widening. Erskine explicitly linked his Great Books proposal to his ambition to acculturate the increasing number of immigrants and ethnic students at Columbia, an ambition that links Erskine as well as Freeburg and Patterson to the Progressive projects of Americanization.[53]

The Great Books tradition, as mediated through Columbia University, would have a long and direct influence on the moral character of Hollywood, especially as Hollywood attempted to align itself with the values of middle-class America. Freeburg and Patterson, for example, did not limit themselves to teaching screenwriting and film appreciation. They both served as members of the National Board of Review, evaluating the moral content of films. As late as 1939, Erskine could only grudgingly bring himself to applaud the films of his college friend William de Mille. That same year, however, Erskine went to Hollywood himself for six weeks to host a radio show, and he returned several times in the 1940s to write about the film industry, to discuss turning his own novels written in the 1920s into films, and, some speculated, to be considered as a replacement for Will Hays as head of Hollywood's moral center, the Motion Picture Producers and Distributors of America. In the late 1930s, Erskine's most famous student, Mortimer Adler, helped divert efforts to condemn film as a cause of criminal behavior, a corrupter of children, and a generally amoral industry. After starting the Great Books program at the University of

Chicago, Adler began working with Hays and the director of the Production Code Administration, Joseph Breen, as an adviser and ghostwriter. Through his own publications and lectures, Adler functioned as an official public advocate for film as a moral, aesthetic object.[54] Under the mandate of general education, Freeburg, Patterson, Erskine, and Adler all intervened in discussions of the film industry to shape public opinion.

The initial application of the Great Books philosophy to film, however, relied on a less overtly prescribed method of reading film. For both Freeburg and Erskine, the cultivated individual's test of greatness was repeated study of primary texts, and, as we saw earlier, Freeburg looked forward to the day when films like phonographs would be appreciated in homes, a statement that also bears echoes of Erskine's armchair reader. To facilitate repeated study and to carve a cultivated public out of the crowd, Freeburg ran his film club and started a "photoplay museum" in addition to offering courses. These methods of removing film from the movie theater encouraged an experience of film unmediated by either expert knowledge or the pull of the crowd. It required only the self-reliance of the reader/viewer placed directly before the work of art. The film school, film club, and film museum thus became testing grounds in which the individual and the work of art reciprocally gave each other value. But, again, this was far from Lindsay's model of a film institution, and the comparison is instructive. Lindsay too sought a venue that would provide unmediated access to films as works of art, harnessing a new popular medium of expression for the cause of a renewed representative democracy. In Lindsay's ideal film museum, spectators would have been encouraged to converse with each other and arrive at an interpretation that reflected the views of the people rather than the experts. The Columbia film museum, on the other hand, came out of the tradition of general education and backed the nineteenth-century model of the civilizing institution in which the individual came to realize the timeless moral lessons embodied in works of art.

CONCLUSION

Sometimes the specifics of Columbia's film program seem opaquely embroiled in long-forgotten debates. We no longer fear the flammability of film, and Hollywood has since successfully shed its working-class connotations. At the same time, however, these interlocking histories add up to an image of film education that set the stage for intellectual and institutional frictions that have continued to keep Hollywood and American universities at arms length. At Columbia, film served as an emblematic element of popular culture. Faculty and administrators included film in university curricula as part of larger plans to redefine the social function of American universities adapting to the growing ethnic diversity of students and the mounting consumer culture. American universities may now depend on corporate partnerships, ethnic diversity among students, and preprofessional curricula. But many of the factors that have continued to make film at once desirable and awkward for universities—its popular appeal, its promise of making academic work relevant beyond specialized circles, and its potential to attract corporate involvement in higher education—also drove and plagued early attempts to invent film education.

Nevertheless, Columbia's film program had a direct influence on the design of university film programs. The idea that a university film program could aid in the professionalization and hierarchical control of filmmaking labor became (as we will see in the next chapters) the primary motivation for Lasky, Zukor, and other Hollywood producers to promote film programs at Harvard and the University of Southern California in the late 1920s. And in the mid-1930s, the Museum of Modern Art's Film Library took over Columbia's established film program to define its own influential model for film education. In 1938, Columbia's Extension School established a Division of Film Study in collaboration with MoMA's Film Library. More than two decades after the first Columbia film courses, the focus on scripts over films seemed archaic. But the larger objectives of the film program—to reach out to the undifferentiated crowd and transform them into a cultivated public—remained at least partly intact.[55] MoMA's staff also shared the Columbia faculty's desire to use film to define a national public. By the late 1930s a number of urban universities offered both technical training in filmmaking skills and film appreciation courses, though film was by no means common to American university curricula. Columbia's administrators, however, envisioned its 1938 collaboration with MoMA as a prototype that would follow in both the generalist and specialist traditions.

While the courses were still offered through the adult education division, film education and its relation to the film collection were reconceived with a double mission, and Columbia offered two very different film courses. One course, "Motion Picture Parade," continued the task of using film to reach out to a diverse public beyond the ivy walls. The director of Columbia's Division of Film Study, Russell Potter, invoked the "universal popular appeal" of film, and he saw the return of film education indebted to the establishment of MoMA's "entirely disinterested" collection.[56] This Populist rhetoric of unmediated mass exposure to film was also emphasized in the brochures, which minimized the importance of the lectures presented before each film. "These discussions will be definitely popular, rather than academic," the brochure assured potential students, " . . . [and] always the emphasis will be, not on talk, but on the movies!"[57] In the Great Books tradition, students were promised direct access to selected important texts. Also in the Great Books tradition, once audiences were corralled into the hall, they were exposed both to didactic lectures on how to read a film and to lectures which used film as a jumping off point to discuss morality and politics in the generalist mode. During the second semester of the course, for instance, MoMA's film curator Iris Barry used one class lecture to critique the "great man" theory of history as she saw it evidenced in biographical films and to make a plea for more films that represented the quotidian experience of the past.[58]

Columbia and MoMA's second course, "Fine Arts Em1-Em2," was also offered through the extension school, but it was taught in a small room in MoMA's Film Library offices rather than in a large lecture hall at Columbia. In contrast to "Motion Picture Parade," "Em1-Em2" was designed to train experts in film technique, history, and aesthetics. Potter qualified his claim that MoMA's film collection was "entirely disinterested" with the assertion that it had also been "intelligently directed." Invoking the role of specialists in the creation of the Film Library, Potter saw the second course as a sort of backroom in which community leaders could be exposed to advanced discussions and trained as film experts.[59] The "handpicked" group of future film specialists included two film critics; the chair of the Wesleyan University Fine Arts Department; the executive head of the Legion of Decency, Father McClafferty; a South American government official, Dr. Hermogenes Garavito of Columbia; a "rich girl"; and several students from the degree-granting undergraduate schools of Columbia University, New York University, and City College. The course also included a film projectionist, who was there as an ad hoc sociologist to share his "varied experiences with the motion picture public."[60] Where film education had, in the past, been confined to moral guidance and vocational training and it had remained outside the province of the university proper, Potter assured us that the Columbia University undergraduate in the class was given credit toward his degree. One mission of the film school and collection remained the moral and political education of a mass public through controlled exposure to a medium of popular culture. But MoMA assumed a second educational mandate: to train a class of film experts. The next chapter turns to the struggle to identify who would be included in the class of film experts.

3

MANDARINS AND MARXISTS
HARVARD AND THE RISE OF FILM EXPERTS

A class of experts is inevitably so removed from common interests as to become a class with private interests and private knowledge, which in social
matters is not knowledge at all.
— John Dewey, *The Public and Its Problems* (1927)

We pin our hopes on the sporting public.
  Make no bones about it, we have our eye on those huge concrete pans,
filled with 15,000 men and women of every variety of class and physiognomy,
the fairest and shrewdest audience in the world. . . . The demoralization of
our theatre audiences springs from the fact that neither theatre nor audience
has any idea what is supposed to go on there. When people in sporting estab-
lishments buy their tickets they know exactly what is going to take place.
— Bertolt Brecht, "Emphasis on Sport" (1926)

The producers are experts.
— Theodor Adorno and Max Horkheimer, *The Dialectic of Enlightenment* (1944)

A LTHOUGH FILM INDUSTRY leaders since Edison had paid lip service to
placing films in universities, it is surprising that Hollywood producers and Columbia University faculty members found enough
common ground to put a plan into practice, especially as early as 1915.
After the establishment of the Columbia program, both movie producers
and Ivy League professors continued to hold on to the hope that a university film school and film collection could help them influence the successful film industry, even if the two groups continued to have different
motives. More than a decade passed before Jesse Lasky and Adolph Zukor
embarked on another collaboration with a university. When they did, they
joined a larger group of moguls who looked to Harvard University to help
find some method of postponing the impending unionization of
Hollywood talent and stabilizing an industry on the verge of new expansion and conglomeration. In the late 1920s, the Hollywood moguls were
on the verge of the transition to sound; they were encountering increased
resistance in international markets; and they were attracting new Wall

Street investors. The moguls hoped Harvard's business school and art history department would be able to roll film art and commerce into a neat and manageable package that could be useful on all three emerging fronts. The Harvard professors, for their part, hoped to redefine their fields and their institution through the inclusion of film. As it had at Columbia, the inclusion of film promised to redefine the class and ethnic makeup of the university, although at Harvard the background of the professors and not the students was at stake. In the end, we will see, the producers decided to take the lessons of their Harvard experiment back to California. They started their own institution of film art, the Academy of Motion Picture Arts and Sciences, and they teamed up with the University of Southern California, which was closer to home. But the brief Harvard film collaboration created a generation of film lovers among Harvard's students, and this film generation went on to find a permanent place for film in American museums, universities, and, eventually, wartime government agencies.

This chapter examines two documents in order to explain how a few isolated Hollywood/university projects in the 1910s and 1920s led to full-scale institutions of film art in the 1930s. One document is a 1927 proposal to start a film division within Harvard University's Fogg Art Museum. The other is an outline for a film library and film school composed by the Marxist critic Harry Alan Potamkin and published in the Harvard-affiliated journal *Hound and Horn* in 1933. Taken together, these two documents mark a break in the intellectual history of museums' and universities' courtship of Hollywood. D. W. Griffith, Vachel Lindsay, and the Columbia film faculty, however dubious their intentions may have been, envisioned exoteric film libraries, film museums, and film schools that would have allowed mass publics to have a hand in defining canons of film. Harvard's and Potamkin's plans, in contrast, were explicitly designed to proffer selective taxonomies of film rooted in the ideologically charged methodologies of, respectively, elite art connoisseurs and Marxist cultural critics. The class positions of the planners may have been different, but they shared a desire to bring film into the province of experts rather than a universal or even a narrowly defined public.

Taken individually, the two documents chart a passage in the politics of film art. As we will see, a direct lineage can be traced from the Fogg agreement to the Potamkin proposal and eventually to the Academy of Motion Picture Arts and Sciences, the Academy Awards, and the Museum of Modern Art's Film Library. But the role envisioned for the film expert changed at each stage. This chapter argues that the designs of these various film institutions were tied to larger attempts to redefine class politics in America. Harvard's development of an elite film appreciation, for example, aided its art department's concurrent overthrowing of a regime of connoisseurship based on birthright with one dependent on acquiring the appropriate evaluative skills, and therefore more inclusive. Potamkin, in contrast, designed a carefully organized Marxist film library intended to unravel the hidden structures of the film industry. With Brechtian logic (as suggested in the epigraph), Potamkin saw the film library and the film school as a necessary step in the creation of a classless audience of experts analogous to sports fans. Both of these extreme possibilities were, in turn, modified at the Museum of Modern Art and the Academy of Motion Picture Arts and Sciences through negotiations with commercial, government, and nonprofit organizations. The progression from the Fogg plan to the Potamkin plan reveals how expert knowledge and class politics—precisely the factors that had been submerged in earlier discussions—came to the foreground of the struggle to place film in the hands of American cultural institutions.

HOLLYWOOD'S COLLECTION; OR, MIGHT THE ACADEMY AWARDS HAVE BEEN HELD AT HARVARD?

The plan for the Harvard Film Library[1] developed out of a course on film being taught at Harvard's Graduate School of Business Administration. The Business School's classes were taught using the case study method developed for law school curricula, and in 1927 Harvard alumnus–film producer Joseph Kennedy (father of John F. Kennedy) was asked to invite Hollywood leaders to speak about the different phases of their industry: financing, distribution, advertising, and so on. After hearing about the Business School course, a university administrator, James Seymour, suggested to the associate director of the Fogg Museum, Paul Sachs, that the Fogg might use the opportunity to add some films to its holdings. Sachs discussed the idea with enthusiastic members of the art history department and, using Will Hays and Kennedy as liaisons to Hollywood, Sachs quickly negotiated an agreement for the acquisition of films.[2] The project never moved beyond the drafting of what I will call the Harvard Film Library Agreement, but the Fogg set a precedent for cooperation between the film industry and private institutions that proved influential in the establishment of later film organizations, most directly the Academy of Motion Picture Arts and Sciences and the Museum of Modern Art.

As they had in the creation of the Columbia program, the professors and moguls had different designs on the Harvard project. But the film library was not an entirely empty or malleable concept. The Harvard Film

Library Agreement resulted from collaboration, and it is the nature of collaboration for each participant to contribute and want something different. The Harvard Film Library Agreement can be read as a palimpsest with marks left both by Hollywood producers and by the faculty of Harvard's Department of Fine Arts. In search of what each wanted from a film collection, let's look at the agreement from the film industry's perspective first, because it provides an enlightening comparison with Columbia's courses and collection.

The Harvard course was the first Hollywood-supported university endeavor in America since the Columbia program, and both projects involved several of the same representatives from the film industry, including Lasky, Zukor, and DeMille. Again, Hollywood leaders imagined that a university film program could be used to control the public perception of film and to solidify the hierarchy of labor relations in Hollywood. That is, the university was once again part of an effort to professionalize the film industry. In the interim between the Columbia and Harvard film courses and proposed collections, however, the nature of film as a commodity had changed and so had the management needs of Hollywood moguls.

On the surface, the Film Library Agreement was simply a method of obtaining a Harvard endorsement for films to extend the length of their profit-producing lives. In contrast to discussions of morality and authorship that permeated the Columbia courses and photoplay museum, financial concerns remained on the surface throughout the discussion of the Harvard Film Library. The Harvard Business School's courses were one indication that the film industry was evolving from an entrepreneurial field to a mature business. In Kennedy's opening remarks, for example, he insisted that the development of "depreciation tables" and "estimates of residual values" were the key to transforming movies into stable investments. Kennedy complained more than once about the brief theatrical runs of individual films, warning at one point:

> In our business, quick sales are necessary. You can never put your product on the shelf. It will not keep. Its value is perishable in the sense that it is worth more when it is first released than it will be six months later. Hence the struggle is to get playing time—dates. You are always running a race with the calendar. The minute the picture plays in a given territory, it looses value there and your opportunity is gone. (*The Story of the Film*, 17)

From this fear of the shelf as a mark of expiration it was a small leap to the following justification for a film library, which, it was suggested, possessed the power to endow films with aesthetic and commercial value even as they sat still:

> [Film's] weakness, no less obvious, is its transiency. Where nothing stands still, nothing endures. The careers of the motion picture actors are generally brief; those of the majority of plays almost ephemeral. The circulation of a popular picture is immediate and world-wide. Twenty million people may witness it in a year. But this vast diffusion is paid for by a corresponding brevity. The scenario writer and the director see his finest work flash upon the screen and fade away, perhaps into oblivion; whereas some book, of which a bare handful of copies was sold while the author lived, may be read and treasured a thousand years afterward.
>
> To prolong this abbreviated life, to rescue and preserve the best of these too perishable creations, some almost incredibly rich in significant beauty, is the avowed purpose of the Harvard film library. (*The Story of the Film,* vi–vii)

The overstatement here might undermine the analogy: that the "finest work" of filmmakers enjoyed by millions should be preserved as long as "some book" that only a handful of people cared about a thousand years ago. But reading the two passages together the point is clear: a film library appeared to be the perfect meeting of commerce and art. The recognition of aesthetic and preservation value had the potential, as a by-product, to increase and extend commercial value.

Beneath this predictable discourse of art and legitimation, however, structural changes in the film industry and at Harvard subtended the desire for a film collection. The alliance between Hollywood and higher education that resulted in the Harvard course coincided with a nodal point in the development of the film industry, as had the Columbia courses. In 1927 the major movie studios sat on the brink of the sound revolution, in the middle of a rapid expansion into international markets, and toward the end of a decade of labor disputes. Kennedy had only moved from Wall Street to Hollywood a year earlier, but he had already positioned himself at the center of the complex consolidation of the Hollywood studios that attended these corporate metamorphoses. In the two years between the Harvard course and the stock market crash, Kennedy moved into top positions at the RKO studios and the Pathé distribution exchange. In those positions he played important roles in both Hollywood's transition to sound and its increased international expansion. Kennedy alluded to his future plans when pressed by a Business School student during the question period: "We are on the eve now of big consolidations . . . ," Kennedy hinted to the crowd of students and faculty. "Ours is an industry that lends itself to consolidation, and they are all contemplating it at the present time."[3] But aside from this one cryptic admission (the context doesn't make it any clearer exactly who "they" are), the economic motivations behind the Harvard film courses and library are only evident when we look more deeply into its institutional context.[4]

From the Business School's perspective, the film course fit smoothly into its case study method. Starting in the 1920s, case studies allowed the Business School's classes to serve as unofficial consultants to many American industries adapting to the demands of a growing consumer culture, a service for which the Business School often benefited financially. In particular, William Leach has shown, "Harvard courted—explicitly—the corporate marketing and merchandising sectors of the economy. Its evolution was intertwined in the 1920s with the development of America's new mass market commercial economy."[5] Kennedy, in particular, intervened in many aspects of film marketing, and he developed a distinct studio style in the process. Kennedy's production company, the appropriately mercantile-sounding Film Booking Office, specialized in low-budget genre pictures targeted to an underserved lower-middle-class audience. On the whole, Kennedy sought to turn filmmaking into a stable business with quantifiable commodities. "Bankers have lately become interested in the business," he explained in his Harvard address, "because now they can get a balance sheet to their liking from [every studio]."[6] At the time he spoke to the Business School, Kennedy's most immediate concerns were the lack of financial expertise among studio accountants and bureaucratic impediments to overseas expansion. He used the course pragmatically as a recruiting forum for students capable, in the long-term, of facilitating the transformation of movie-making into a financially sound business and, in the short term, developing corporate strategies to adapt to unyielding European protectionism (tariffs, quotas, etc.). Kennedy appealed to the Business School's emphasis on marketing and, employing one of Will Hays's many catch phrases, Kennedy explained the importance of the film industry as a "silent salesman" for American products in foreign markets. After a digressive tirade about European quotas, Kennedy launched into his well-placed recruitment speech and called on the students in the audience to study film's effect on international markets as their life's work.[7]

The other speakers performed less comfortably before the academic audience, and their motivations are less obvious than Kennedy's move to solicit trained business school personnel and help usher in a corporate era in the movie business. The various Hollywood leaders may have agreed to participate in the course because they were flattered by the attention from Harvard or content to be doing a favor for the well-connected Kennedy. But the other moguls' most immediate interest was the unionization of film talent. They used the opportunity to reinforce Kennedy's explicit call for professionalization and to test out the educational and managerial goals of the Academy of Motion Picture Arts and Sciences. The Academy was legally incorporated only one week after the last Harvard film lecture, but it had been in the works for at least six months. Several of the participants in the Harvard lecture series were official founders of the Academy (DeMille, Lasky, Harry Warner, and Milton Sills), and others benefited directly from the Academy's activities. On closer inspection it becomes clear that the collaborative educational effort in Cambridge was linked to management concerns back in Los Angeles.

Ostensibly founded "to take aggressive action in meeting outside attacks that are unjust," to "promote harmony and solidarity among the membership," and a host of other vague, lofty goals,[8] the Academy managed and effectively postponed the impending unionization of Hollywood actors, writers, and directors. Stagehands, electricians, and other crewmembers had been unionized several months earlier in the Studio Basic Agreement.[9] The Academy's members arbitrated labor contracts, but that was only the most direct manifestation of their management role. In order to defer the unionization of the Hollywood workforce, the Academy took several steps to define film industry jobs as skilled artistry rather than labor. The ultimate goal of the Academy was to oversee the Hollywood workforce from training to retirement, and the most public and disarming sign of this process was the establishment of the Academy Awards in 1929. To be sure, the Academy Awards served many purposes including general industry legitimation and advertising for the nominated films. But the award ceremony resembled nothing so much as a well-publicized annual meeting of a professional organization, complete with a chicken or fish dinner in the years before it became an unabashed performance.

Seen this way, the Academy Awards assisted in the definition and installation of the division of filmmaking labor and art undertaken by the Academy. It is telling for instance that the award categories changed considerably in the beginning, as product categories and professional descriptions were refined. The first ceremony (cohosted by William de Mille) awarded separate prizes to the best picture (*Wings*) and the best "unique and artistic picture" (*Sunrise*), separating commercial fare from prestige art films. The acting awards that year were given on the basis of several films, a body of artistic work, rather than a single outstanding performance, a job. Janet Gaynor won the first best actress Oscar for *Sunrise, Seventh Heaven*, and *Street Angel*. The awards separated "below the line" workers from the artists who wrote, directed, and acted in films, effectively distinguishing the unionized laborers from the artists.

A less well-known element of the Academy's oversight of moviemaking labor is its sponsorship of film courses at the University of Southern California. These courses, the foundation of USC's prestigious film program, took up the task of professionalizing filmmaking that Columbia had mishandled in the 1910s. The courses also took over the studios' burden of training filmmakers. After two years of planning and experimentation that began with the Harvard course, USC offered a broad-based "Introduction to the Photoplay" in collaboration with the Academy. USC's course initially employed the lecture format and industry breakdown of the Harvard course. William de Mille's lecture for the USC course updated the discussion of the photoplay he had begun at Columbia and his brother Cecil had delivered at Harvard. USC's film curriculum quickly developed from its one all-inclusive prototype course into specialized programs of instruction on the arts and crafts of film production. USC began granting degrees in cinematography to its very first film students; bachelor's of science degrees in cinematography were awarded in 1932 and master's degrees in 1935.[10]

The Harvard courses were an acknowledged model for the Academy's USC courses,[11] and the Harvard Film Library Agreement, we will see, was a model for the Academy Awards. The same participants were behind both endeavors, and both arose out of the same complex negotiation of labor relations and commodity value in Hollywood. As a result, the fine points of the Agreement indicate a larger structural diagnosis of the Hollywood film industry in the late 1920s.

Kennedy and the other film producers injected both their economic and managerial objectives directly into the Harvard Film Library Agreement. The Agreement demonstrates both film producers' fear of losing control of the commodity once it entered the collection and their desire for the value a film collection might confer. To begin with, the writers of the Agreement went to great lengths to prohibit Harvard from reaping any financial reward from the exhibition of its films. It was stipulated that films could only be shown to "members of the Harvard community" and that no ticket sales or loan of films were permitted. The Agreement went so far as to insist that the film prints continued to belong to the production companies even after they were deposited in the Harvard vault.[12] This arrangement extended the business practice of renting film prints to exhibitors and licensing the rights to show films for a fixed period of time—a sales policy that almost entirely replaced the out-right sale of film prints by about 1915. By licensing the right to show films publicly (as you might a play) rather than selling film prints and all they contained outright (as you might a painting), the film became a perform-ance text, both legally and metaphorically detached from the film as a ma-terial object. Placing Harvard in the same position as an exhibitor, the Agreement turned the Film Library into just another venue for film exhi-bition, albeit a venue for older and exemplary films. In this way, the Harvard Film Library would have been reduced to the level of an early re-vival house. The producers thus insured that even if Harvard's Film Library succeeded in altering the exchange value of films, the use value remained entirely under the control of the producers.

Interestingly, while ownership and value were carefully defined, the questions of materiality that had been central to the Columbia negotia-tions were glossed over. The Agreement swept aside the still unsolved question of flammability with a brief statement that if fire risks prevented the storage of films in the Fogg Museum's vaults, they would somehow be stored safely in the Widener Library (the main campus library) or at the Business School.[13] By the late 1920s, the film collection seemed more use-ful in valuing the artistic content—what we might now call the intellec-tual property—of the films than their materiality.

The film producers' protection of their interests did not stop with fi-nancial regulations; they wanted control of the aesthetic criteria as well. An introductory note sets out a preliminary aesthetic guideline: "the har-monious synthesis of pictorialism, narrative, dramatic, and histrionic qualities."[14] But even this innocuous standard was withheld in the more formal Agreement, which reads: "The Committee will follow the advice and wishes of the industry in the matter of deciding whether the reasons for the selection of awards will be stated publicly, sent to producers of the films, or held as confidential by the [selection] Committee."[15] This overzealous provision—that discussions of harmonious synthesis must be kept confidential—suggests two important factors to remember when an-alyzing the rhetoric of the Agreement. First, the language throughout in-dicates the producers' desire to take control of the reception of films. Second, on almost every point of the Agreement, the film producers out-negotiated the Harvard professors, who are rarely given any power in the document.

The representatives of the film industry may have been tentative about relinquishing films or even the right to publicly discuss them, but they were also enticed by the collection's promise of celebrating Hollywood in a way that would later be taken up much more efficiently by the Academy of Motion Pictures Arts and Sciences. The Harvard Film Library, for instance, would have been entirely American in scope. This is uncharacteristic for both the Fogg Museum's collection and Harvard's Department of Fine Arts, which were principally devoted to European art. Making clear that films would be allowed into the collection only because of their aesthetic and not historical or national importance, it was nevertheless agreed that, "For the time being, foreign films will not be considered by the [selection] Committee."[16] The collection thus suggested to the public that only American films—and here they meant Hollywood films—were worthy of preservation. The grudging phrase "for the time being" points to what must have been the Fine Arts Department's frustration with the Hollywood bias.

Moreover, the Harvard Film Library would have had a unique temporal structure that reinforced the Academy's efforts to present filmmaking as a professional industry. The acquisition of films was to follow two organizational criteria. First, it would have been a collection of the past, "recording the evolution of the moving picture from its beginning to the present day." Second, it would have been a collection of the perpetual present, "selecting annually those films which are deemed worthy of preservation as works of art."[17] This temporal structure suggests an art form that had reached its final stage of evolution: films before 1927 were identified as worthy of preservation because they marked stages of development; films from 1927 onward could be evaluated purely based on aesthetic merit.

The Film Library's historiographical intervention throws a new light on the public effect of the Academy Awards, which similarly contributed to the idea that the film medium had reached maturity. Indeed, the competition to allow films into the Harvard collection can be seen as an inchoate Academy Awards. Consider as further proof the description of the acquisition process in points 12–15 of the Film Library Agreement:

12. Committee shall publish regularly and send to the various organizations in the industry notices of plans for each year. . . .
13. It is contemplated that a series of showings of the selected films will be made at the University during the spring of each year. . . .
14. The Committee shall be at liberty to recognize special merit in the production or direction on the part of individuals to individual firms.
15. The selection of each year of films for preservation in the archive will include formal notification by the Committee of the firm which has made any of the films chosen. (*The Story of the Film*, 361)

A nomination process, annual screenings of selected films, recognition of individual merit in production, formal notification of the production companies—all of these elements of the selection process suggest that the Harvard Film Library was intended to perform the function assumed only two years later by the Academy Awards. In both undertakings Hollywood found formats that could be used to define films as enduring works of art and celebrate the skilled artistry that went into making them, two goals that simultaneously helped sell old films and postpone unionization.

The idea of the film library prefigured but was not entirely replaced by that of the award ceremony. A film collection was deemed an essential element of the Academy's activities, and, from its inception, the Academy planned to establish its own collection of films and related documentation. By the end of 1928, the Academy had acquired a skeleton library of documentation from donations (a library that remains a valuable historical resource). That same year the Academy also considered starting a collection of films, but getting hold of film prints proved to be more difficult than acquiring paper materials. The Academy unsuccessfully tried collecting films that had been reedited for classroom use, thus differentiating their educational collection from the commercial market. By the 1930s the Museum of Modern Art's Film Library had established relationships with major studios, and the Academy had to be content to organize screenings of classics sent to them by MoMA. During World War II, as we will see in chapter 5, both MoMA and the Academy established film libraries to aid in the production of pro-American propaganda.[18]

A CULT OF AUTHENTICITY: ELITISM AND EXPERTISE

This chapter hasn't yet addressed the issue of social class, the importance of which only emerges fully when we look at the Film Library Agreement from Harvard's perspective. As it was for Hollywood, 1927 was a pivotal year for Harvard's Department of Fine Arts. The inauguration of Paul Sachs's museum course and the dedication of a new building for the Fogg Museum were two indications that 1927 marked the final replacement of the moral evaluation of art with a museum-focused method of empirical connoisseurship rooted in the aesthetic practices of art collectors. This museological method, known widely by the 1930s as the Harvard Method or the Fogg Method, relied on skilled observation informed by historical, archaeological, and stylistic data. The Fogg Method included Bernard Berenson's exacting connoisseurship as well as Chandler Post's meticulously documented 12-volume *A History of Spanish Painting*. Along with three or four other universities,[19] Harvard initiated a professional field of art history in America and the skills that defined the profession. The Fogg disseminated its method to great effect by circulating lecture slides and textbooks to other university art history programs and training a generation of art historians and museum curators.

The development of an empirical basis of art connoisseurship entailed more than just a methodological shift. It was also a form of self-fashioning for a still unsettled American elite. As Paul DiMaggio has shown, after the Civil War the first unified culture elite in America—the Boston Brahmins— cohered principally by rallying around the Boston Museum of Fine Arts, the Boston Symphony Orchestra, and other local cultural institutions. (Divisions within wealthy urban populations doomed every attempt to start a major public museum in America before the 1870s.) In DiMaggio's language, these cultural institutions contributed to the invention of an American upper class by forging an *organizational base* for the separation of high and popular culture and their respective audiences.[20] The Fogg Method of museology was part of a transition *within* the sphere of Brahmin high culture. It changed the organization of cultural institutions, supplanting genteel art appreciation—traditionally the province of WASPs—with a method of connoisseurship that belonged to a new American elite comprised partly of the children of Jewish bankers and in- dustrialists. The new members of Harvard's Department of Fine Arts fre- quently belonged to German Jewish families who both merged with and divided the Boston Brahmins. Patrician art historian Arthur Kingsley Porter, to take an example of a schism caused by the change, decided to resign from Harvard and retire to a castle in Ireland, "out of a growing, publicly expressed abhorrence of democratization in American universi- ties and in political and economic life in general."[21]

The Film Library Agreement raises some important questions about the changing Boston upper class. As a general rule, the new elite was as concerned with separating high art from popular culture as its predeces- sors. Indeed, if the Fogg Method ushered in a significant change in the ob- jects of art historical scholarship and appreciation at Harvard, it was a move from classical sculpture and Gothic architecture to Renaissance painting and architecture. Nevertheless, the Fogg did briefly entertain the idea of incorporating popular culture qua film into its move toward in- stalling specialized skills as the criteria for inclusion in an elite class. It should be clear from the above reading of the Film Library Agreement that the plan failed to progress largely because the Hollywood leaders re- fused to relinquish any power to the university and eventually decided that

FIGURE 3.1 The faculty of Harvard University's Department of Fine Arts in the Fogg Art Museum Courtyard (1927). Standing (*from left*): Meyric R. Rogers, Langdon Warner, George H. Edgell, Arthur Kingsley Porter, Chandler R. Post, Martin Mower, Kenneth Conant; seated (*from left*): Paul J. Sachs, George H. Chase, Denman Ross, Edward W. Forbes, Arthur Pope.
(Courtesy of Fogg Art Museum, Harvard University Art Museums)

they could achieve their goals without Harvard. Still, by investigating the Department of Fine Arts in some more detail, we can begin to understand what the art historians sought to gain from the inclusion of film in their new museum. This history is particularly important to the political genealogy of the inclusion of film in America museums. Paul Sachs's venture to add a film collection to the Fogg Museum didn't progress very far, but he instilled a model of expertise that his students carried into the successful formation of museum film departments in the 1930s.

Like the Columbia film program, the competition between German and English models of the university drove film and art education at Harvard. Even as the research model of the German university began to leave its first imprints in America in the 1870s, Harvard hired the quintessential nineteenth-century generalist, Charles Eliot Norton, as its first lecturer in fine arts. A disciple of Ruskin, Norton's art historical investigations made up only one element of a larger social mission. In an oft-quoted description, Norton's son caricatured his father's courses as "lectures on modern morals illustrated by the art of the ancients."[22] Before becoming a teacher, Norton had had an unusual career that included stints as editor of both the *Nation* and the *North American Review*. He hesitantly accepted the university post offered by his cousin, Harvard president Charles Eliot, and although Norton went on to train a generation of university professors, he continued to think of himself as a public intellectual, publishing, speaking, and exerting influence beyond the classroom. Norton was, to be sure, a fussy Anglophilic aesthete, contemptuous of the masses he sought to educate. Noblesse oblige and not egalitarianism led Norton to view art and literature as tools for the moral and political education of "the people," a phrase he used to mean " 'not a political body forming a state' but 'a moral community, already organized and governed by moral principles.' "[23]

As we have seen, the Ruskin-Norton tradition of moral education inflected Vachel Lindsay's musings about a new film institution, and it provided the foundation for implementing film study at Columbia.[24] The Harvard Film Library Agreement, by contrast, was bound up with the move away from moral education and toward archaeology, connoisseurship, and skilled expertise. Paul Sachs's 1927 museum course at the Fogg signaled the completion of this paradigm shift. Sachs had offered makeshift versions of his museum course twice before to a total of six students. During the 1926–27 academic year, however, over thirty students enrolled in the museum course, including future director of the Museum of Modern Art, Alfred Barr. The museum course became a staple of the Harvard curriculum, and Sachs went on to place many of his students in key curatorial and directorial positions in museums throughout the United States. In addition to Barr at MoMA, some of Sachs's most prominent students held directorships at the National Gallery and the innovative Wadsworth Atheneum in Hartford. Sachs actively forged alliances with museum trustees and successfully made his course into the compulsory entrée into the old boy network of museum professionals. This network, in turn, entrenched Fogg museology throughout American art museums.[25]

Sachs's class identification was a constituent rather than an incidental element of his pedagogical method. A member of the Jewish banking family that founded the firm Goldman Sachs, Paul Sachs—like Aby Warburg a generation earlier—left a preordained banking career to pursue his avocation, art history and collecting. Only a generation later, a philanthropic career in the arts was encouraged in children of Jewish-American bankers, stockbrokers, and retailers. Many of Sachs's students, including future founders of MoMA's Film Library Lincoln Kirstein and Edward M. M. Warburg (Aby's nephew), came from such backgrounds.[26] Sachs's move into the world of art collecting and scholarship followed the familiar path: the appropriation of WASP culture as a form of social advancement. One of his proudest achievements, for example, was moving into Shady Hill, Charles Eliot Norton's family estate in Cambridge. But Sachs did not only bear similarities to a social type, he played a role in the institutional formation of that type. By aiding in the replacement of genteel art appreciation — a condition to which one was born — with a codified system of connoisseurship that had to be acquired, Sachs's museum course helped to redefine the organizational base of high culture and create a new and somewhat more inclusive standard for permission into the elite realm of tastemakers.

At the core of this transition was an overturning of the nineteenth-century museum's use of copies of artworks for educational purposes. The Fogg Museum and its subsequent reconstruction reveal this shift in thinking about originals and copies. The Film Library — and this is counterintuitive — was part of an effort to restore the importance of original works to the study of art.

It is only when wealthy alumni, including Edward Forbes, who eventually became director of the Fogg, and Paul Sachs himself began to bequeath original works that the Fogg Museum redefined its role as a teaching museum. Forbes represents a sort of interstitial phase between Norton's emphasis on copies and Sachs's insistence on originals. Forbes considered photographic reproductions best suited to "the study and comparison of facts relating to art and artists," but he thought originals equally desirable for their ability to "inspire" young artists and scholars.[27] Sachs's museum course went much further and helped to mount an object-oriented art criticism that revolved around a cult of authenticity. In place of Norton's moral evaluation supported by the use of copies, the Fogg Method, exemplified by the figures of Bernard Berenson and Paul Sachs, was premised on the empirical observation of originals and the accumulation of supporting data. Many students remembered Sachs placing them before a table of three objects and being asked to identify the one worthless piece in the group. In training his students to be curators, Sachs asked them to assume the position of the private collector and cultivate an owner's relation to the objects in the collections they supervised. Sachs presented himself as the model collector-curator, frequently holding courses in his home, Shady Hill, and using examples from his own collection while teaching. Agnes Mongan, who became Sachs's assistant, remembered him taking objects off the shelf in his house and placing them in students' hands. "It would stir you deeply," Mongan recalled, "[because] you could never go into a museum and touch a work of art, you could never feel it that way." To consummate the owners' relationship to the object, every student in the museum course was required during the semester to buy a work of art.[28]

The construction of a new Fogg Museum building—which opened the same year that the Film Library Agreement was drafted—reinforced Sachs's model of curatorship and object appreciation. In one of the last exhibitions held in the old Fogg, a 1926 show of modern art, the catalog demonstrated embarrassment over its use of reproductions. The catalog assured visitors that the exhibition contained "facsimiles reproduced so miraculously that under glass it is impossible to detect them from originals."[29] Remedying the embarrassment over its reproductions, the new Fogg was designed for the expert contemplation of original works of art. In Carol Duncan's examination of American museums' contempt for its public in the 1920s, the most blatant elitism she finds is in a review of the new Fogg building. In the article, Charles Loring of the Boston Museum of

FIGURE 3.2   Paul Sachs with students in the Naumberg Room of the Fogg Art Museum (1943 or 1944).

(Courtesy of Fogg Art Museum, Harvard University Art Museums. Photographed by George S. Wooddruff)

Fine Arts (which had recently banished its own collection of plaster casts) openly expressed his disdain for museums that attracted a wide public. In a celebration of the move away from reproductions, which represented for him "the emphasis on quantity as against quality," Loring applauded the Fogg's obfuscating method of displaying original works. The Fogg reminded him of "a very rich and exclusive metropolitan club house," with "nothing to lure the average man in the street off the street."[30]

How then did the Fogg, with its emphasis on authenticity, uniqueness, and expert knowledge, come to consider building a collection of film, a mass art form that seemed to be ontologically without originals? One explanation is that the Film Library Agreement was proposed at a time when the Fogg was testing the purview of connoisseurship. If the basis for class distinction became expert knowledge rather than birthright, then the type of objects became less important than the ability to draw a hierarchy within the field of objects. One example of such boundary testing is the introduction of modern art at Harvard, still a scandalous move in Boston at the time. In addition to the Fogg's show of reproductions of modern paintings in 1926, Sachs supported the Harvard Society for Contemporary Art, a groundbreaking exhibition venue founded by undergraduates Lincoln Kirstein, Edward Warburg, and future director of the National Gallery John Walker III. The Society allowed Sachs to keep modernism at a distance even as he experimented with expanding Harvard's art historical purview.[31]

The same faculty and students that pushed for the Fogg to bring modern art into its orbit also suggested the inclusion of film.[32] Professor of Greek Chandler Post, who taught the first course on modern art at Harvard, was the Department of Fine Arts' most avid filmgoer. He regularly took his students to the movies, and he was involved at every stage of the development of the Film Library Agreement. When Paul Sachs asked his student most interested in modern art, Alfred Barr, how the museology curriculum could be improved, Barr responded with a long letter suggesting a multidisciplinary program that included lectures on film and vaudeville by cultural critic Gilbert Seldes. (This letter is often considered the first indication of Barr's later plan for MoMA as a multidisciplinary museum.) In 1927 the Fogg Method was tested officially in the waters of popular culture, as the Film Library Agreement attempted to apply the Fogg criteria to Hollywood film. As a result, we can reread the Agreement—which from the perspective of Hollywood moguls redefined Hollywood artistry and commodity status—as a gesture toward extending the Fogg Method of museology to film.

First, Harvard sought to solve the copy/original problem by acquiring two prints of each film: "one will be available for possible exhibition before students and other University groups; the other will be set aside for permanent preservation in the archive."[33] The exhibition print clearly fulfilled the function of the annual award competition and allowed for repeated study of films. The preservation print demonstrated a mode of ownership that exceeded Hollywood's concentration of value on exhibition. The inert "permanent" print would remain in pristine original condition even as other copies wore from use. Of course the archival prints would have decayed but that wasn't a consideration here. The award ceremony itself, while it buttressed Hollywood producers' efforts to define film industry jobs, also suggested the method by which to evaluate films: the film producers wanted to limit Harvard's ability to publicly declare its aesthetic decisions, but the Harvard art historians still "hoped that it will be possible to use as the criterion of choice the harmonious synthesis of pictorial, narrative, dramatic, and histrionic qualities."[34] If the method of evaluation was only indicated in abbreviated form, the Fogg's representatives were able to insist that, in line with the Fogg Method, the Film Library would collect archaeological material (film stills, scripts, criticism and other "cinematographic literature") to augment the study of objects. And in keeping with the Fogg's production of art history textbooks, the published volume of lectures and the Film Library Agreement were intended to be "material on which a textbook might be based, a starting point for systematic research."[35]

All of these conditions sought to make film into an object more like sculpture or prints, which could also have multiple copies. Film itself, however, was never a priority for Sachs or the Fogg. Instead, film represented a symbolic object of consumer culture that Sachs and his followers used to theorize the museum. As we will see in the next section, the Fogg's contribution to the history of the film museum was not a fully articulated method of film study but the encouragement it gave its students to include film and popular culture into the work of museum professionals.

The Fogg's cultivation of expertise and its cult of authenticity represented only one pole of 1920s museology. A brief comparison with one of Sachs's competitors reveals that the future of museums was at stake in the Film Library Agreement. John Cotton Dana (whose career was discussed in chapter 1) founded a competing museology program at the Newark Museum in 1925. A Progressive reformer, Dana fought against the idea that the museum should be run by experts, and he concentrated instead on increasing the utility of museums for public education. To make museums more relevant and enticing to the working class, Dana campaigned for the incorporation of popular culture and quotidian objects into the museum. In place of the expert, he purposed a model of the museum worker who assisted rather than led the public:

> The students will not be expected during the first year of study to attempt to equip themselves for *expertness* in science, art, or industry. Rather they will equip themselves for *actual practice* in making the contents of the museum interesting and, above all, helpful to the community it supports.[36]

Dana's vision of the curator was similar to his vision of the librarian, whose job was to help make the design of the collection as transparent as possible. Significantly, there was a strong gendered division to Sachs's and Dana's methods. Dana taught classes comprised entirely of women, whom he thought best suited to the selfless task of facilitator required by museum work.[37] Sachs's ideal expert, on the other hand, invoked the masculine model of the individual collector as hunter in the marketplace. Starting in the 1880s, Rémy Saisselin has argued, men and women were perceived as having different relationships to objects in the marketplace: "women were consumers of objects; men were collectors."[38] Both schools turned out leaders of the museum world, and at the Museum of Modern Art, Sachs trained most of the MoMA men while curator of painting Dorothy Miller and several other women came from Dana's program.

In response to attempts like Dana's (or Vachel Lindsay's or Victor Oscar Freeburg's) to make museums more popular or to press them into the service of general education, Sachs replied that museums existed not for entertainment but as immaculate examples to "give [the public] some sense of excellence." He warned curators to "resist pressure to vulgarize and cheapen our work through a mistaken idea that in such fashion a broad public may be reached effectively." Elsewhere, Sachs tried to reconcile his defense of the museum as an elitist, scholarly institution with its use in general education. "One should never forget," he conceded, "that in America at least, the museum is a social instrument highly useful in any scheme of general education. . . . The primary need of museums is guidance through the scholar's approach."[39]

The two poles of museum work exemplified by Sachs's and Dana's courses came together in the 1930s. A synthesis of Sachs's method of connoisseurship and Dana's celebration of the quotidian can be seen in such MoMA exhibits as the 1935 "Machine Art Show." The displays of gears, dental instruments, and typewriter carriages, for example, answered

Dana's call to connect the museum to the everyday life of the public. Yet in deference to Sachs's model of connoisseurship, the show's objects were judged, in what was partly a publicity stunt, by experts on the aesthetic qualities of machinery: philosopher John Dewey, pilot Amelia Earhart, and Museum of Science and Technology official Charles Richards. Both Dana's populism and Sachs's elitism, however, were challenged in the political debates of the 1930s.[40]

COMMUNISM AND THE FOGG'S PROGENY IN THE THIRTIES

There is no evidence that the Fogg Film Library acquired even one film, but Harvard's Department of Fine Arts did produce a generation of art historians, patrons, and curators devoted to film. Transplanted to New York in the 1930s, a group of Sachs's students continued to experiment with the idea of starting a film library before they eventually went on to found the enduring film department of the Museum of Modern Art. This group of former Fogg students was centered around the ambitious editor, patron, and organizer Lincoln Kirstein and included Edward M. M. Warburg, Julien Levy, Philip Johnson, Chick Austin (at the Wadsworth Atheneum in Hartford), and Alfred Barr. Hilton Kramer has called them "the aesthetic generation" to recuperate what he polemically interprets as their apolitical formalism.[41] Kramer's assessment isn't entirely off the mark, but a subtler characterization of the group's political and aesthetic inclinations can be found in Thomas Bender's consideration of their place in the intellectual geography of New York City. Bender labels the group "civic intellectuals," and he calls their milieu, only half ironically, "uptown bohemia." For Bender, the civic intellectuals were separated from the downtown New York Intellectuals by more than the theater district. Where the downtown intellectuals were frequently communists and fellow travelers, educated at City College and interested in literature, their uptown counterparts had Harvard degrees, less radical politics, and predilections for the visual and performing arts.[42] If these two groups of New York Intellectuals, when taken as a whole, formed a mutually defining binary, their various attempts to collect, exhibit, and sell film as art reveal moments at which the boundaries between the uptown and downtown intellectuals threatened to collapse, moments when the civic intellectuals defined their class politics and taste through encounters with downtown Marxism and communism.

The Harvard Film Library seems to have been planned in an institutional vacuum, responding only to the narrow demands of Hollywood and Harvard. When we look at it on a wider scale, however, we realize that the

Harvard Film Library was conceived on the cusp of a period rife with attempts to start film collections and museums in Europe and the United States. Between 1927 and 1933, short-lived film museums, repertory film theaters, and film lending libraries appeared in Paris, London, Moscow, and New York. To some extent, these short-lived endeavors followed the international explosion of art cinemas and film journals in the 1920s. In a prescient observation, Gilbert Seldes dubbed the art cinemas of the mid-twenties "cinema museums" because they gave life to older or unprofitable films.[43] Seldes's definition became even more apt by the end of the decade. The financial barriers to sound-film production and government control of the film industry in Germany all but erased avant-garde filmmaking, and theaters that had been devoted to screening the latest avant-garde films began to show repertory programs of the past decade's masterpieces. In Paris, theater manager Jean Mauclaire and film critics Jean Mitry and Léon Moussinac argued for a permanent bibliothèque and cinémathèque. But even the most serious attempt to raise funds for a Cinémathèque nationale in 1933 failed to produce a collection.[44] At approximately the same time, but in very different circumstances, the Amateur Cinema League in New York began a lending library of amateur and avant-garde films to support low-budget film production.[45] These various attempts to start non-commercial film institutions didn't grow smoothly out of 1920s film culture nor did they consolidate an accepted history and obvious canon of films. Rather, a few victors emerged from an intense six- or seven-year contest to establish film institutions and claim a film canon.

On the American front of this contest, the civic intellectuals are the pivotal link between the Harvard Film Library Agreement and the Museum of Modern Art Film Library. Though reared at the Fogg, the civic intellectuals reimagined the film museum through an engagement with trans-Atlantic film culture. As leaders of New York's cultural life, they looked for models to replace the eremitic Fogg Method of connoisseurship. Lincoln Kirstein, for example, wrote of returning to a Ruskinian model of public education, but one that focused on the visceral experience of art rather than its moral consequences. It was a period of development and contradiction for Kirstein, who described his rereading of Ruskin as a process rather than a solution. "Directly from Ruskin," he remembered, "would develop, burgeon, and then rot my interest in most of contemporary art."[46] Before becoming a leading patron of modern art and dance in the mid-thirties, Kirstein devoted most of his energy to publishing *Hound and Horn*, the literary journal he had started as an undergraduate, and writing criticism for other publications. *Hound and Horn*'s pages are an important barometer of the intellectual trials of the civic intellectuals in the 1930s, and it is in *Hound and Horn* that Kirstein eventually published Harry Alan Potamkin's plan for a Marxist film school and film library.

A self-proclaimed Wildean, Kirstein followed Oscar Wilde's innervating call to see the "Critic as Artist." A character in Wilde's fictional dialogue announced with an uncharacteristically Hegelian view of human consciousness, "There was never a time when criticism was more needed than it is now. It is only by its means that humanity can become conscious of the point at which it has arrived."[47] As film critic for the journal *Arts Weekly*, Kirstein echoed Wilde and suggested that the debates of film critics were more important to "human interest" than the revolutions in film production or avant-garde style they commented on. This emphasis on the reception of films would lead almost immediately to discussions of film collecting, film museums, and film libraries.

For a politicized model of film reception, Kirstein looked to Soviet and French film culture. As he wrote in one introspective review:

> There are several healthy things about a militant intelligentsia, such as the Parisian. They inspire a ruthless competition. They forbid a personal, almost martyred isolation of ideas. They insist on "human" interest. When all is said and done, the interest one may have in the texture of materials, in the rhythms of shifting surfaces, in the perfection of photographically reproductive values is inferior, less full of implication and reference than human beings in action, expressing attitudes toward *progressive facts of existence*.[48]

This passage is both more cryptic and revealing than it at first appears. At its core, the passage attempts to reconcile the debate that preoccupied *Hound and Horn* and left-wing criticism more generally in the early 1930s, a debate that pitted a humanist insistence on a transhistorical human consciousness against a Marxist doctrine of historical progress.[49] On the one hand, *Hound and Horn* published T. S. Eliot's, Bernard Bandler's, and Alan Tate's calls for artistic continuity with "tradition" and the American agrarian past. On the other, the journal endorsed the Marxism of proletarian fiction and Constructivist murals and films. One *Hound and Horn* editor dismissed the humanism/Marxism debate as "a Tweedledum-Tweedledee affair,"[50] but Kirstein responded to it by attempting an absolute synthesis of the two positions. In the paragraph above, for example, the phrase "progressive facts of existence" was meant to recall Soviet realist films and a historical-materialist idea of progress. In his writings from this period Kirstein frequently supported Soviet realism to the exclusion of all other styles. The early Soviet sound film *The Road to Life* (1931) moved him to describe Hollywood as a "disease" by comparison and European art film as "even worse, because there more is attempted." Moreover, he professed, "*The Road to Life* compels our highest homage to the direction that conceived it and to the government that made it possible."[51] In a similar response to the 1932 version of Sergei Eisenstein's *Qué Viva México!*—a film Kirstein tried to buy the rights to the following year—he directly defied his intellectual mentor T. S. Eliot's insistence on "Tradition and the Intellectual." In response to Eliot's reported statement, "I am incapable of being convinced [of the justification of communism] by the arts of the cinema," Kirstein responded, "Fortunately, I *am* capable of being convinced by the arts of the cinema."[52] In each of his moves to embrace communist art and ideology, however, Kirstein attempted to reconcile this position with an insistence on the humanistic ideal of the individual genius. Using Eisenstein as an example, Kirstein argued that individual talent thrived under communism. Indeed, all the civic intellectuals celebrated Eisenstein as an example of the communist-genius.[53] And, above all, for Kirstein the personal experience of writing criticism became the ultimate humanist response to Marxist art and politics.

In the politically charged debates of the early 1930s, Kirstein's form of eclectic and synthetic criticism was difficult to sustain unchallenged. A clarification of Kirstein's and *Hound and Horn*'s allegiances was forced to the table in a *New Republic* review of Kirstein's first novel *Flesh Is Heir*. The reviewer, Granville Hicks, accused the editors of *Hound and Horn* of practicing dilettantish "leisure class" politics. After some soul-searching, Kirstein responded to Hicks's attack by confirming the accusations. He took the advice of the now disaffected Bandler to keep the journal aloof from political engagement, and he defended *Hound and Horn* purely in terms of the aesthetic quality of its submissions. At the time, Kirstein's retreat from politics may have been partially a result of his growing interest in bringing ballet to America, an interest that led him to a romantic view of the great ballet culture of pre-Soviet, Tsarist Russia. It is also important to note that the Popular Front movement, which united the heterogeneous left against fascism, was still a few years off.[54]

If Kirstein ultimately shied away from taking a political stance himself or for his little magazine, film (and mural painting) remained the exception. Even after the *New Republic* incident, *Hound and Horn*'s film criticism consistently followed Marxian methodologies: examples include Alfred Barr's reading of German war films as reflective of national consciousness,

Kirstein's typological celebration of James Cagney, and Harry Alan Potamkin's unswerving Marxist analysis of the political conditions of film production and reception.[55] In addition to publishing Marxist film criticism, Kirstein supported several attempts to start film collections as political interventions. In the same *Arts Weekly* article discussed above, Kirstein mentioned another direction (in addition to criticism) that a "militant intelligentsia" might take. Kirstein announced that his former Harvard classmate, Julien Levy, had, "been informally show[ing], for all interested, several films, the foundation for a film library, which Mr. Levy is collecting to display on request."[56] Levy's attempt to incorporate a film club and a film collection into his important art gallery led to another encounter with communism and a test of his politics similar to the trial *Hound and Horn* went through in the pages of the *New Republic*.

Levy had been an avid moviegoer since he joined the group of students who regularly accompanied Chandler Post to the movies at Harvard. As a gallery owner and dealer in New York, Levy's inventive exhibitions of European avant-garde painting and photography earned him a reputation for consistently surprising the New York art world. In 1932, as Levy remembers the story, he decided to incorporate film into his gallery as one more surprise. In 1931 he traveled to Paris in search of a screening of Luis Buñuel and Salvador Dali's banned Surrealist film, *L'Age d'or* (1930). When Levy finally found an illicit screening of the film in a Paris suburb, he discovered that the film created pandemonium in the theater, inciting the audience of Sorbonne students to violence. Levy interpreted the reaction as a direct expression of political agitation provoked by the film. Later, recalling this as a moment of revelation, he declared: "It was the first time that I had been forcibly brought to realize that the artist, for example, might be considered a moving factor in immediate politics."[57] Levy's belated enthusiasm probably resulted from accounts he had read as much as the actual scene. *Un Chien andalou* (1929) and other Dada and Surrealist films had been met, at first, with right-wing attacks and general riots. But by the time Levy happened upon the *L'Age d'or* screening, audiences expected outbursts and protests as they might at hockey games or soccer matches.[58]

Convinced of their revolutionary political potential, Levy returned to New York determined to show *L'Age d'or* and other films in his gallery. The films, he thought, would help both to politicize the reception of modern art in New York and, at the same time, introduce film into the burgeoning market for modern art collectors. Levy felt assured that collectors would buy films by name-brand painters like Marcel Duchamp, Fernand Léger, and Salvador Dali, and he speculated that "if a collector's market could be organized, I thought to persuade other painters to experiment in the medium." Levy diagnosed Hollywood as "show[ing] signs of unpleasant bloat," and he mistakenly thought avant-garde films (he called them "extra-Hollywood films") about to take off. If Levy had successfully created a dealers market for avant-garde film, it might have prevented a decade of atrophy in avant-garde film production, but Levy's collecting and marketing ambitions were derailed by the humanist/Marxist debate.[59]

To avoid potential problems with censors or theater licensing, Levy decided to start a subscription film society modeled on the prominent London Film Society. In October 1932, Levy and seven other directors met to design the film programs. Like so many other attempts to start film societies and collections at that time, the founders felt burdened by the potential permanence and ideological weight of their decisions. Also like similar endeavors, their film society led a fleeting existence, folding after five programs in as many months.[60] At the first meeting of the selection committee, a disagreement over the criteria for choosing films led to the replacement of three of the seven directors. Since we have only Levy's account of the incident, the anecdote is limited to what it reveals about his own political development. According to Levy, at that first meeting the film critic Harry Alan Potamkin "very vehemently urged that we show Communist films, and Communist films only."[61] This firm position resulted in an immediate standoff between Potamkin and journalist Raoul Roussy de Sales. Levy saw the confrontation as another symbolic contest between Marxism and humanism, and his allegiance was clear. Levy caricatured Potamkin as "the little Communist director," and he nicknamed Potamkin's strongest ally in the group of directors, Dwight Macdonald, "the tall director." In opposition to this communist duo, Levy found in de Sales the humanist ideal: "His intelligence was tempered by a skepticism and a fastidious heritage which placed him beyond prejudice, in the position of a privileged spectator. . . . In this age he represented for his country the *homme d' esprit.*"[62] When Levy, who had most of the subscribers behind him, sided with de Sales, Potamkin resigned and took Macdonald and a third director with him. In their place, Levy appointed three new directors, two of whom were concurrently in the process of starting a film library at MoMA: Lincoln Kirstein, and former organizer of the London Film Society Iris Barry. To Levy's surprise, the large museum felt threatened by his small film society, and MoMA censured its employees' involvement.[63]

The stakes of film collecting and noncommercial exhibition were higher than Levy imagined, and the urgency to establish an American center for film art was growing. The civic intellectuals remained the foundation for the establishment of such a center, but they flirted with different political models of the film institutions before the Museum of Modern Art Film Library was born.

EVERYONE'S A CRITIC: HARRY ALAN POTAMKIN'S MARXIST FILM LIBRARY

Levy's inclusion of Harry Alan Potamkin on the directorial board of his film society is as important as Potamkin's swift expulsion. By the time of the film society skirmish, Potamkin had already firmly established himself as the favorite film critic of the civic intellectuals. If Levy and Kirstein viewed film as a medium that demanded a political commitment that they were unwilling to shoulder, they imported Potamkin from downtown (sometimes uneasily, as we have seen) to fill that role.

Potamkin's inclusion in the ranks of the civic intellectuals is unusual because he was also the favorite film critic of the downtown New York Intellectuals. Never a Communist Party member, Potamkin served as executive secretary of the party's most prominent organization of fellow travelers, the New York John Reed Club. Before his untimely death at thirty-three in 1933, Potamkin rose quickly in circles of Marxist criticism. He served as a delegate to the International Bureau of Revolutionary Literature in Kharkov, contributed to the *New Masses* and other radical publications, and published a biography of Lenin for children. When *Hound and Horn* tormentor Granville Hicks collaboratively planned a compendium of American Marxist criticism, the projected table of contents contained the most obvious leaders of Marxist thought: Sidney Hook on philosophy, Meyer Schapiro on fine arts, Harry Alan Potamkin on film, and a dozen or so other essays.[64] Yet like his John Reed Club associates William Phillips and Philip Rahv, founders of the *Partisan Review*, Potamkin must be considered a "radical modernist," who tried to incorporate the experimental style of 1920s modernism into politically committed art and literature of the 1930s.[65] Potamkin had been an aspiring modernist poet in the early twenties and continued to write about modernist film for the journal *Close-Up* and other publications. As both proletarian political radical and Ivy League modernist (he attended the University of Pennsylvania although he eventually graduated from New York University), Potamkin had the rare ability to straddle the divides of uptown and downtown intellectual life. In a revealing obituary, the *Nation* compared the radical Marxist Potamkin to both the Fogg's most famous student and to *Hound and Horn's* intellectual mentor: "Potamkin revealed in his reviews and articles a familiarity with the motion picture, past and present, as complete as to inspire the same implicit confidence in his authority as a Bernard Berenson writing on Florentine paintings, or a T. S. Eliot writing on Elizabethan poetry."[66]

Kirstein befriended Potamkin and offered him the opportunity to publish some of his most ambitious and mature pieces of Marxist film criticism. In keeping with the journal's auteurist party line, however, all of Potamkin's *Hound and Horn* essays were studies of directors: Eisenstein, G. W. Pabst, and Vsevolod Pudovkin. Even after *Hound and Horn*'s retreat from political criticism, Kirstein published posthumously Potamkin's notes for a film school and library, a document that points toward a new and unrealized phase in Potamkin's career. But Kirstein was careful, in an obituary-cum-disclaimer, to separate *Hound and Horn* from the political implications of the document. "He believed in 'the Revolution,'" Kirstein wrote of Potamkin, "and he was impatient with those of us who could not see that it would come by way of historical channels which he felt determined by Marx."[67]

Potamkin had begun to think about the possibility of an American film school and library only a few months before his death. His emphasis on education and collecting resulted from a critical stance toward the culture of 1920s film clubs—another indication of the complex transition from the film clubs of the 1920s to the film institutions of the 1930s. "The film club," Potamkin came to realize, "has its ultimate justification only when it recognized itself as an educational forum,"[68] and he envisioned a school and library that could inaugurate a new stage in the development of spectatorship. Recalling Brecht's discussion of the sports spectator,[69] Potamkin argued that even the consummate movie fan and film club devotee had none of the expert knowledge of the typical baseball spectator. Where Kirstein and Levy saw the film club and library supporting the insular critical discourse of a film "intelligentsia," Potamkin wanted the same institutions to create a mass audience of critics. He sought to transform "the movie fan [who] is strictly a fan," into an expert comparable to the sports fan who is also, "a critic of sport."[70]

To be sure, Potamkin's film criticism was itself a product of the film club movement. Still an aspiring poet in 1926, Potamkin arranged to spend his honeymoon in London and Paris in the hopes of meeting the great modernist writers. Instead, he discovered the London Film Society and the ciné-clubs in Paris. He returned to the United States devoted to film criticism and, more specifically, to "little cinemas" or art cinemas, the more commercial American version of film clubs.[71] Potamkin's attitude

toward film clubs changed in the early 1930s when he took part in founding two of New York's first subscription film societies: the Film Forum and
Julien Levy's film society. Levy's condemnation of Potamkin's aggressive
partisan didacticism only indicated Potamkin's own discomfort with the
format. Even as he participated in their importation to New York,
Potamkin declared the film society and film club antiquated and elitist;
they needed to be replaced with institutions capable of transforming the
mass public through a critical engagement with film.[72]

In a series of essays, Potamkin fleshed out a Marxist critique of both
Hollywood and film club spectatorship that eventually led to his notes for
a film school and library. Analyzing the interplay of attractions and distractions that we associate with the film theory of his contemporaries
Siegfried Kracauer and Sergei Eisenstein, Potamkin (coming to very different conclusions) investigated the failings of Hollywood cinema.
Product giveaways at movie palaces, product marketing, and other extratextual attractions, he complained, were only the most vicious and material elements of the equally commercial attraction of Hollywood films: "As
attractions these [promotional giveaways] are a means of bolstering the
boxoffice; as influences they inveigle the audience." Where Kracauer
found the glitter and excitement of the movie palace useful distractions
from absorption in the film, Potamkin read all of these distractions as participants in the production of transitory, empty experiences:

> The movie is at present constructed to be momentarily effective. . . . Try to
> think back to pictures that had important subject matter, and see if they are
> memorable in your mind. You will find it is very difficult to remember mo-
> tion pictures for their point, their idea, because they are so built as to assure
> a response from the audience at the moment. (*The Compound Cinema*, 217)

Developing his own critical vocabulary, Potamkin wrote that the momentary attractions of movies and movie palaces added up to a "grand ritual"
of Hollywood spectatorship. The "ritual" made spectators into unthinking
"fans" hungry for more spectacle. Commercial cinema succeeded in in-
doctrinating customers when it made "the audience uncritical." He concluded: "It is my contention that not until the audience ceases being a part
of the ritual does it become an audience. In a ritual there is no audience
because the fan is part of the ritual" (217–18).

Potamkin's goal was the same as Lindsay's and Freeburg's even if his
vocabulary and ideology were different: to create critical filmgoers and citizens. Where Lindsay and the theorists of the Columbia film program ex-

pected their film institutions to create critical viewers through controlled and repeated exposure to film, Potamkin's plan was much more programmatic. He wanted to find an institutional form of promoting the insights of film criticism.

Film clubs and little cinemas, in Potamkin's assessment, were only slightly better at bringing about a critical audience than Hollywood. Choosing his words (i.e., *audience* and *spectator*) very carefully, Potamkin mused: "I would say, then, that the film club is to the audience generally what the critic is to the spectator, that is, the film club provides the critical audience" (218–20). The film club's promotion of a critical distance appealed to Potamkin, but he objected to the class makeup of the film clubs. Film clubs replaced commercially induced "fanaticism" with elitist "cults." These "cults," as Potamkin used the term, "arise from dissent with the ritual or they may arise from exaggeration of certain points in the ritual." The cults of the film club—the adulation of Chaplin or the contemplation of *cinema pur*, for instance—ended, he argued, in either the feigned populism of the "intelligentsia" or in the irrelevance of a formalist avant-garde (217). Partly as a result of his interaction with Kirstein and Levy, Potamkin came to see a vast separation between the "fanaticism" of the everyday moviegoer and the specialized viewing skills of the self-proclaimed "film intelligentsia": "The movie-fanatic is part of a grand ritual. He does not specialize in the adulation of the rudimentary. That is left to the elite, the effete, the intelligentsia of cinema" (227).

The problem for Potamkin was how to extend the critical expertise that came with exaggeration and dissent to the mass public. His solution was a film school and library. Like the planners of the Fogg Film Library, Potamkin wanted to counteract the "momentary" experience of the cinema with an institution that encouraged repeated viewings in a critical framework. But where the Fogg planners wanted film history preserved so that it could endure,[73] Potamkin wanted it preserved to be more politically effective (217). Dissatisfied with the elitism of the film club model, Potamkin found inspiration in attempts to forge official film cultures through state-controlled institutions. He cited programs in Moscow, Leningrad, and Berlin as well as the British government's report, *The Film in National Life* (1932), which concluded with a proposal for a national film archive (589).

Potamkin was also familiar with the Harvard Film Library Agreement. He even wrote a critical review of the published volume (534–35). And it is not a coincidence that Potamkin's analytical diagram bears some striking resemblances to the Fogg plan, which was conceived in part by the leaders of the film industry he loathed ("Accident and opportunity made them magnates" [534]). Potamkin revised the Harvard plan to conform to a historical-materialist approach to film history. When the time came to sketch the plan of his film school and library, Potamkin drew up a taxonomy that gave a visual order to world film production. Where the Fogg Film Library took the form of a contractual agreement, Potamkin's diagram looked more like an Enlightenment tree of knowledge or Brecht's famous list comparing the epic and the dramatic theater.[74] The catalog was designed to lay bare the structure of the film production and its reception for the mass public and, ultimately, to educate (and create) the critical audience he desired. Potamkin's notes offer the most radical image of what a Marxist film library might have looked like. It is necessary to read Potamkin's notes closely, in all of their illusory density, to grasp the urgency and importance the organization of a film collection and an alternative film institution had in the early 1930s (see fig. 3.3).

Potamkin died before he could explicate his own plan. But his writing gives us many clues to help read the document. In addition, Walter Benjamin's analysis of the relation between historical materialism and collecting mass-produced objects (specifically film, newspaper caricatures, and stamps), written a few years after Potamkin's diagram and under the influence of Brecht, helps to unlock the function of Potamkin's proposed film library. Benjamin argued famously that mechanical reproduction—whose avatar for him was film—diminished the cult value of works of art. Unlike Potamkin, Benjamin concluded that the film spectator was already an expert akin to the sports spectator. "It is inherent in the technique of film," Benjamin wrote, "as well as that of sports that everybody who witnesses its accomplishments is somewhat of an expert."[75]

But like Potamkin, Benjamin's Marxist analysis of film also left room for the possibility that cult value could be returned to objects through their revaluation in collections. In a footnote to "The Work of Art in the Age of Mechanical Reproduction," Benjamin qualified his argument, that film destroyed the cult value of art, noting that the collector "always retains some traces of the fetishist, and . . . by owning the work of art, shares its ritual power."[76] In Potamkin's plan as well as in the Harvard plan, the position of the individual collector remained the ideal stance toward mechanically reproduced objects. But where Paul Sachs sought to place the curator in the privileged position of the collector, Potamkin wanted every spectator to see film from the vantage of the individual collector.

Both Benjamin and Potamkin sought an alternative to what they read as the inherently ruling class politics of collecting. The Harvard plan's iso-

A Library of the Motion Picture
Categories for a Catalog

The two main categories:
1. Foreign Films
2. Domestic Films

I. *Films*

A.
1. Dramatic
2. Ethnological
3. Experimental
   a. abstract
   b. absolute
4. Educational
5. Industrial
6. Documentary (news-film)
7. Animation

B.
1. Popular
2. Innovations in style and technique (principles of film-making)
3. Individual Performances
4. Individual direction
5. National Sequences—Swedish, Italian, etc.
6. Industrial Sequences (Fox, Metro, etc.)
7. Subject matter—folk films, gangster, prohibition
8. Serials
9. Shorts:
   a. travelogue
   b. vaudeville
   c. sport film
   d. dramatic
   e. private and experimental
10. Pivotal masterpieces

II. *Scenarios*
(By well known or significant authors, or of worthy films)

III. *Designs*
A. Stage sets
B. Designs for costumes

IV. *Stills*
(see categories in note 1)

V. *Books, Magazines, and Pamphlets*
A. History
B. Novels made into films
C. Legal aspects
D. Source material

Source: Harry Alan Potamkin, *"Notes on the Film: A Proposal for a School of the Motion Picture,"* Hound and Horn *(October-December 1933): 140–143.*

FIGURE 3.3 Harry Alan Potamkin's taxonomy for a Marxist film library, designed to uncover the workings of the film industry for its patrons, was published in Lincoln Kirstein's *Hound and Horn* in 1933.

lation of great directors and harmonies within artworks falls into the category Benjamin, following Engels, calls "cultural history." "Cultural history," for Benjamin, preserves the interests of the ruling class. In art appreciation it celebrates "unities" and "great geniuses" by appealing to illusory "universal" rather than class-based ideas of beauty. This history of triumphs, Benjamin argues, represses the political circumstances that allow some art and artists to be preserved on the backs of "the unnamed drudgery of their contemporaries." "There is no document of culture," he aphoristically restated the same point, "which is not at the same time a document of barbarism." "Cultural history," Benjamin continues, disguises its preservation of the powerful by claiming to address a general, classless public rather than acknowledging its specific class politics. In the end, "Cultural history, to be sure, enlarges the weight of the treasure which accumulates on the backs of humanity. Yet cultural history does not provide the strength to shake off this burden in order to be able to control it."[77] For both Benjamin and Potamkin, the historical-materialist collection contained the potential to reveal the class politics of art.

Benjamin set up the image of the collector as cultural historian as an uncomplicated straw man against which to describe the collector as historical materialist. The historical-materialist collector, for Benjamin, is involved in a class-directed, destructive project; the historical-materialist collector reorganizes the fragments of the past to make them politically useful for the present; and "the historical materialist explodes the epoch out of its reified 'historical continuity.' "[78] The importance of the collection for Benjamin is its ability to liberate "things from the drudgery of being useful" and place them "into the closest relation to things of the same kind."[79] Potamkin's plan called for both the fragmentation of film history and the reorganization of those fragments into a politically transforming order.

In the end, Potamkin's fragmentation and reordering of film and the film industry separated his plan from its predecessors. Potamkin's plan immediately divided films into two categories: domestic and foreign. Clearly, Potamkin did not intend to celebrate Hollywood films. Nor did he, as a proselytizer for left-wing documentary and avant-garde production, consider Hollywood to be synonymous with "domestic" film. It is more likely that the national makeup of Potamkin's schema referred not to U.S. film production at all but simply implied that a film collection should represent a national film industry to its respective national audience. Potamkin's critical work consistently attempted to integrate theories of production and reception into a larger national framework. Surveying national cinemas on a tour of Europe, Potamkin never discussed the

Italian film *Cabiria* (1914), just for example, without also positioning it in relation to the Italian film industry, Italian fascism, and his (in this case unfavorable) impressions of Italian movie audiences.[80] Potamkin's film library fit smoothly into the national program of his criticism.

Within the overarching national categories, Potamkin placed in opposition popular (i.e., commercial) films (column B in his diagram) and films not made explicitly for profit (column A). In the column of noncommercial films, the subcategories stand alone without further breakdown or elaboration: e.g., "ethnological," "educational," "animation." The exception to this rule is the category of "experimental" film, which is subdivided into "abstract" films and "absolute" films. This is an important distinction for Potamkin, who frequently objected to the "absolute" or "pure" film's quest for media specificity. Filmmakers and theorists interested in isolating the unique properties of film, he often complained, engaged in a dogmatic and socially irrelevant formalism. The "abstract" film, in contrast, encompassed for Potamkin the political engagement of the 1920s avant-garde. In general, all of Potamkin's categories were designed to separate the politically relevant elements of films or the film industry from the elements that seemed to veil their politics as formalism or entertainment.

If the subcategories of noncommercial films needed little further explication, the field of commercial film was broken down into constituent parts to uncover a variety of hidden connections between films. Instead of the typical genre breakdown we might expect to find, Potamkin was barely interested in complete films at all. Instead, most of the categories culled groups of related scenes from within films, slicing through film history with a variety of different methods. One group, for instance, contained scenes that were revealing of individual national traits while another category, termed "industrial sequences," compared institutional traits of studio styles.

Looking at fragments rather than at films in their entirety disrupts films' ability to circulate as distinct commodities. The fragmentation of films to uncover national and institutional connections worked to interfere with the commercial market for films. As opposed to the importance the Harvard plan placed on the unity of individual films to bolster and extend their market value, Potamkin's emphasis on fragments reduced the significance — and therefore the exhibition value — of individual films as commodities.

Potamkin's "exploding" of film history into fragments, to use Benjamin's term, is important. But so is his reassembly of those fragments. Potamkin's taxonomy was generally ahistorical in approach. He devoted almost the entire diagram to sketching a synchronic, ahistorical topography of the cinema, emphasizing formal, industrial, and cultural divisions. In Potamkin's plan for a film library, only a single category, "pivotal masterpieces" was devoted to the history of film. This format replaced an evolutionary historiography of film with a structural analysis of cinema that revealed to the film library patron the complex network of determinants that came to bear on the final film product: national traits, industrial limitations, individual artistry in direction and acting, and so on.

It was a Marxist reworking of Harvard's proto–Academy Award ceremony. Instead of offering a history of film's development, Potamkin's collection would have inculcated in a mass public the specialized critical skills of the film intelligentsia: the cult of individual elements that came from repetition and dissent. Moreover, Potamkin planned to solidify this transfer of expertise to the mass public by making the documentary material (scripts, critical literature, and stills), the same material Harvard wanted to save for art historians, available to the critical audience. He also wanted the film library to be incorporated into a larger mission of film education that would have included a film school as well. In the film school and library, the intelligentsia's critical knowledge of film and the film industries would have been transferred to a mass audience.

Ironically, Potamkin's plan was published in a little magazine read exclusively by members of the culture elite he was trying to supplant. It is impossible to predict what would have happened if Potamkin had lived, but it seems clear that his tenure as an honorary member of uptown bohemia had ended. The downtown Marxists at the Workers Film and Photo League and the New School for Social Research, not the civic intellectuals, teamed up in 1933 to open the commemorative Harry Alan Potamkin Film School. But the school lasted for only one year, and it neither employed Potamkin's vision nor did it include a film library.[81] Like their other encounters with communism and Marxism, Kirstein and the civic intellectuals flirted with but rejected Potamkin's plan for a film institution. Instead, as leaders of the Museum of Modern Art and founders of its Film Library, the civic intellectuals replaced Potamkin with a new expert, Iris Barry, who seemed at first, we will see, more firmly grounded in the elitist camp of high modernism.

What is interesting about Harvard's and Potamkin's plans are not only their attempts to place film at the service of class politics but the importance they placed on film as a medium for transforming American politics. Although neither of these plans was directly put into practice, they reveal the poles of the debate that drove the Fogg's progeny when they were finally given the opportunity to start an American national film institution in the mid-1930s.

4

IRIS BARRY, HOLLYWOOD IMPERIALISM, AND THE GENDER OF THE NATION

> If cinema is historical, so is pleasure. If cinema is ideological so is pleasure. Hence the question: Can pleasure be instrumentalized, institutionalized, used and abused, exploited, transformed, and made "political"?
>
> —Thomas Elsaesser, "Film History and Visual Pleasure" (1984)

> We go to the cinema and do not know or ask what it is: yet there must be something in common between Buster Keaton's *Sherlock Jnr.* and a travel picture like *The Epic of Everest.*
>
> —Iris Barry, "*The Epic of Everest* at the Scala" (1924)

IN 1933 the director of the Museum of Modern Art's Department of Architecture and Design, Philip Johnson, met the British film critic Iris Barry (born Crump) at a party in New York, most likely held at the apartment/salon of their mutual friends Kirk and Constance Askew. Johnson promptly offered Barry a job starting a library at the Museum of Modern Art. Barry had some experience as a librarian; she had worked for a short period in the library of the School of Oriental Studies in London. But the post was, more accurately, a form of patronage for a writer who traveled in the same transatlantic circles as Johnson, Lincoln Kirstein, and Alfred Barr.[1] These circles included Ezra Pound, Wyndham Lewis, and other modernist writers and artists associated with Kirstein's journal *Hound and Horn.* Alfred Barr was in Europe on an extended sabbatical when Johnson appointed Barry librarian. When Barr returned to New York, he recognized the opportunity—with a film expert already on staff— to push again for the film department he had been planning since MoMA's inception. After years of campaigning, Barr finally persuaded the museum's trustees and the Rockefeller Foundation's administrators to investigate the viability of a film department, and in 1935 MoMA established a film library with Barry as its curator and her then husband, John Abbott, as its director.

In the right place at the right time, Barry was absorbed into the significant momentum to start a film department in the young but already influential museum. As a member of the same coterie as the Harvard circle, Barry's was hardly a radical or unfamiliar voice. Once she joined the project, however, Barry became the most important individual in the development of the Museum of Modern Art Film Library, and she became central to American cultural institutions' aggressive intervention in the production and circulation of film during World War II and the cold war. Before turning to her work at MoMA, however, it is necessary to look at Barry's early career as a film critic in Britain. Her early career not only illuminates Barry's personal biography, it reflects the widespread mobilization of film in the pursuit of nationalistic responses to the very real threat of Hollywood imperialism.

Galvanized by the spread of American culture in the 1920s, Barry emerged as a staunchly anti-American political film theorist. After moving to America in the 1930s, however, she changed from an anti-American modernist to a champion of the global spread of Hollywood and American culture. Barry's personal transformation is intertwined, in many ways, with cultural institutions' changing relationship to film. The 1920s saw the rise of film clubs, film societies, and art house movie theaters that grew out of communities of film lovers, artists, and critics. The film society movement was part of a response to Hollywood's post–World War I dominance. Dadaists, for example, found art in the repeated showing of select Hollywood films, and Soviet critics sought to mount a national cinema style based on a reinterpretation of Hollywood editing techniques. Cinephiles often had radical political ambitions for their film venues. By the 1930s, however, museums, libraries, foundations, and government agencies in the Soviet Union, Europe, and the United States began to take film very seriously as political propaganda, and many of the cinephiles of the 1920s were suddenly thrown into positions of real political power.

Barry's inclusion in the group of founders for MoMA's Film Library solidified the links between the Harvard group, Pound-Eliot modernism, and the culture of European film clubs. Barry spent almost a decade as a protégé of Ezra Pound, occasionally publishing derivative imagist poetry in modernist "little magazines";[2] she was a founding member and organizer of the London Film Society (1925); and she published regular film

columns in London papers between 1923 and 1930. Barry's collecting
agenda and political perspective as curator of MoMA's Film Library were
informed by her viewing in these contexts and were contingent upon the
web of personal contacts she developed throughout the European film
community during the 1920s.

But the continuities between Barry's activities in the 1920s and her later
work as a curator are more than just personal. As we will see, Barry's vision
of film history rested on theoretical propositions developed in London in
the 1920s and revised (though not abandoned) in New York between the
1930s and the 1960s. Reading Barry's early writings and their context reveals that her interests in establishing a canon of films, a narrative of cinema's development, alternative spaces for film exhibition, and eventually
a circulating film library all stemmed from a desire to reposition film as a
medium of public opinion. More specifically, Barry sought to use film as
a means of transforming both gender and national identities. Through
Barry we get an image of the film curator, collector, and policymaker not
as passionate individual in the Romantic mode but as a socially conscious
member of the filmgoing public.

Indeed, throughout her career as a film critic, Barry identified herself as
a member of the public. She entered the film world as an amateur, or at
best a buff. After the unsuccessful publication of her first novel, the autobiographical *Splashing into Society* (1923), John St. Loe Stratchey, a
friend's father, gave Barry a regular film column in the London paper he
edited, the *Spectator*. There is nothing in Barry's earlier writings or in her
autobiographical notes written in the 1960s to suggest that she took her
moviegoing hobby seriously before that point.[3] But Barry quickly grew into
an eloquent theorist and critic of the phenomenology of spectatorship, the
state of British cinema, and the influence of films on society. Instead of presenting herself as a highbrow slumming in the movie theater, as did so
many European intellectuals in the 1920s, Barry highlighted the typicality
of her moviegoing habits to corroborate her insights into the "mind of the
spectator" (a favorite phrase of Barry's). She defined herself as a "pleasure
loving member of the public" and later reminisced about the "intoxicating
+ vaguely forbidden" atmosphere that drew her to movie theaters as a girl.[4]
Throughout her career as a critic and curator, Barry remained a
participant-observer in the audience more than an aesthete or connoisseur.
Writing from the perspective of the spectator, Barry became interested in
cinema as a form of *mass influence* and *"vicarious experience."*[5] She identified filmgoing variously as a psychoanalytic salve, an educator, and a drug
that had the ability to transform individual and mass identities.

Barry's personal reflections on the cinema developed in response to two larger shifts in 1920s film culture. The first was the formation of a British national cinema. Within a nationwide debate about how to improve the moribund postwar British film industry, Barry actively participated in the movement to establish a national tradition of modernist art cinema in Britain through alternative exhibition venues modeled on French film societies and repertory theaters. Barry's involvement with the London Film Society functioned as both a springboard to and a rehearsal for her role as curator at MoMA. It also provided her with an opportunity to theorize how an alternative exhibition venue might reshape national cinema industries and national identities.

The second shift Barry responded to was the reassessment of cinema by modernist women writers in the late 1920s. Along with her contemporaries and Bloomsbury neighbors H. D., Virginia Woolf, Bryher (Annie Ellerman), and Dorothy Richardson, Barry theorized what she saw as a new relationship between gender, beauty, and experience as mediated by cinematic representation. In the end, Barry's readings of film as a gendered medium also influenced her views on how film might best be used as a tool in the formation of national identities. Reading Barry as an interlocutor in both nationalist and feminist discourses on the cinema helps to explain her later role as curator at MoMA and decisions that have become mystified under the rubric "art."

AMERICANIZATION AND ENGLISHNESS

Iris Barry began to write about cinema at the same moment that the British film industry was trying to rebuild itself in the wake of World War I. Like France, Italy, Russia, and Germany, Britain dramatically cut back film production during the war. After the war, Britain emerged, also like most of Western Europe, primarily as an importer of American films. At the nadir in 1926, approximately 95 percent of films on British screens were American.[6] But whereas Germany, France, and the Soviet Union developed national styles and industries that achieved footholds in the world market, British film production continued to founder throughout the 1920s. In the eyes of many British commentators, the blame lay in the omnipresence of American films, which seemed part of a larger American cultural and economic imperialism, or what had been known since the Paris Universal Exhibition of 1867 as Americanization.[7]

The protean discourse of Americanization in Britain has, of course, often reflected British anxieties as much as American conquest. Nineteenth-century literary critics Matthew Arnold and Edmund Gosse, for example, worried that American-style mass literacy and democracy would unhinge the hierarchical transference of literary canons and place the burden of taste in the hands of an insufficiently prepared mass. After World War II, writers on both the political left and right—including George Orwell, Evelyn Waugh, and Richard Hoggart—united in a cultural conservatism that decried the dissolution of both elite literary culture and native working-class cultures as they both competed with a vulgar and homogenizing (yet somehow irresistible) American consumer culture. By the 1960s, according to Dick Hebdige, American popular culture had become so pervasive that British youth could express alternative identities only by recombining the iconography of American popular culture.[8]

In the period we are concerned with here, the 1920s, the fear of Americanization was pitched largely in economic terms and focused primarily on the success of the Hollywood film industry in Britain. The rapidly expanding Hollywood hegemony seemed both a harbinger of total economic and cultural imperialism and a process still early enough in its development to be controlled. As a result, the British Parliament, film industry, and press debated the best means of improving the quality and success of British films and establishing a British national cinema with an international presence to challenge Hollywood. The proposed solutions (some of them implemented) included increased isolationist policies (e.g., quotas on American film), economic incentives for studios and for exhibitors who showed British films, and schemes for fostering a uniquely British aesthetic.[9]

In her film columns in the *Spectator* (1924–1929) and the *Daily Mail* (1925–1930), Barry was just as likely to discuss hard numbers and government film policy as aesthetics, and her taste in films developed in dialogue with a range of national concerns. In most cases, Barry shared the general feeling that the American film industry posed a threat, certainly to the British film industry but to Britain's position as an economic and imperial power as well. It is surprising in this context to discover that the woman who organized "A Short Survey of American Film, 1895–1932" and "Some Memorable American Films, 1896–1934" as MoMA's first two film programs, and who did so much to enshrine American film at the center of film historiography, at first considered American silent film to be an unfortunate, transitional stage in film development.

Moreover, before she moved to the United States in 1932, Barry had little of the cultural understanding necessary to evaluate American films. It is only a slight exaggeration to say that throughout the 1920s Barry watched Hollywood films as ethnographic representations of American life. In one review, she went so far as to describe Hollywood domestic melodramas as, "travel picture[s] of American life."[10] Barry felt so far removed from American language and customs that she added a glossary to the American edition of her book *Let's Go to the Movies* so that Americans could translate such mundane words as *zip* (pep), *sweets* (candy), and *pub* (saloon). It was with more than a little self-directed irony that after settling in New York Barry published an article declaring, "Hollywood Is Not America." "Everyone in Europe," she wrote, "has been told so often how thoroughly he is in danger of being Americanized by the movies that it is astounding to come here and find that movies do not represent America in the least."[11]

Barry's anti-American feelings of the 1920s may have been tempered after she moved to New York, but the British and European nationalism that led to her antipathy toward Hollywood cinema nevertheless form the roots of Barry's view of film as principally a national art. One of Barry's earliest articles, published in the trade journal *The Bioscope*, set out a position that she would maintain throughout the 1920s. In part responding to Vachel Lindsay—whose *The Art of the Moving Picture* had recently been reprinted in Britain and whose language Barry often appropriated—Barry addressed the question "A National or International Cinema?" In this article, Barry argued that discussions of film as an international language or an "esperanto of contemporary human emotion" had been misguided. She agreed that films spoke clearly across national borders, but she also insisted that the films themselves, like other art forms, always bore the imprint of their country of production.[12] Elsewhere, Barry clarified this position, suggesting that films were symptomatic of national identity—a position that links her with Alfred Barr's and Siegfried Kracauer's writing on film while at MoMA.[13] In a heuristic attempt to differentiate national cinemas—a game she would refine in later articles—Barry listed essential traits of different countries. In her schema Americans made action films "because they understand suspense"; France made serious melodramas that reflected the melodrama of its law courts; "Sweden contributed pictorial parables, because legend and parable colour all their art." But Barry couldn't find a thread to unite British films. She suggested that because many popular British novels were character studies, Britain might find its national form in the elaboration of character.[14]

In other places, Barry attempted to define national traits by tempo and tone rather than subject and genre: "Shall I say that American films are slick and speedy, English films pedestrian, German films ponderous,

Swedish films severe, French films blustering?" Barry insisted that national traits were somehow institutionally instilled and transcended context and individual artistry. Americanness, for example, remained intact, "even when an American film is made in Italy . . . or when it is made in the States with a German director, French photographer and a Babel of actors."[15] National identity and style, in other words, were simply there to be recognized by critical eyes—like Barry's. Her columns continually asserted her ability to identify proper national traits through films, and she aimed to train a public of readers to do the same.

In addition to reading films as symptomatic of national identity, Barry analyzed their reception as a form of cultural exchange. Barry took for granted what had become a truism for both Americans and Europeans by the early 1920s: that the dominance of American films promoted an international embrace of American lifestyles, values, and, most visibly, commercial products. The head of the Motion Picture Producers and Distributors of America, Will Hays, orchestrated much of the discussion of Americanization. To shift public concerns away from Hollywood's erosion of American morals and toward its aid to American industry, Hays spoke widely and unabashedly about film's role as a "silent salesman" for American goods. "Every foot of American film," he boasted, "sells $1.00 worth of manufactured products some place in the world."[16] In another speech Hays claimed, "The motion picture carries to every American at home, and to millions of purchasers abroad, the visual, vivid perception of American manufactured products."[17] Hays's catchy soundbites infiltrated discussions of film around the world. Barry's contemporary, the British film critic C. A. Lejeune, observed in a discussion of films as "ambassadors of commerce": "Go where you please, in any city of the world, and you will see women emulating the make-up and hairdressing of Greta Garbo; young men dressed in the George Raft tailoring cut, shop windows advertising the soap used by Claudette Colbert, or the cosmetics favored by Mae West, while dashing young continentals greet you with the hand-salute of Gary Cooper."[18]

As Tom Ryall has demonstrated, questions of the deterioration of British sovereignty, trade abroad, and prestige came to hang on the fate of the film industry during Parliament's debates in the 1920s.[19] Barry echoed the common rallying cry that "trade follows the film," and in a series of articles on "The British Film Situation," written while the House of Lords was considering new film policy, Barry articulated fears that an American cultural imperialism was stunting the British economy and eroding British military imperialism:

A popular entertainment such as the moving picture is not, however, in the same case a mere commodity. That Britons should eat Argentine meat does not mean that the *morale* of the nation is endangered. But a preponderance of foreign films is another matter: it is as though throughout the land all newspapers, magazines and books, were foreign, describing almost exclusively foreign events and reflecting almost wholly foreign ways of thought. The American films are not consciously propaganda, but they continually remind the vast (and impressionable) cinema audiences of the sky-scrapers, factories, army, aeroplanes, ballrooms, universities, great open spaces, cattle, and so forth which exist in the United States, and never recall that the Empire also contains manufacturing towns, landscapes, armies, and virile men. And we begin to like this no better than Americans would like it if every picture theatre of theirs showed nothing but British films. It is not only that we see few British films at home; we also expect few. Our Dominions and Colonies and the other nations of the world are not made aware of England as they are aware of America. This is bad alike for our prestige and trade which "follows the film."[20]

This paragraph is one of Barry's most pessimistic statements on the Americanization of Britain, yet it reveals the centrality she placed on film's role in shaping public opinion and influencing national identity. In other places, Barry refined the formulation expressed in this paragraph: that American films functioned like propaganda influencing the passive mass of spectators. She began to have more faith in spectators' critical abilities. But she consistently worried that overabundance of American images masked and emasculated the iconography of British identity by precluding Britain's ability to represent itself.

Barry's analysis of Hollywood's influence was actually less extreme than some of the positions voiced in the popular British press or in the House of Lords. One peer, the Viscount Arthur Lee of Fareham, tried to associate the Americanization engendered by Hollywood with anxieties about communist conspiracies. Hollywood films, Lord Lee claimed, are "used by Bolsheviks to stir up trouble." The writer who reported this claim in *Harper's* magazine explained the logic:

American film actually imperils the safety of great empires. It does this, so its critics say, by lowering the prestige of the white man in the Orient. . . . It is here that the Bolsheviks are said to enter into the equation: using cheap melodrama to undermine the prestige of white governments at home.[21]

This *Harper's* article confirms Barry's assessment that cultural imperialism was perceived to be a direct threat to military imperialism. The *Harper's* article also offers another perspective because its author, Charles Merz, was writing for an American audience. Merz evaluated the British reaction to Hollywood films for American business practices, and he found the opposite of Will Hays. Merz concluded that by threatening British imperialism, Hollywood undermined its role as a "silent salesman" and "foreign ambassador." As a result, Merz called on Hollywood to decrease the overt American nationalism and moral transgressions in Hollywood films that insulted and offended other nations.[22]

Despite Barry's agreement with pessimistic diagnoses of the effects of American films, she disapproved of efforts to limit the export of American film to Britain, by far the most popularly supported solution in Britain. When she did endorse government intervention in the functioning of the film industry, she did so only when the policies seemed to bolster the British industry without hampering relations with the United States. In questions of policy, Barry was almost solely interested in exhibition. Significantly, her career as a film critic began with a series of articles responding to an initiative called British Film Weeks. Arranged by the British National Film League, British Film Weeks were blocks of time in which theaters across Britain reserved space exclusively for British films. These occasions provided British production companies with an opportunity to gain access to theaters from which they were excluded because of "blind" and "block" booking arrangements between U.K. theaters and U.S. distributors. In other words, exhibitors agreed to show whichever films distributors provided in order to secure deals with the most popular studios. In 1926 Barry took a more active role in determining government policy when she represented Britain at a conference of exhibitors in Paris sponsored by the League of Nations. The conference's goal was to establish a pan-European response to the American invasion of film screens, but no consensus emerged.[23] When Barry eventually supported the quota legislation of a 1927 bill, she did so only because she was convinced that the limited quotas were pro-British and not anti-American.

Why did Barry oppose strict limits on the influx of American films? On the one hand, she feared that exhibition circuits would collapse without a steady stream of American films. *"Take away American films,"* she warned, *"you close the cinemas."* Overly aggressive quotas might diminish the central role of film as a form of entertainment and communication. As Barry wrote in 1925, "at the moment the cinema is American and little else."[24] On the other hand, Barry was less troubled by the dominance of American cinema or a global Americanization than most of her contemporaries. America impressed Barry as an economic force, but she was skeptical of the merits of its films and the culture they presented.

In the 1920s, Barry thought of America as an "unsophisticated" but bustling nation. [25] She attributed the success of American films to the efficient industry of Hollywood producers, not to the quality or mass appeal of the films. Barry was not immune to what she referred to as the "lesser glories" of Hollywood cinema: John Ford and Tom Mix westerns, Felix the Cat, and Norma Talmadge.[26] But these were pleasures for the habitual filmgoer like herself who had to cull moments of pleasure from the hours of dreck. When, in an unusual encomium, Barry declared the preeminence of American films, her compliment was preceded by a comical string of qualifications: "Now while it is true that many films of American origin are deplorable, that they are vulgar and sensational and even dismally stupid, it is also true that we owe the present vitality of the cinema as a whole to Americans, and that their best films are the best in the world."[27] But when Barry found space in her columns to recommend a Hollywood actor, director, or film to her readers, she always celebrated and called attention to European émigrés in Hollywood: Charlie Chaplin, Ernst Lubitsch, Greta Garbo, and Reginald Denny, among others. When analyzing *Hotel Imperial* (1926), a film financed by Paramount Pictures, directed by Swedish filmmaker Maurice Stiller, and produced by the recent German émigré Erich Pommer, Barry attributed anything interesting in the film to the "German influence" and all elements of bathos to Hollywood. After decrying the saccharin ending, Barry grumbled that even with so many talented non-Americans involved in the production, "Hollywood wins."[28] This kind of tunnel vision caused Barry to see German influences in everything she liked, even justifying her affection for Douglas Fairbanks's films by claiming that they had incorporated elements of German expressionist style.[29]

On the whole, however, American films seemed so middling to Barry that, more than simply opposing quotas, she *encouraged* the spread of American cinema, because she was sure that Hollywood only undermined the process of Americanization. Barry suspected that after a decade of Hollywood dominance audiences were growing weary of American films and that the films themselves were devolving into self-sustaining simulacra of American life:

> I cannot help feeling that the prestige of America is lower because of the cinema, than it would have been without. It is hard to retain one's respect for a

nation so constantly put before our eyes, as it is almost always on the screen, in an unenviable whirl of surreptitious cocktail-drinking, graft, bad taste, hideous domestic architecture and vile manners. Our good sense tells us that it is the motion picture community, not the United States that is reflected."[30]

Barry further became convinced that with the help of an ongoing public debate about the value of Hollywood films, British filmgoers would eventually develop a critical perspective and distance themselves from Hollywood entertainment. Barry responded to "the theory that the public wishes almost exclusively to be entertained with rubbish," with the announcement that "there is not only no such thing as 'the public,' [but] the success of mediocre American films is simply the success of the cinema as a form of entertainment."[31] Like Vachel Lindsay, Victor Oscar Freeburg, and Harry Alan Potamkin, Barry concluded that film as a medium had not yet found its public and that its nascent audience was not yet film literate. As a result, she restaged the political and economic debates about Americanization on an aesthetic field.

As a reaction to Hollywood, Barry used her columns to promote what we would now call a *camp* appreciation of Hollywood films. In a weeklong survey of London film theaters and audiences, Barry observed that spectators like her "positively enjoy tearing a bad film to bits, so long as they do not get too many [bad films] or feel the badness is deliberate. The professional critic, indeed, feels while overhearing the often unexpected and very shrewd comments of those sitting near, that almost every filmgoer is, purely for his or her own amusement, a critic."[32] Written in 1928, this passage suggests that Barry gauged attempts to dislodge American film's hold on British audiences through the development of a critical audience more effective than control over the circulation of films.

In addition to lamenting the mediocrity of American films, Barry encouraged audiences to attend films made by what she referred to as the "continental school": Swedish, Danish, French, and especially German films. Throughout the 1920s Barry frequented the New Gallery Kinema and other London theaters that specialized in European films, and she frequently used her columns to promote German films. Her most enthusiastic praise was reserved for *Die Nibelungen, Warning Shadows, Metropolis,* and Lotte Reiniger's *Prince Achmed.* In her review of *Warning Shadows,* for instance, Barry claimed that Weimar cinema

has in fact "given cinema a soul," though it is a neurotic soul [another of Barry's attempts to diagnosis national identity through film]. America is feeling this influence and assimilating it. There is everything to hope for, but the next few years we shall probably often need to look back to these 'high-brow" Continental pictures and refuse valiantly to be soothed by the hypnotic murmur that because films are made to please a vast undifferentiated public, they must necessarily be vulgar and cheap.[33]

Barry clamored to be heard over the "hypnotic murmur" that facilitated the complacent acceptance of Americanization. She urged British filmmakers to follow the example of Germany and develop a distinct style that both spoke to its national identity and differentiated its films in an international market flooded with formulaic Hollywood genre films. In one impassioned plea Barry declared, "Films which are 'different' must be made."[34]

Yet in the above passage Barry does not criticize Hollywood's assimilation of national styles. Barry's was not an Arnoldian, a priori opposition to the cultural imperialism of mass media. On the contrary, she seems pleased that "continental pictures" improved Hollywood films. She did not think, however, that the success of "continental pictures" or criticism alone could bring about mass changes in British production or the taste of spectators. For that, Barry helped launch the influential London Film Society, which promised to launch a stronger British national film industry.

THE MINORITY, THE MASS, AND THE FILM SOCIETY

As her film criticism makes clear, Barry did not occupy the typical stance of a European intellectual toward Hollywood. She neither reveled in the action, comedy, and stars of American films as did the Surrealists nor did Barry dismiss Hollywood with a wholesale condemnation of mass culture as would F. R. Leavis, Theodor Adorno, and Max Horkheimer.[35] Instead, Barry attempted to forge a minority of middlebrow tastemakers, and in so doing she broke with her mentor Ezra Pound's aristocratic view of culture. Barry not only wrote *about* popular culture but she wrote from *within* popular culture. Barry's most visible forum, the *Daily Mail*, was the most successful lower-middle-class newspaper in England at the time.[36] Indeed, Pound had explicitly warned Barry away from the *Daily Mail* at the beginning of her tutelage. "The main thing being," Pound wrote to the budding poet Iris Barry, "to have enmagazined some mass of fine literature which hasn't been mauled over and vulgarized and preached as a virtue by Carlyle, *The Daily Mail, The Spectator, The New Witness*, or any other proletariat of 'current opinion.' "[37] By writing for the *Daily Mail* and the slightly more upscale and politically engaged *Spectator*, Barry withdrew from the literary coterie of the little magazines and embraced a position equivalent to the organizers of the Book of the Month Club or reviewers for the book section of the *New York Herald Tribune* (which Barry would write for after moving to New York).[38] As a middlebrow tastemaker, Barry saw herself actively directing popular culture to create a national public.

If in the 1920s Barry wanted Britain to compete with Hollywood with minimal government intervention, she strongly supported changes that encouraged the formation of a national style and the cultivation of a public able to discern stylistic differences. To advance the industry and wean audiences from American films, Barry became actively involved in the British film society movement, a move that was in many ways a precursor to her activities at MoMA. Far from being a turning away from the political and economic implications of Americanization, the film society movement's

FIGURE 4.1   *Praxitella* (Iris Barry) by Wyndham Lewis (c. 1921).
(Courtesy of the Wyndham Lewis Memorial Trust. © Wyndham Lewis and the estate of the late Mrs. G. A. Wyndham Lewis)

creation of noncommercial exhibition venues represents an alternative strategy for developing a national film culture and, ultimately, national pride and prosperity.

Within a contentious environment of emerging alternative or minority film cultures in Britain in the 1920s, Barry joined with a group of intellectuals, aristocrats, and cinéastes to found the London Film Society in 1925. Many historians have chronicled the wave of film criticism, film clubs, and experimental film movements that characterized British film culture in the 1920s.[39] Within that climate, the London Film Society occupied a clearly delineated position. It was separated from the collective of modernist writers and filmmakers associated with the journal *Close-Up* on one side, the organization of socialist film clubs on another side, and the mainstream film industry on yet a third. The London Film Society was modeled directly on the example of the Vieux-Columbier theater in Paris, one of the first theaters in Europe devoted exclusively to screening experimental film. The London Film Society's other direct antecedent was the London Stage Society, which had introduced landmarks of experimental theater to Britain since 1899. The London Film Society was dedicated to screening films that had little chance of making it to British screens, either because they were not commercially viable or because they had not passed British censors. (The London Film Society bypassed the censor's restrictions by operating on a subscription basis rather than selling tickets.)

Other European film clubs were smoothly incorporated into the functioning of their national film cultures, and Soviet workers' clubs proved integral to the formation of a Soviet national film culture. American film clubs too enjoyed a brief vogue, although they proved all but innocuous compared to the Hollywood behemoth.[40] Yet all segments of British film culture perceived the London Film Society as a threat. The commercial film industry worried that it would derail the careers of talented filmmakers and lead them on noncommercial paths. One of the society's founders, Adrian Brunel, even had to resign from the society's council in order to continue working in the film industry.[41] Despite hostility from the commercial film industry, however, the London Film Society sought to jumpstart a popular British national cinema by "fertilis[ing] British film ideas" and nurturing a public for non-Hollywood films. The number of successful filmmakers associated with the London Film Society, including Alfred Hitchcock, John Grierson, and Anthony Asquith, indicates that it did at least partially achieve its goal.[42]

On another front, the growing movement of workers' film societies in Britain, which were organized directly for political purposes, accused the

London Film Society of being apolitical. One tract complained that the Film Society and the larger discussion of film as art represented a conspiracy to "eliminate social content" from film culture.[43] But this too misconstrued the intention if not the effect of the Film Society. The Film Society's chairman, the aristocrat Ivor Montagu, was a socialist when the society began in 1925, and he joined the Communist Party in 1929. Montagu went on to be president of the Communist Party in Great Britain and a successful Soviet spy. As recently decrypted Communist Party communications reveal, Montagu (code name Nobility) functioned undetected as a leader of the Soviet spy ring in Britain.[44] He started the Film Society after a life-altering trip to the Soviet Union in 1925, and his primary motivation for starting the organization was to introduce and promote films that had been censored for political reasons by the reactionary British Board of Film Censors. One ongoing mission of the Film Society was to screen banned Soviet films.

The practice of showing banned films, in turn, drew threats of lawsuits from a different segment of the British press, which claimed that the Film Society sought to "communise" the country. In response to these accusations, Montagu resigned from the Film Society's council in 1929 when it appeared that his political affiliations—as a member of the Communist Party and vice chairman of the Workers' Film Federation—might compromise the society's growing influence. Foregrounding aesthetic and technical goals allowed the Film Society to show politically engaged films in an environment that viewed all films as political statements first and as art and entertainment second.[45] Still, it would be wrong to suggest that the Film Society continually changed in the light of criticism to match some clear and unswerving mission. Rather, the society tested the limits of an alternative exhibition in the emerging national film culture.

In the *Spectator*, Iris Barry frequently complained about the mystifying decisions of the censors, especially when they banned films for political rather than moral reasons.[46] Ivor Montagu was a practicing film critic himself and a regular reader of Barry's columns. Aware of her positions on national cinema and censorship, Montagu and the actor Hugh Miller approached Barry with their idea for the London Film Society. Barry had been a film critic for little over a year, but she enlisted the few friends she had made who might prove useful, John Stratchey and theater owner Sidney Bernstein. She hosted a party in the small Bloomsbury basement flat she shared with her first husband, the poet Alan Porter. The party evolved into the first meeting of the Film Society's council, and without remuneration or an official title, Barry continued to help organize programs and advertise the Film Society in her columns. At least at first, Barry neither traveled enough nor had the personal contacts to find new films for the organization. She functioned generally as an enthusiast and devoted attendee.[47]

Limited information on the Film Society makes it impossible to establish Barry's exact role in the organization's workings,[48] but we can identify two ways in which her association there helped shape Barry's later career as MoMA's film curator. First, the Film Society offered Barry her first exposure to many films and filmmakers, including Sergei Eisenstein, Carl Dreyer, and Alfred Hitchcock, among others. It is important to remember that Barry had been a "member of the public" until 1924. As she admitted in her book *Let's Go to the Pictures* (1926), before that point she had seen only one of the handful of Russian films released in London (*Polikushka* [released 1922]), and she had missed many important films including Griffith's *The Birth of a Nation* (1915), though that didn't stop her from discussing *Birth* in her columns. It would be overly programmatic to suggest too close a correspondence between the agenda of the London Film Society and MoMA's later functioning, but it is clear nevertheless that the former exposed Barry to monuments of film history and to a community of European filmmakers, theorists, and producers who would reappear throughout the history of MoMA's Film Library. As Barry's correspondence while curator of MoMA's Film Library reveals, her major source when choosing films for the museum was her memories of film screenings at the London Film Society on Sunday afternoons. Barry's work for the London Film Society also proved essential to her important collecting trip through Europe and the Soviet Union in 1937. The doors that were opened are entirely the result of personal contacts she forged through the Film Society, including Eisenstein, Jean Benoit-Lévy, Charles Laughton, and Fritz Lang. In the Museum of Modern Art Film Library's first years, the London Film Society occasionally acted as a feeder for films and traveling filmmakers, including Paul Rotha, who briefly worked at MoMA's Film Library, and an unsuccessful attempt to bring Soviet documentary filmmaker Dziga Vertov to New York.[49]

Second, and more important, the Film Society provided Barry with an opportunity to reflect on the function of an alternative exhibition space, such as the one she would later create at MoMA. In her discussions of the Film Society, Barry seemed to smooth over the many controversies and contradictory positions and policies. Barry saw the Film Society as the clear and inevitable foundation of a national film industry, and she expanded and nuanced Montagu's promotional rhetoric. Barry adopted a model that resembled one put forward by the French filmmaker, theorist, and ciné-club zealot Germaine Dulac.[50] Like Dulac, Barry employed an evolutionary model of film development: "When the first films were made the public loved them. But were those same films put out to-day, no one could bear them. What has happened? Continuous improvement and un-tiring experiments have gone on, imperceptibly of course."[51] For both Barry and Dulac, avant-garde and mainstream film formed a dialectic of cinematic development. Barry had little appreciation for the avant-garde on its own terms; she dismissed it as irrelevant. Barry complained, for example, that *Ballet mécanique* (1924) was "meaningless," and although René Clair and Francis Picabia's film *Entr'acte* (1924) amused her because it contained a loose narrative sequence (a chase), Barry felt "confident that there is no future whatsoever for films of this kind" unless they aid in the production of narrative films.[52] As a result, Barry celebrated attempts to press avant-garde and Hollywood films into the service of modernist national cinemas through the use of alternative exhibition spaces.

As a result of her involvement with the London Film Society, Barry began to identify "a second cinema" that she considered an experimental laboratory to be used by the commercial film industry. In an article promoting the Film Society's opening—a text that resembles a manifesto in its utopian language and calls to action—Barry implored the British film industry to look to the avant-garde, which she referred to as an "increasingly self-conscious form of expression in a new medium . . . a new kind of beauty . . . the uncommercial, the ideal part of the cinema."[53] She argued that it "would *pay* the commercial cinema to support and encourage the non-commercial element,"[54] as French and German studios did, in order to develop differentiated national styles. She listed films as different as Douglas Fairbanks's *Don Q: Son of Zorro*, Chaplin's *The Gold Rush*, and F. W. Murnau's *The Last Laugh* as exemplary hybrids of commercial successes and avant-garde experiments. In subsequent articles, Barry thought the London Film Society effective in its stimulation of the British film industry, and she often celebrated its most obvious protégé, Alfred Hitchcock, who attended the Film Society and as a result incorporated American, German, and Soviet styles into his films.[55]

Throughout her career, Barry continued to believe in the power of al-ternative exhibition spaces like the London Film Society and the Museum of Modern Art Film Library to influence national film industries, nation-al identity, and public taste. This belief stemmed in part from her en-gagement with the larger changes in British film culture and a growing in-ternational interest in film collecting and alternatives to commercial exhibition. In addition to the rise of film societies and a film press, for instance, a series of British institutions and government studies beginning in the mid-1920s led to the creation of the British Film Institute and the British National Film Archive concurrently with the incorporation of MoMA's Film Library in the mid-1930s. The British National Film Archive can be traced directly to the 1932 report of the Commission on Educational and Cultural Films titled *The Film in National Life*, which was an important influence on Harry Alan Potamkin's own class-based proposal for a film library.[56] It should be no surprise then that after moving to New York, Barry immediately joined Julien Levy, Kirstein, Potamkin, Dwight Macdonald, and several others in their effort to start a New York film society, or that she helped found MoMA's Film Library. As curator and later director of the Museum of Modern Art Film Library, Barry became more sympathetic to Hollywood films and filmmakers. And her distaste for avant-garde film grew even stronger. Both of these changes resulted from a shift in her politics, which we will return to in chapters 5 and 6. In her role as MoMA's film curator, Barry continued to emphasize the centrality of noncommercial spaces of motion picture exhibition in the production and control of national identities. But she did this from an entirely pro-American position.

"IT EXISTS TO PLEASE WOMEN"

Barry thought experimental and mainstream film production worked together to advance modernist national cinemas, but she considered public taste the primary force guiding film style and content. *Let's Go to the Pictures* was written with the intention of encouraging spectators to patronize better films and thus encourage the production of better British films. Barry strongly believed that public taste drove film production. "The cinema runs after the public," she wrote, "it does not spring from it."[57] She expected the Film Society and her columns to give the inarticulate audiences both a lexicon for evaluating films and a forum in which to demonstrate a predilection for emerging and distinct national cinemas. "It is 'up to' the public," she wrote, "to hasten this differentiation."[58]

One segment of the public, in particular, interested Barry: women. Barry estimated that women made up three-quarters of British cinema audiences, and from the beginning of her journalistic career, she recognized that her frequent moviegoing linked her to a broad social formation. On one level, Barry's writing about women reproduced the turn-of-the-century discourse that viewed mass culture as a feminine realm and high or avant-garde culture as its masculine counterpart. In this vein, Barry grouped film with popular literature and theater made for women's consumption:

> Now one thing never to be lost sight of in considering the cinema is that it exists to please women. Three out of every four of all cinema audiences are women. I suppose all successful novels and plays are also designed to please the female sex too.[59]

By identifying cinema as a site for the production of women's pleasure, Barry referred to the sentimental genres targeted (and marketed) to women as well as to the space of the movie theater, which represented a new social sphere for bourgeois women. If bourgeois women had been denied the safety that allowed men unprecedented mobility in the nineteenth-century city, the relative propriety of the movie theater offered women a site for a new—if virtual—mobility.[60] Barry wrote about her own transgressions, sneaking off to see films while growing up in a provincial farming town. After moving to London in her early twenties, Barry delighted in the newly discovered freedom of urban filmgoing. She attended eight films a week (two on Sundays) even before becoming a professional critic.[61]

Barry saw this new social sphere as a radical forum with the potential for influencing the already captive audience of women. She considered the gaze of film spectatorship to be a form of "vicarious experience" as important to the formation of gender identities as real experiences. Theorizing the effect of film on women spectators, Barry began to carve out progressive and regressive canons from film history, and she encouraged the extension of those traditions she thought expanded women's horizon of experience.

Ultimately, Barry's writings on gender can't be separated from her analysis of the process of Americanization, which itself assumed a multivalent gendering in Barry's writings. As we saw earlier, in her pessimistic diagnosis of Americanization, Barry worried that representations of a prosperous America preempted Britain's ability to display a strong self-image ("manufacturing towns, landscapes, armies, and virile men").[62] In this way, according to Barry's analysis, the United States emasculated Britain in the eyes of both British and colonial movie audiences. To remedy the situation, she advocated injecting a reinvigorating dose of avant-garde experimentation, a formula that at first seems to reinforce the gendering of modernism as masculine.

But Barry also worried that, in addition to emasculating British cine-

ma, the overwhelming flow of romantic melodramas from America con-
stricted the realm of "vicarious experience" available to women spectators.
In this context, American films assumed a repressive feminine character as
well as a dominating masculinity. In response to what Barry perceived as
cinema's detrimental feminization of its audience, she prescribed the
same cure she suggested as a remedy for Britain's national cinema problem. Barry advocated fostering a modernist cinema which, she argued,
would contain more complex representations of gender identities than
Hollywood melodrama. Along the same lines, Barry championed travel
films (what we would now call ethnographic films) to expose women spectators to an even greater range of "vicarious experiences." From this perspective, modernist European films and orientalist travel films assumed a
feminist (through not feminine) function in addition to possessing a masculine cant.[63]

Barry's feminist position rested on her theory of film spectatorship as
experience. The future curator of film at the Museum of Modern Art rejected the widespread discussions in the 1920s of film as art (Rudolf
Arnheim, Louis Delluc, etc.) and of film as a cognitive instrument (Vertov,
Jean Epstein, *Close-Up,* etc.). Instead, Barry adopted metaphors that explained spectatorship as transporting and transformative: as a surrogate re-
ligion, a daydream, and a drug. "The Cinema," she wrote,

> is the great wrong-resolving agent of our time. . . . It is primarily something
> to banish care, even reflection, even consciousness. The cinema is a drug.
> That it has on certain grounds and for certain reasons an aesthetic value is
> more or less accidental. It is not designed to be an art, but a comforter.[64]

In a familiar formulation, Barry linked the "second-hand" emotions transferred though film inversely to the strictures and demands of industrial society and consumer culture. She saw the movie theater as a respite for
housewives and laborers.

Barry's reflections on women spectators overlap with those of her
Bloomsbury neighbors: Dorothy Richardson, Virginia Woolf, H. D., and
historical novelist–film critic Bryher. Dorothy Richardson, for example,
shared Barry's view of film as "comforter" and "narcotic." But where
Richardson found solace in the idea of spectators, "escap[ing] from cease-
less association . . . becom[ing] for a while citizens of the world,"[65] Barry
was critical of the content of those largely American, synthetic dreams.
She was also always aware that the abstract concept of *spectator* referred
most concretely to women.

Barry argued that Hollywood melodramas simply reproduced "popular opinion," which she defined as "a lot of lies boosted in the form of soothing syrup by the printing press and the film factory, to give people false dreams for fear they kick at true facts."[66] This opposition between "false dreams" and "facts" is central in Barry's discussion of spectatorship. Barry interpreted marriage narratives as being ideologically symbolic — like folk tales, she suggested. And she equated the "false dreams" of Hollywood narratives with dominant social conventions, both of which seemed to her to end inevitably in marriage. Barry complained of Hollywood films having "too much plot" and she devoted a chapter of her book *Let's Go to the Pictures* to a critique of "this marriage business" — a phrase that encompassed, for her, the Hollywood film industry, the trajectory of film narratives, and the traps of conventional notions of gender.[67] (It is probably not incidental that at the time she wrote this, Barry's marriage to Alan Porter was beginning to break up.)[68]

On the side of facts, Barry suggested that Hollywood narratives did not always dupe spectators; rather, they culled moments of beauty, pleasure, and truth from the visual details of films by separating them from the confines of narrative. "Even in the crudest films" she observed, "something is provided for the imagination, and emotion is stirred by the simplest things — moonlight playing in a bare room, the flicker of a hand against a window."[69] Here, again, Barry emphasized film's stimulation of emotion and pleasure, and her identification of the practice of viewing and even feeling visual detail against the grain of the narrative links her with a range of women's writings on cinema from the same period. We find echoes of it in Virginia Woolf's and H. D.'s ruminations on the expressive beauty of film's infinite visual specificity. Virginia Woolf, for example, described the film spectator's synesthetic absorption in detail as "the eye lick[ing] it all up instantaneously."[70]

Feminist film theorists have expanded on Barry's observations, suggesting that as a historical phenomenon of women's spectatorship, this selective viewing indicates the play of extratextual information that spectators brought to film viewing. Both exposés of popular stars in fan magazines and product tie-in advertising, they have claimed, further corroborate the speculation that women focused on visual details in excess of narrative. The heightened attention women spectators paid to visual details has been seen as resistance to the identification of classical film spectatorship, on the one hand, and another incarnation of the industrialized glance used to pick out products in the whirl of the shop window, on the other.[71]

As a participant-observer, Barry was less concerned with the reason for women's resistance to Hollywood narrative than with the possibilities it opened up. In the table of contents for *Let's Go to the Movies*, Barry both summarized her diagnosis of the problem with Hollywood cinema and promised a cure:

> —The Cinema exists to please women—The question of wedding bells— Some films which ignored them—A fierce digression on "this getting married business"—Do we really want so much love stuff?—How to get rid of it—

Barry theorized movie theaters not only as spaces for the acquisition of experience but also as an escape from society and training for reentry into streets, homes, and factories (much as Walter Benjamin and Siegfried Kracauer would). Barry saw the cinema as a truly revolutionary new realm for the simulation of experiences women were denied in the real ranks of English society. The actively resistant or at least restless form of spectatorship Barry observed in women spectators convinced her that women wanted better films or, as she says, "better dreams." As a result, Barry was led to take an active role in influencing film production, public taste, and popular conceptions of film history. Indeed, her interest in identifying canons of film and in developing alternative exhibition spaces grew directly out of her desire both to expand women's experiential realm through film and to bolster Britain's national cinema in the light of Americanization.

In her book *Let's Go to the Pictures*, Barry produced long lists of films she considered the basis for a progressive women's cinema. Barry's lists, as we might expect, included films of emerging national cinemas (mostly German and French), which, she argued, had successfully replaced Hollywood's marriage narratives with filmmaking styles that spoke to a range of gender identities in addition to national identities. Her lists of feminist films included the same modernist films she identified as successfully differentiating themselves from Hollywood: *The Golem, The Niebelungs, The Last Laugh, The Wheel*, and *Les Misérables*, among others. "Never in any of these [films]," Barry observed,

> is "love and marriage" the theme. Even in *The Niebelungs* the love of Siegfried and Kriemhild is only one little thread in the great canvas of magic and war hatred. *Warning Shadows* and *Nju* were again tales of married life, not of the business of getting married. They assumed no conventions, were plain tales of emotional crisis, such as occur, or might well occur, in any home. They were truth and not fiction. *The Last Laugh* had no love interest

at all: it was a character study, and so at the heart was *The Street*. Character is what counts in all of them, not marriage lines.[72]

Barry asked what happens when women become consumers of modernism? And she concluded that exposure to modernist films stretched the experiential realm of women moviegoers beyond the "marriage business" of Hollywood and, in turn, beyond socially circumscribed gender identities.

Barry also endorsed ethnographic films because, she argued, they too expanded audiences beyond the truncated world of romance in Hollywood narrative. Barry argued that ethnographic films challenged "moderns with our highly-specialized and therefore limited experience of life." After viewing the travel films *Grass* (1925) and *Moana* (1926), for instance, Barry called for a "return to nature," and in another instance she fetishized "the soft movements of bare brown limbs" in *Cannibals of the South Seas* (1917, though Barry saw it in 1924).[73] Fatimah Tobing Rony has described picturesque representations of early travelogue films, such as the ones discussed by Barry. For Rony this picturesqueness frames the films' subjects through a protected and nostalgic mode of address that virtually inscribed the power structure of colonial viewer and colonized subject.[74] Rather than a latent set of viewing relations, however, it is precisely the picturesque distance that Barry called attention to and found so empowering for English women who had been denied the protected social mobility of men. In a related orientalist context, Barry spoke of identifying with Lady Mary Wortley Montagu's tales of transgressing English gender stereotypes on trips to Turkey. Barry dubbed Lady Montagu the first New Woman, and in 1928 Barry wrote a popular biography of Lady Montagu, which reads like an extended metaphor for Barry's description of cinematic experience. The biography demonstrates how Lady Montagu remained distanced and cloaked from Turkish society, yet she returned to England transformed and with increased power because of her orientalist experience.[75]

In Barry's emphasis on both modernist national films and ethnographic films, her proposal for a progressive, feminist cinema followed directly from her thesis that, "The cinema helps us lead complete lives, in imagination if not in fact."[76] What is important here is not only Barry's insight into "the mind of the [1920s] spectator," but the fact that Barry thought of film collecting, canon formation, and noncommercial exhibition as means for shaping national and gender identities. Barry took part in the same debates about the social and political uses of film collections and film education that occupied Vachel Lindsay, Victor Freeburg, Frances Taylor Patterson, Harry Alan Potamkin, and the other early theorists of civic film institutions. But unlike these other theorists and advocates, Barry was later placed in an unusually powerful position to implement her theories of film's role in the creation of national and gender identity.

CONCLUSION: IRIS BARRY IN AMERICA

Barry's nationalism and feminism form a bridge between her activities in London in the 1920s and her later roles as curator, government adviser, and international organizer of film archives. Barry's commitment to modernist national cinemas and what she termed "the film of fact" (a larger designation that encompasses travel films and other forms of documentary) continued throughout her career. When we look over the familiar lists of German or French films Barry circulated in the early MoMA programs, it is striking how many titles overlap with Barry's lists of national/feminist films.

But Barry also changed as a result of her new circumstances and affiliations. After moving to New York, Barry's anti-American sentiments, the foundation of all of her early theorization, were converted relatively quickly to American nationalism, a reversal that isn't easily explained. Her newfound admiration for the American landscape and its ethnic communities eventually grew to a point that would have made Vachel Lindsay blush. In one paean Barry wrote of the United States:

> I am not going away again. I have seen the red earth of Virginia with its smoky woods and hills, most of New England, the year round in New York, cock-fighting in Maryland, a fiesta in New Mexico, have peered at the moon through Mt. Wilson's telescope. Life here grows on one increasingly. Portuguese villages in Connecticut that Cézanne might have designed, proud, poverty-stricken Huguenot families on Staten Island, the crowds seething on the beach in Far Rockaway, yachts on the Sound, the heliotrope windows through which Bostonian looks upon life—all this is America but not all of it.[77]

The poetic rhetoric of this unpublished article continued with a reverie of American modernity:

> I dislike relics and ruins. Here we are now, with all that past in all of us, in our minds, more of it to soak up as we (heaven send me [sic] may) keep our interests lively. The past is not in buildings and monuments. We do not have to study every missal to know something about the Middle Ages nor visit the battlefields of Troy to know what the Greeks were. History is alive in the

minds of men. . . . We are living today and today is on tap in America, more generously on tap than anywhere, easy to taste and enjoy.[78]

Barry didn't give in to the power of the American landscape and culture that she fought against in her columns. Instead, as these lyrical images of a uniquely American time, space, and people reveal, Barry replaced a fear of American homogenization with an admiration for American diversity.

As MoMA's film curator (we will see in the next two chapters), Barry changed her politics as a result of the rise of fascism and communism in the 1930s. She became a committed cold warrior and worked to promote the global spread of democracy through American films. She turned against the avant-garde, which she now saw as a dangerous rather than a welcome threat to Hollywood. And she repackaged American film so that it would be palatable to European audiences, a task she was singularly prepared for.

Barry worked for the cause of Americanism, but she remained a figure divided by circumstances. The painter Marc Chagall may have best captured the complications of Barry's relationship to film in an undated sketch he drew of her. In the sketch, we see a divided Iris Barry, half man/half woman, clutching a miniature Charlie Chaplin. Barry seems to be trapped inside the iris of an eye, clearly a pun on her name but also an implication of how Barry influenced the life of people around the world: through the eye. Barry is presented to the viewer both straight on and in profile, a cross section of Barry as a film curator as it were. We see a masculine Barry, in profile, with the hat and suit she always wore in the museum. This masculine Barry is presenting the miniature Chaplin. This is the Barry who grew to power in a world of political influence dominated by men and who actively worked to promote American film. But facing us we also see a feminine Barry, lurking behind the hat and the suit. The feminine Barry seems to be dressed as a Russian peasant, embodying not just displaying Russian film. The feminine Barry stares directly out of the sketch. She stares at *us*, asking us to reconcile the two Barrys—the professional curator-politician and the cinephile who watched films to take on new and potentially liberating identities.

FIGURE 4.2 Marc Chagall, Untitled (sketch of Iris Barry), n.d.
(©2004 Artists Rights Society [ARS], ADAGP, Paris)

5

THE MUSEUM OF MODERN ART AND THE ROOTS OF THE CULTURAL COLD WAR

The Movies Come from America
— Title of Gilbert Seldes's 1937 book[1]

As the Museum of Modern Art is a living museum, not a collection of curios and interesting objects, it can, therefore, become an integral part of our democratic institutions — it can be woven into the very warp and woof of our democracy.

— John Abbott (paraphrasing Franklin Roosevelt) on Lisa Sergio's *Column of the Air*, WQXR (July 2, 1940)

ILM MUSEUMS, libraries, and collections were first theorized and tested in the name of nationalism, as interventions either for or against the spread and preservation of American culture after World War I. They were realized (we will see in this chapter and the next) when the definition and dissemination of American culture became an important element in the war to defend democracy against the threats of communism and fascism. As a result, film museums, libraries, and collections found their enduring, nationalistic function during World War II, and they became full-blown weapons in the cultural cold war.

Much of the debate about the role of museums as purveyors of American culture during the cold war has rightly focused on the unofficial cooperation between the Museum of Modern Art (MoMA) and the Central Intelligence Agency. The debate on this issue still rages, and it has become a productive subfield of art history, occasionally driving high-profile books thanks to the ongoing declassification of intelligence records.[2] But if there are lingering questions about the secret details of

MoMA's crucial role as a disseminator of American propaganda during the cold war, it is simply because the collaboration between museums, the media, and the U.S. government were so ingrained by the 1950s that they needed few written contracts.

There is nothing so clandestine about the relationship between MoMA, government intelligence agencies, and Hollywood during World War II. When we look at the creation and development of MoMA's film department, we realize that the collaboration between these three American institutions really begins in the 1930s when government propagandists, themselves between wars, took on the task of uniting MoMA and Hollywood, among other commercial and cultural institutions. From the mid-1930s through the end of World War II, MoMA's film department worked under direct contract for the communication research wing of the Rockefeller Foundation and later for government intelligence agencies, making the world safe for democracy and Hollywood, two terms that became almost synonymous with MoMA's help.

The current chapter is the story of how, to put it bluntly, MoMA, Hollywood, and various government agencies teamed up to define and take possession of the idea of America. Several overlapping forces contributed to their success. On a national front, MoMA's trustees and Hollywood's public relations arm, the Motion Picture Producers and Distributors of America (MPPDA), cooperated on a campaign to paint their organizations as quintessential American institutions in the light of criticism and the threat of censorship, respectively. MoMA's cautious board of trustees embraced Hollywood as the font of American modernism in order to stave off the impression—created by a few badly received exhibits—that their museum was out of touch with American modernist art. Hollywood producers were openly receptive to MoMA's overtures because, at the time, the moral character of American film was under scrutiny. Hollywood freely opened its vaults to MoMA, hoping the museum could imbue Hollywood film with a sense of history and stature deserving of a major American industry. By the time the Japanese invaded Pearl Harbor, we will see, MoMA and Hollywood had so perfected the art of selling America and selling themselves as American that their transition from private institutions to government propaganda contractors was almost imperceptible.

While Hollywood and MoMA fought public relations battles at home, the Soviet Union and almost every European country established film collections as a means of building national traditions of mass culture. These traditions of mass culture were in turn mobilized in radio and film propaganda campaigns. With the support of MoMA and Hollywood, the

American war effort found its own method of creating a national film collection and utilizing the successful U.S. art and film markets for political ends. This process of identifying traditions of American mass media relied, to a large extent, on the emerging field of communication studies, supported almost entirely by the Rockefeller Foundation. The same names appear frequently when we examine the many Rockefeller Foundation-funded organizations that resulted from the interaction of MoMA, Hollywood, and government agencies from the 1930s on. Rather than a labyrinthine system of distinct projects, these organizations were simply different names for the same ongoing mission: to integrate American media and politics.

"THE MOVIES COME FROM AMERICA"

The Museum of Modern Art's first few months of existence proved a whirlwind followed by a thud. In May 1929 three wealthy art collectors, Abby Aldrich Rockefeller, Lizzie Bliss, and Mary Quinn Sullivan, invited A. Conger Goodyear, another collector and former museum administrator, to lunch. Goodyear came to their attention when the Albright Gallery in Buffalo dismissed him from its presidency for purchasing a Picasso nude, *La Toillette* (a painting that the Albright proudly displays today). The three women posed the idea of starting a museum of modern art to Goodyear, and the four of them quickly assembled a preliminary board of trustees and asked art historian Paul Sachs to handpick a director from his museology class at Harvard. Sachs surprised everyone when he chose 27-year-old Alfred Barr Jr., who was teaching art at Wellesley College while still a doctoral candidate in art history at Harvard. Barr's youthful enthusiasm set the tone for the museum. He immediately went to work on an ambitious, Bauhaus-inspired plan for a multidepartmental museum that included departments of architecture and design, film, and photography. By September, MoMA had acquired a preliminary museum charter from the State of New York, and the small core of trustees and staff planned a November opening—just six months after the first seeds of the museum had been planted. Then, on October 29, the stock market crashed. Nevertheless, MoMA opened as planned ten days later. The trustees had been apprehensive about Barr's multidepartmental plan even before the crash. In the unstable economic environment, they were relieved that MoMA was still a modest gallery of painting and sculpture tucked away in two rooms on the twelfth floor of the Heckscher Building at Fifth Avenue and 57th Street. The more ambitious plans for MoMA were put on hold.[3]

During the first few years of the Depression, museum attendance around the country increased unexpectedly as middle-class Americans looked for inexpensive forms of entertainment, education, and air-conditioning. MoMA's trustees began to see the importance of a popular rather than an exclusive museum during economically difficult and, later, war-torn times. Gradually, all the departments in Barr's original plan were added to what became the full-fledged museum. But each department appeared with a newly conceived function, designed to fit into MoMA's evolving passage from elite tastemaker to lighthouse of American identity. Looking back from 1941, Barr concluded that his multidepartmental plan had achieved new relevance as U.S. institutions were called on to defend democracy in the face of communism and fascism. "In connection with the multidepartmental plan," he wrote cryptically, "there are certain theories which bear upon the social usefulness of the Museum in a democracy and therefore upon the Museum's strategy of survival."[4] If Barr was unwilling to divulge those theories, it is clear from the development of its film department that MoMA rose to prominence as an integral link in the network of private and government institutions that harnessed visual art and mass media to promote representations of America and Americans during and after World War II.

MoMA was neither the first gallery of modern art in New York nor even the first New York gallery to be named the Museum of Modern Art (that claim belongs to Catherine Drier and Marcel Duchamp's Société Anonyme: Museum of Modern Art). The trustees' and staff's responses to the events of its first two decades, however, made MoMA not only the pre-eminent museum of its kind but redefined the role of a museum in a democracy and consumer culture. At the intersection of corporate public relations and government propaganda, MoMA pioneered a model of the patriotic, corporate museum that has become more closely associated with the Guggenheim Museum, the Smithsonian Institution, and other museums that handle their corporate and government ties much less smoothly than MoMA.

To be sure, no change in MoMA's design occurred by accident or entirely as a result of external forces. MoMA's board of trustees could boast some of the greatest business families of the early twentieth century (Rockefeller, Warburg, Sachs, and Whitney), and the museum itself was run much like a corporation, with a publication division, a system for conducting market research, and, by 1933, an in-house public relations department. When the staff and trustees considered starting a film department, for example, trustee John Hay Whitney privately funded a survey of university presidents, museum directors, and chairs of university art departments to gauge the demand for traveling film programs; 84 percent of the responses they received were favorable.[5] And before each department curator prepared his or her regular reports to the trustees, they studied detailed analyses of attendance figures, scrupulous financial reports, and copious newspaper clippings to quantify the effect of their exhibits. Two years after its inception, the film department had counted references to its activities in over 1,300 publications.[6] MoMA was unusually conscious, for its time, of its public image, and each new department, as a result, was designed to reinforce, refine, and propagate the MoMA "brand" at the same time that that brand came to be linked with a sense of American accomplishment and creativity.

Indeed, American propaganda and commercial public relations had been two names for the same activity since World War I when journalist George Creel directed the U.S. Committee on Public Information, more commonly known as the Creel Committee. Creel defined propaganda as government-sponsored public relations in his history of the Creel Committee, *How We Advertised America*. And the book, in turn, became the foundational text for both the fields of propaganda analysis and public relations.[7] To advertise America during the World War I, Creel recruited top public relations experts from the emergent profession, including Ivy Lee, the Rockefeller family's personal image consultant, and Edward Bernays, an expert in the psychology of persuasion with the unmatched credential of being Freud's double nephew (on both his mother's and father's side). The Creel Committee emphasized the importance of reaching the public on an emotional rather than a purely informational level, and to this end the committee employed Hollywood filmmakers to add empathy to their propaganda efforts. In addition to overseeing film content, Creel deployed some of his four-minute men, named for the length of their rousing patriotic speeches, to speak in theaters before or after a movie. After World War I, Creel's protégés moved back to the private sector and spread the gospel of persuasion they had honed while government employees. Ivy Lee returned to the Rockefellers' employ and achieved international prominence; at the time of his death in July 1934, Lee's work for the German Dye Trust earned him the obituary headline, "Rockefeller Aid Nazi Mastermind," suggesting again the overlap between the political and commercial fields of persuasion. Edward Bernays went on to pioneer the field of commercial public relations, emphasizing, among other things, the potential of museums to act as advertising for design firms in his 1928 book, *Propaganda*.[8]

MoMA's board of trustees employed Bernays to help with their initial endowment drive. A few years later they heeded Bernays's advice and established a department of architecture, the first department to be revived from Barr's plan. The trustees agreed to launch the department in the summer of 1932 after MoMA's blockbuster "Modern Architecture: International Exhibition"—the show that introduced the label "international style" to the public vocabulary—demonstrated that architecture and design could increase the size of the museum's public. With Bernays's help, the exhibit landed on the front page of the *New York Times*, and after that Barr hired a full-time public relations officer for the museum.[9] The architecture department realized a position Barr articulated in a pamphlet, *The Public as Artist*: "Art is a joint creation of artist and public."[10] It was up to MoMA, he came to see, not only to create an audience for modern art but also to shape the taste of the nation as a whole. It was both a grandiose and profitable epiphany. Extending this new national mission, the "Modern Architecture" show was MoMA's first traveling exhibition. In his pamphlet, Barr illustrated the weblike extension of influence the traveling exhibitions brought the museum; the show reached every corner of the country and the globe, and it directly penetrated the commercial market in ways a standing museum exhibit never could. The exhibit stopped at Bullock's Wilshire department store in Los Angeles in addition to other museums. By the time MoMA staged its Surrealism show a few years later, it had perfected its marketing strategies, arranging for endless store window placements and product tie-ins.[11]

MoMA considered starting a film department at the same time that it established its architecture department, but the process took a few years longer than expected. Despite initial resistance to the idea, the film department would prove to be central to MoMA's vision of its true civic function. Even after MoMA's modest opening, Barr continued to push for a film department, taking trustees to the movies and clarifying the idea for them in an internal report.[12] Personally, Barr was interested in introducing European film to art lovers. "It may be said without exaggeration," he complained, "that the only great art peculiar to the twentieth century is practically unknown to the American public most capable of appreciating it."[13] After seven months of research, however, MoMA officials announced slightly altered plans. MoMA had no interest in European art film, executive secretary Alan Blackburn Jr. assured the National Board of Review: "We are interested in the picture you see every time you go to a motion picture house, in the commercial product mainly and chiefly." The film department, at this stage in its planning, was intended to do for film what the architecture department had done for industrial design: shape public taste as a method of reforming American mass-produced art. "It is just as much the responsibility of the public," Blackburn continued, "to have a fine national art."[14] In preparation to assume the task of teaching film literacy where Columbia and Harvard had left off, MoMA hired Iris Barry to be the museum's librarian, a holding position until she could run the film department. But the plans changed drastically.

Over the next few years, MoMA's staff realized that film possessed something far more valuable than a means of reaching a greater share of the middle class. Rather than refining public taste in films, MoMA embraced Hollywood cinema whole, as already a quintessentially democratic, American modernist art form. Of course this is how we view Hollywood's classic years today, as America incarnate. But it is not clear that that would have been the case without MoMA's particular mode of embracing film and its staff's tireless efforts to promote MoMA's position.

MoMA's film department (at first called the Film Library) was finally begun with a local ambition: to answer the persistent criticism that MoMA couldn't connect with American modernism. MoMA's first shows of American painting and sculpture were the least successful and most controversial of its first years. MoMA displayed four shows of American painting and sculpture during its first fourteen months: "Paintings by Nineteen Living Americans," "Homer, Ryder, and Eakins," "Painting and Sculpture by Living Americans," and the descriptively titled "Forty-Six Painters and Sculptors Under Thirty-Five Years of Age," which closed after only two weeks. After the poor turnout for these exhibits, MoMA didn't devote another show exclusively to American art until its ill-fated and now infamous 1932 exhibit, "Murals by American Painters and Photographers." In the 1920s, the mural emerged as an important American art form, though of course it was a politically charged form influenced by Soviet Constructivist aesthetics and Marxist ideology.[15] Lincoln Kirstein, who was by that time a member of MoMA's advisory committee, and Julien Levy, who championed photography in his gallery, curated the mural show. In the same year that Kirstein and Levy threw the communist fellow travelers out of their film society (see chapter 3), they championed the left-wing art of the muralists included in the show. The most controversial piece submitted for the exhibit was Hugo Gellert's " 'Us Fellas Gotta Stick Together'—Al Capone." Gellert's mural placed J. P. Morgan, John D. Rockefeller Sr., Herbert Hoover, and Henry Ford next to Al Capone, machine gun in hand. The trustees were shocked by this depiction of political corruption and refused to include it in the show. They eventually relented after other artists threatened to pull their work from the exhibit and Nelson Rockefeller—after conferring with his father and J. P. Morgan— came to Gellert's defense.[16] The mural remained in the show, but the subsequent controversy that it drew in the press was enough to make the trustees wary of overtly political art altogether. Unlike the other trustees, Rockefeller came to see film and art increasingly as political representations but, at the same time, his anticommunism hardened steadily. When confronted with a similar situation only two years later, Rockefeller, in a now famous incident, asked Diego Rivera to remove Lenin's head from a mural commissioned for Rockefeller Center. Rivera refused, and the mural was eventually destroyed.

With film, the museum's administration thought they had found something incontrovertibly and uncontroversially American. MoMA not only attached itself to the success of Hollywood, but its Film Library played a key role in defining film as *the* American art. The Film Library's first director, John Abbott (Iris Barry's second husband), generated support for the project by lecturing on film as "an original native American art."[17] And the Film Library's first two traveling programs demonstrated its American focus: "A Short Survey of the Film in America, 1895–1932" and "Some Memorable American Films, 1896–1934." The dates on the programs reflect a deal MoMA struck with the studios: the Film Library agreed to show films only after their commercial run—gauged at two years—was over, and more recent films were added to these programs after their two-year commercial life had passed.

These first programs were "devoted principally to the American film or to foreign films having an immediate influence in America."[18] The format suggested that American narrative film was the inevitable outcome of the first few decades of international experimentation with film styles. This evolutionary narrative was reinforced by the Film Library's immensely popular contribution to MoMA's "Three Centuries of American Art" exhibit at the Musée du Jeu de Paume in Paris (1938) and by its contribution to MoMA's "Art in Our Time" exhibit at the 1939 World's Fair in New York. The Paris exhibit confirmed the power of film to display America at its best and, at the same time, it highlighted the inherently controversial act of displaying American painting and sculpture as "modern" in Paris. One French critic summed up the situation when he quipped that he would "give all the paintings in the United States for a few meters of American film."[19] Film Library publications and books endorsed by and researched at the Film Library also attested to the centrality of American film, most notably Gilbert Seldes's *The Movies Come from America* (1937)

FIGURE 5.1 Fund-raiser for the Museum of Modern Art Film Library at Mary Pickford and Douglas Fairbanks's home, Pickfair. *Left to right*: Frances Goldwyn, John E. Abbott, Samuel Goldwyn, Mary Pickford, Jesse Lasky, Harold Lloyd, Iris Barry. *(Author's collection)*

FIGURE 5.2 Founding the Film Library (1935). *Left to right*: John Abbott, Iris Barry, John Hay Whitney (seated), A. Conger Goodyear, Nelson Rockefeller. *(Author's collection)*

and Lewis Jacobs's *The Rise of the American Film* (1939). Iris Barry, now promoted to the position of film curator, condensed the museum's collective position in her preface to Jacobs's book. "Film," she exclaimed, "has become essentially an American expression and its history is part and parcel of the national life."[20]

Of course that is exactly what Barry had been complaining about for over a decade as a British film critic. Barry, however, made several surprising about-faces in the 1930s. Shortly after Philip Johnson hired her as MoMA's librarian, Barry renounced her earlier Hollywood grievances and declared, "Hollywood Is Not America."[21] This change was presumably the result of her experiencing real Americans for the first time, even marrying one. During World War II and the cold war, Barry's resistance to America and Hollywood weakened even further. In another dramatic turn, she entered the ranks of the staunchest defenders of liberal, American democracy, and she devoted the remainder of her career at MoMA to championing American film and to proving precisely that Hollywood is America, or at least a utopian fantasy of American ideals necessary in the struggle for global democracy.

As MoMA's film curator her job was to defend Hollywood as an alternative to Nazi Germany and Stalinist Russia. But there is no evidence that Barry simply and wholeheartedly assumed the Film Library's jingoistic mission right away. In an essay she published the same year Jacobs's book came out, for instance, Barry expressed an equivocal view of the Film Library's party line:

> The United States has contributed a veritable Mississippi of films. What is more, whether by good fortune or by accident, this country has undeniably contributed a very large portion of what is genuinely cinematic: the film is largely and typically an American Expression.[22]

This image of a Hollywood leviathan, important in spite of itself, is much closer to Barry's earlier distaste for American film. But Barry's personal evolution and the Film Library's safe Americanism both became unexpectedly politicized during the 1930s. Several forces, we will see, pushed Barry and the Film Library into their entrenched roles as warrior and weapon in the cultural cold war, including government demands and anticommunist redbaiting. But the reason for MoMA's politicization may be much more fundamental: producing and exhibiting films in the 1930s, 1940s, and 1950s was an unavoidably political act. With the rise of mass politics in the 1930s, film became increasingly useful to the U.S. government's opinion-building campaigns. Linked to this aestheticization of politics was the politicization of Hollywood films, from the censorship battles of the 1930s to the blacklist of the 1950s. Washington and Hollywood, as a result, became inseparable.

NO LAUGHING MATTER: THE SOCIOLOGY OF FILM

Despite its increasing politicization, MoMA tried hard to appear neutral at first by promoting the film staff as sociologists rather than tastemakers or ideologues. We are so used to renting videos and watching vintage movie channels today that it is surprising to realize how ephemeral films seemed in 1935, and how resistant the Film Library's first audiences were to films made just two or three years earlier. The most common observation reporters made about MoMA's early programs was that audiences tended to laugh at silent films. MoMA's revival of Paramount's 1911 *Queen Elizabeth* with Sarah Bernhardt attracted typical headlines: "Laughs Greet Film Bernhardt Made to Insure Immortality"[23] and "Resurrect Film of Sarah Bernhardt, Tragedy and Audience Roars with Laughter!"[24] Reporting on the opening of MoMA's Film Library in *New Theater and Film*, Robert Stebbins hypothesized that audiences had been conditioned to laugh at silent films by popular compilation reels called *Screen Souvenirs*, which strung together clips of old movies with mocking commentary on the sound track.[25] Of course 1930s audiences didn't need any more reason to laugh at decades-old films than we do today.

Film Library publications continually combated the laughter by insisting on the sociological rather than the artistic importance of film. One *Film Library Bulletin* explained, "As a medium which exercises a powerful influence on society and is peculiarly characteristic of our culture, [film] concerns students of sociology as profoundly as it concerns students of the fine arts."[26] Another journalist echoed MoMA's press releases in order to put the laughter in historical perspective: "MoMA considers films to be social documents, so they don't laugh at old films, viewing films as documents will prevent laughter of a 1956 audience [at a 1936 film], 'Why, even Shirley Temple will be grown up.' "[27]

At this point, MoMA's sociological approach to film was relatively undefined. The invocation of sociology served largely to exempt MoMA from sticky aesthetic debates, on the one hand, and to disavow political responsibility for presenting European and Soviet films during the regimes of Hitler, Mussolini, and Stalin on the other. The Film Library encountered the inverse problem of the Department of Painting and Sculpture.

Apart from some laughter, MoMA's programs of American film were undeniably successful. In the Film Library's first year alone, the American programs were seen by 125,000 students and rented by seventy-six institutions.[28] The Film Library's presentation of films from communist and fascist countries, however, attracted unruly controversies, which required utilization of all the museum's public relations resources in order to be contained.

The Film Library's first foray into presenting foreign films as *foreign films* rather than as influences on American film came when MoMA was invited to show political documentaries to an audience of diplomats, government officials, and reporters on May 10, 1936, at the Mayflower Hotel in Washington, D.C. The event premiered *The Plow That Broke the Plains*, the Resettlement Administration's documentary about the physical deprivations of the Dust Bowl. President Roosevelt and several prominent Hollywood directors had already screened the film and given it their personal endorsements, but distributors worried about handling a film they saw as "a propaganda film for the Roosevelt administration."[29] Rather than combat the claim, the Film Library reinforced it. The evening's program included government-produced or -supported films from Britain, France, and the Soviet Union as well as the controversial film of the Nazi's 1934 Nuremberg rally, *Triumph of the Will*. *The Plow That Broke the Plains* concluded the program as America's contribution to the burgeoning field of world propaganda. John Abbott addressed the audience and attempted to explain the reasons why documentary film had become an important tool of mass politics in the 1930s, and why America needed to catch up to other countries in documentary production. Advances in documentary technique, he argued, were making film "more sociological" and as a result documentaries were "being employed increasingly by governments, and by public bodies, desirous of explaining graphically to a wide public the social and economic problems that confront them, and the solutions to those problems being attempted, or to be desired." Abbott made a subtle plea for the importance of film museums in a world in which visual education was surpassing oratory and the press as political communicators. Documentaries, he concluded, weren't sufficiently entertaining for commercial exhibition but, freed from commercial demands, museums could take on the role of demonstrating "how the new film of reality is being used today, all over the world, to bring the new world of citizenship before the public imagination."[30]

Once MoMA's staff saw the Film Library in this role, it set out to present other national cultures to America through film in addition to circulating visions of America abroad. Just ten days after the Mayflower screening, Abbott and Barry embarked on a whirlwind collecting trip to London,

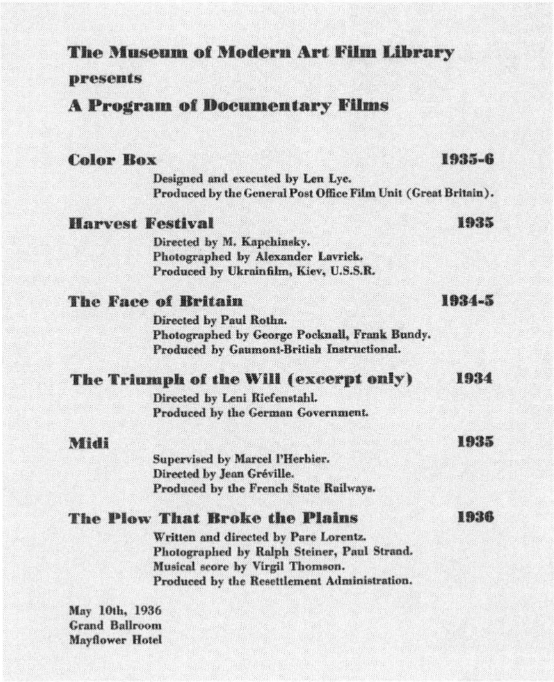

The Museum of Modern Art Film Library
presents
A Program of Documentary Films

Color Box   1935-6
        Designed and executed by Len Lye.
        Produced by the General Post Office Film Unit (Great Britain).

Harvest Festival   1935
        Directed by M. Kapchinsky.
        Photographed by Alexander Lavrick.
        Produced by Ukrainfilm, Kiev, U.S.S.R.

The Face of Britain   1934-5
        Directed by Paul Rotha.
        Photographed by George Pocknall, Frank Bundy.
        Produced by Gaumont-British Instructional.

The Triumph of the Will (excerpt only)   1934
        Directed by Leni Riefenstahl.
        Produced by the German Government.

Midi   1935
        Supervised by Marcel l'Herbier.
        Directed by Jean Gréville.
        Produced by the French State Railways.

The Plow That Broke the Plains   1936
        Written and directed by Pare Lorentz.
        Photographed by Ralph Steiner, Paul Strand.
        Musical score by Virgil Thomson.
        Produced by the Resettlement Administration.

May 10th, 1936
Grand Ballroom
Mayflower Hotel

FIGURE 5.3 Invitation to Mayflower Hotel screening (1936).   *(Author's collection)*

Paris, Hanover, Berlin, Warsaw, Moscow, Leningrad, Helsinki, and Stockholm. On the return trip, they visited Berlin, Paris, and London again. They drew on Barry's acquaintances from the London Film Society and Alfred Barr's contacts to meet with a who's who of international filmmakers, from G. W. Pabst and René Clair to Alexander Korda and S. M. Eisenstein. They drew on the Hollywood contacts of John Hay Whitney—MoMA trustee, Technicolor stockholder, and president of Pioneer Films—to meet with the studios' international representatives. They drew on Nelson Rockefeller's political contacts to meet with State Department and embassy personnel. And, finally, they encountered for the first time an emerging community of sympathetic film archivists from countries soon to be combatants in World War II as well as partners in the FIAF (La Fédération Internationale des Archives du Film, or the International Federation of Film Archives), founded in 1938.[31] The network of film allies they cultivated on their collecting trips would prove instrumental to the Film Library's unanticipated role as clearinghouse for the production, circulation, and decoding of political propaganda.

FIGURE 5.4 Iris Barry in Berlin (1936).   *(Author's collection)*

The generosity of the foreign archives exceeded Barry and Abbott's ex-
pectations. It seemed that every country in Europe was establishing a film
collection at the same time as MoMA, each one identifying and preserving its own national film tradition. And every new archive was willing to
trade films for copies of Hollywood's already recognized canon of classics.
Abbott and Barry were most surprised by the cooperation of the German
Reichsfilmarchiv. In 1933, Hitler and his minister of propaganda, Joseph
Goebbels, established the Reich Film Guild, charged with "aryanizing"
the German film industry. And in 1935 the Nazis banned the screening of
all films made by or with the help of Jewish filmmakers before 1933. Alfred
Barr—traveling through Germany at the time—had been so disturbed by
a Goebbels rally he attended, that he translated and published excerpts
from the speech in *Hound and Horn*, along with an extended analysis of
the evolving propagandistic meaning of German war films.[32] In Berlin,
however, Abbott and Barry were given open access to the archives, filmmakers, and bureaucrats. They glimpsed Goebbels at a screening at the

Reichsfilmkammer, and the infamous director of *Triumph of the Will*, Leni Riefenstahl, told Barry of her desire to travel to New York to study the Film Library's collection. Barry discovered that "contrary to rumor, non-Aryan films of Germany's great silent period 1919–1928 had not been destroyed." And Abbott and Barry were able to secure German films by Jewish filmmakers as well as Nazi films. On a return trip to Berlin, Barry even acquired a print of Eisenstein's Soviet masterpiece *Battleship Potemkin*, struck from the original negative, which Goebbels had purchased in 1933 in order to study its propaganda power.

According to Barry, the only film she and Abbott were denied was Josef von Sternberg's *The Blue Angel*, starring Marlene Dietrich. They were refused the film "on the grounds that it was a pornographic film, showing Germany and Germans in a very unpleasant light and therefore they did not want it to be shown again abroad."[33] *The Blue Angel's* portrait of acquiescent middle-class schoolboys—Siegfried Kracauer later called them "born Hitler youths"—and a proto-totalitarian leader had angered the National Socialists since the film's release in 1930. Klaus Kreimeier has found one review that spewed Nazi hatred: "We see here a deliberate Jewish detraction and vilification of the German character and German educational values. Even Jewish cynicism rarely sinks this low. One need only glance through the names of the film's makers: nothing but Jews with Galician faces that are enough to vomit."[34] Of all the films produced in Germany, however, it is curious that the German archivists withheld only this one. Perhaps openly refusing to release one film contributed to the impression that they were generous with all others, through there is no indication that other films were secretly withheld.

When Abbott and Barry returned to New York, the Film Library's staff assembled the bounty into several series arranged by national film industry: first German, then French, and later Swedish. The Film Library soon circulated six preprogrammed series to schools and film clubs. In addition to national selections, they offered documentary films, animated films, and films starring famous actresses. The Film Library's staff attempted to preempt criticism by reasserting the sociological importance of the films in its catalog and emphasizing the influence of its selection of foreign films on Hollywood. When discussing the German series, Barry took extra care to assure potential renters that "stress is laid in the notes on the influence which the German film in turn has had on world cinema and in particular on American film."[35] This overdetermined armor of Americanism, however, would soon show its fissures.

REDBAITING AND THE SHORT MUSEUM CAREERS OF
JAY LEYDA AND LUIS BUÑUEL

The Film Library's staff sold an interpretation of European, Scandinavian, and later Soviet film as sociological documents of national character. The term *sociology*, however, was still undefined in their literature and seemed simply to suggest that films were educational as well as enjoyable, often despite being enjoyable. But they underestimated just how controversial the act of interpretation could be, even when the method was labeled sociology. Abbott and Barry encountered an unexpected problem on their collecting trip: filmmakers trying to escape from embattled European countries to America. So many German filmmakers had fled their home country, Barry noted in her journal, that she met more German filmmakers in London than in Berlin. During World War II, Barry helped many Jewish filmmakers find employment in America, often at the request of Varian Fry, the heroic liberator of artists the Nazis labeled "degenerate," or at the urging of Erwin Panofsky, the German émigré art historian who served on the Film Library's advisory committee. After the war, the French government awarded Barry the Legion of Honor medal for giving shelter to Jewish filmmakers.

Collecting people turned out to be more contentious than collecting film, and the Film Library's first controversial film analyst was neither Jewish nor a foreign national. In the Soviet Union, Alfred Barr had arranged for Abbott and Barry to meet with S. M. Eisenstein's American protégé, Jay Leyda. Leyda served as interpreter and guide while they were in Moscow, and he and Barry developed an immediate intellectual bond. They talked about the Film Library into the night, and Barry wrote in her journals about her plans to hire him for her staff. Barry convinced Leyda to rendezvous with her in Berlin on their return trip, where he helped acquire films, books, and posters from the new Ufa film studio museum. After three years of struggling with the Soviet bureaucracy, Leyda had grown weary of being an expatriate. When Barry presented a job offer, he agreed to move to New York and help with the Film Library's Soviet and European collections. The Rockefeller Foundation supported Leyda with a $2,500 grant to produce a comparative study of film collections in Europe and America, and he was eventually made assistant to the curator at the Film Library.[36]

In 1940, however, Leyda's tenure came to an abrupt end when internal department politics devolved into a public redbaiting scandal. MoMA could withstand intense infighting in private, but the museum's staff responded quickly and decisively when its public image was at stake. The Leyda incident began with left-wing, anti-Stalinist film critic Seymour Stern's review of notes Leyda had prepared to accompany a screening of the Soviet film *Arsenal* (1929). Stern had been hostile toward the Film Library since its inception; in a letter to the *New York Times*, Stern described the Film Library as "a dilettante organization" and "noxious to creative cinema" even before MoMA had shown its first film.[37] His *Arsenal* review was bluntly titled "Film Library Notes Build 'C[ommunist] P[arty] Liberators' Myth." In the review, Stern quarreled with Leyda's characterization of the significance of the Bolsheviks in the 1917 Ukrainian congress for independence. This historiographical difference hardly warranted Stern's labeling Leyda a "Communist Party partisan 1940 model" and associating him with "Stalinist historians."[38]

The article clearly struck a cord with disgruntled Film Library piano player Theodore Huff, who shared Leyda's title of assistant to the curator. It isn't clear exactly what happened at the Film Library's offices after the publication of Stern's review, but the incident precipitated the resolution of an ongoing debate between Leyda and Huff over the contents of the collection. Huff wanted more American films represented, and he freely alleged that communist politics drove Leyda's curatorial decisions.[39] Barry fired Huff four months after Stern's article appeared, and Huff used his newfound freedom to air all his pent-up hostility toward MoMA. He wrote private letters to Charlie Chaplin and Mary Pickford, informing them about MoMA's mishandling of their films and of films lost in a nitrate fire. He complained that film was secondary to "freakish modern 'art' " at MoMA, and he asked Pickford, "Why couldn't the industry itself have formed an organization to preserve its best films?" In an aside, Huff also took the opportunity to suggest that Pickford adapt the long-running Broadway play *Life with Father* to the screen with either Clark Gable or Spencer Tracy as her costar.[40]

In public, Huff continued the debate with Leyda. The *New Leader*, which had published Stern's original review, reported Huff's side of the story and continued the Leyda redbaiting. The article condemned Huff's dismissal as a victory for "the Stalinist element in control of the Film Library," and explained how

Miss Barry's faithful assistant, Soviet-trained propaganda commissar Jay Leyda, set himself the task of getting rid of Huff at the earliest opportunity. Leyda poisoned the minds of the Library's staff against Huff, at the same time that he indoctrinated every stenographer, secretary, office-boy in the place with Stalinist doctrines.

The article then set its sites on the Film Library directly: "The Film Library is not a liberal institution, operating in accord with traditions of American democracy, but a totalitarian stronghold in the heart of free America."[41] The story might seem comical in retrospect if you know that Leyda went on to be a successful scholar and pioneer of film studies, publishing the definitive history of Russian and Soviet film, *Kino*. But these were not idle claims in 1940, and Leyda resigned from the museum a few weeks later.

The anonymous author of a subsequent editorial in the *New Leader* did more than gloat. The writer used the opportunity to take another stab at the Film Library, claiming this time that Leyda had "ideologically edited" Jacobs's *Rise of the American Film*, allowing the Film Library to support "the first Stalinist 'history' of American film."[42] This attack cut right to the heart of the Film Library's project, and Barry responded directly to the "whispering campaign" with an article in the *Bulletin of the Museum of Modern Art*, which was aimed at the trustees as much as the public. Barry reworked the film-as-American-expression argument, claiming this time that American film was not only the natural outcome of the first decades of film evolution but, moreover, that all film was essentially American at its root. She conceded that France, Italy, and Germany had initially contributed to what became the mature American style of filmmaking. But once a mature style had been achieved, she argued, American films "stimulated film-making in France, the U.S.S.R., and indeed the world over." So, we are meant to conclude, while Soviet films may at first seem to be Marxist, they are stylistically and somehow effectively American. This argument was realized fully in the circulating program celebrating the international influence of D. W. Griffith's films and in Barry's monograph for the series, *D. W. Griffith: American Master* (1940). The Griffith exhibition emphasized, among other things, his influence on Soviet propaganda filmmakers. On the one hand, Barry's argument—that American film became the basis for world cinema—supported the Film Library's founding claim, that film was an organic American art. But, on the other hand, Barry contradicted another of the Film Library's founding principles: that film is a sociological expression and therefore revealing of political and cultural differences.

Ultimately, these contradictions didn't matter. The article was good public relations. Barry reminded her readers that the film programs had outshone painting at the 1938 Jeu de Paume exhibit and that in all its programs, "the Film Library affirmed its unwavering faith in the film as the liveliest as well as the most popular of the contemporary arts and in which the United States is supreme." The article not only atoned for the Film Library's hiring mistakes but also attempted to exculpate the museum as a whole from any claims of un-American leanings. In addition to the claims that MoMA promoted communist films and murals, the museum had also weathered accusations that fascists had infiltrated its board of trustees. The latter claim followed Philip Johnson and Alan Blackburn's brief trip to Louisiana to study the political philosophy of dictatorial senator/governor Huey Long and start a new "Nationalist Party" based on Lawrence Dennis's neofascist book, *The Doom of Capitalism*.[43] The Film Library proved again that it could function as an effective public relations branch of the museum, securing MoMA's place as a patriotic institution through its affiliation with American film.

Barry's arguments, however, weren't persuasive enough to stave off future redbaiting, which became an even more sensitive issue when the Film Library started to function as a government contractor. In 1943 the Film Library's staff came under scrutiny again as the Truman Committee reviewed the budgets of the Office of War Information (OWI) and the Office of the Coordinator of Inter-American Affairs (CIAA), both of which had contracts with the Film Library. When the *Motion Picture Herald* broke the story that the Film Library's budget had been cut, the paper also reported that one unnamed member of the staff would leave. In the next paragraph, the reporter insinuated that filmmaker Luis Buñuel would be that employee:

> It was elsewhere disclosed that Luis Buñuel, chief translator for the Museum, was leaving. He has been a storm center of submerged inquiries and discussions for more than a year, growing out of his left-wing and Surrealist film activities in France some years ago.[44]

Buñuel submitted his letter of resignation four days later.

MoMA had hired Buñuel in 1941 after Barry spent two years unsuccessfully trying to find a job for him in the United States. The Film Library immediately informed the appropriate government agencies that Buñuel would be working for the museum on war-related projects. The State Department, the Federal Bureau of Investigation, and other agencies consequently investigated Buñuel on June 18, 1942. After the presumably smooth investigations, he had been allowed to apply for U.S. citizenship and continue working as a film editor and translator at MoMA. The atmosphere at the Film Library was tense, as always, and Buñuel had his detractors.[45] But there is no evidence that Buñuel's resignation had been discussed or that he was under continued government investigation at the time of the *Motion Picture Herald*'s article. When he did resign, after conferring with Iris Barry, Buñuel blamed the *Motion Picture Herald* entirely for tainting his name.[46]

In his letter of resignation, Buñuel worried more about the impending loss of artistic freedom in America than about his own forced departure from the museum. In order to precipitate Buñuel's resignation, the *Motion Picture Herald* needed only to remind American readers that Buñuel and Salvador Dali's film *L'Age d'or* (1929) had been banned in Paris when the film's irreverent use of Christian iconography led to anti-Semitic rallies. Nevertheless, Buñuel wrote, "The surrealism, to my knowledge, has never been irregular or illegal."[47]

The Film Library's staff did not come to Buñuel's defense and stand up for artistic freedom. On the contrary, World War II further entrenched and greatly refined the Film Library's sociological approach to films as a means of circumventing questions of aesthetics and artistic freedom. From shortly after the Nazi-Soviet Non-Aggression Pact in 1939 until a year or so after the bombing of Hiroshima and Nagasaki, the Film Library's staff devoted its energy almost entirely to defining, distributing, and analyzing what they referred to as "the film of fact." The label primarily designated

FIGURE 5.5 Luis Buñuel at projector with CIAA staff (1940). *Left to right*: Ed Kerns, Kenneth MacGowen, Iris Barry, Gustav Pittaluga, Mercedes Megwiroff, unidentified; *front row*: Walter Brooks, Arthur Kross.

documentary films, but it also included narrative feature films, animation, and any film out of which they could squeeze sociological merit. MoMA's *Films of Fact* catalog, for example, described Buñuel's own outrageous Surrealist documentary *Land Without Bread*—if a film that recombines documentary footage into absurd, comic sequences can be called a documentary—as possessing "great feeling and realism."[48] One wonders if Buñuel snuck the description into the catalog himself as an ironic joke. Promoting *Land Without Bread* as a realistic depiction of the rural Spanish area of Las Hurdes Atlas is a little like selling the carefully choreographed *Triumph of the Will* as stock footage of German life, which, as Thomas Doherty has shown, MoMA did at the same time. MoMA owned the only print of *Triumph of the Will* in the United States, and despite Barry's initial protests, Hollywood and government filmmakers continually raided the print for clips of Nazis in action. These are only the most ridiculous points to which the "film of fact" category was stretched. In general, we will see below, as purveyors of visual representations of both foreign and domestic cultures, the Film Library made significant contributions to military and civilian education during the war. And, in addition, it contributed to a more refined theory of propaganda and the sociology of film, finally clarifying what it meant for film to express national identity.[49]

THE PRACTICE OF PROPAGANDA: MOMA AND THE CIAA

Every department of the Museum of Modern Art contributed to the war effort. More than two dozen trustee and staff members from the museum took leaves of absence to work for either the armed forces or the intelligence community during World War II, including the president of the board of trustees, Nelson Rockefeller. The museum's staff staged exhibits ranging from the predictable "Art in War" to the experimental "Camouflage," an analytic exhibit devoted to the problems of creating effective visual deceptions. MoMA also sponsored painting and war poster competitions and hosted dances for soldiers in its sculpture garden. In addition to these war-related activities, MoMA worked directly for at least twenty-one different government agencies during the war, executing at least thirty-eight contracts for over $1.5 million.[50]

During the Depression, MoMA's staff had enthusiastically collaborated with the New Deal's artist relief divisions of the Works Progress Administration, which proved to be a boost both to the museum's American offerings and its attendance figures. But MoMA's New Deal affiliations couldn't have forecast the extent of its patriotic role during World

War II. The transition from elite gallery of modern painting to propaganda factory resulted from a passing of the generational baton as much as
from external forces. When Nelson Rockefeller assumed the leadership of
what he liked to refer to as "mother's museum" from Abby Rockefeller, he
dragged MoMA from a Rockefeller foray into arts philanthropy into the
new Rockefeller mission of public service. And when Nelson Rockefeller
temporarily left MoMA to head Roosevelt's Office of the Coordinator of
Inter-American Affairs (CIAA) within the State Department, he took several members of the board of trustees with him and eventually enlisted the
entire Film Library.

Rockefeller made film the centerpiece of efforts to improve relations
across the American continents. His office was so effective that it kept its
hold over Latin American film distribution even after the Office of War
Information subsumed most other domestic and overseas government film
divisions. Rockefeller appointed John Hay Whitney to head the CIAA's
Motion Picture Division; he placed a CIAA representative in the office of
the Motion Picture Producers and Distributors of America; and he established a group of film producers, the Motion Picture Society for the
Americas, to look out for CIAA interests in Hollywood. The CIAA film
network then set to work lobbying for positive representations of Latin
America in Hollywood films and encouraging studios to shoot films on location in Latin America. At first, the CIAA film officers limited themselves
to removing offensive material from Carmen Miranda's and Xavier
Cugat's films. But the CIAA soon entered the production insurance business. Rockefeller successfully convinced the Walt Disney Company to
produce films for Latin American distribution, agreeing to reimburse the
studio for losses incurred up to $150,000 and funding a good will tour by
Walt Disney himself. In exchange for Disney's help, Rockefeller agreed to
end a messy animators' strike at the Disney studio. The Disney films made
under this contract, including *Saludos Amigos* (1942) and *The Three
Caballeros* (1944), all turned a profit. But when the CIAA offered RKO
(the largely Rockefeller-owned film studio) an even bigger deal to support
an Orson Welles film project in Rio, the consequences were disastrous.
Although Brazil's Minister of Propaganda may even have initially suggested the project, the notion of Welles filming in the slums of Rio and the development of story lines about *mestizos* or mixed-race Brazilians worried
both Rockefeller officials at the CIAA and studio heads at RKO.
Rockefeller found himself caught between Welles, the Brazilian government, and the studio. With the support of the Motion Picture Society for
the Americas, Rockefeller pulled out of the project, angering everyone in-

volved. A reconstructed version of the film, titled *It's All True*, was finally released to the public fifty years later in 1993.[51]

The Disney and Welles deals were high-profile projects. Most of the CIAA's film work, however, involved the production of documentary films and their distribution to schools and local organizations. The one institution allowed to bid for the position of clearinghouse for CIAA films, the Museum of Modern Art Film Library, coordinated all of this work. In April 1941 the Film Library signed a contract with the CIAA's MPPDA office to produce Spanish and Portuguese versions of American documentary films for distribution in Latin America; the contract remained in effect until June 1945.[52] Barry hired Buñuel under a CIAA contract to oversee the translation and editing of films for Latin American release. One strange yet ultimately banal result of this collaboration between Surrealism and intelligence work was a Buñuel-edited version of *Triumph of the Will* for Latin American distribution. Subsequent contracts for the CIAA, the OWI, and other intelligence divisions required the Film Library to produce, edit, and evaluate American documentary films for foreign distribution and to edit and evaluate foreign documentaries for U.S. distribution. The Film Library adapted 544 reels of film under its CIAA contracts, but Abbott and Barry were less successful at subcontracting film production projects to small, independent film producers. Only a few films were ever completed and several contracts ended in litigation.[53]

Barry and her staff continued to repackage and distribute propaganda films from both Allied and Axis countries for a variety of audiences and purposes. Programs of U.S. technical documentaries, for example, were distributed not only to appropriate military and civilian audiences but to Hollywood filmmakers as well. MoMA joined forces with the Academy of Motion Picture Arts and Sciences to show military documentaries to commercial producers and directors as a means of both stimulating mainstream, narrative features and promoting accurate representations of wartime activities. Two popular films in the genre—*Bomber* (1941), an Office of Emergency Management film about a bomb manufacturing plant, and *Aluminum* (also 1941), which showed the making of aluminum for planes—were screened in Los Angeles for Cecil B. DeMille, Alfred Hitchcock, and producer Walter Wanger more than a month before the attack on Pearl Harbor.[54]

There seemed to be no end to the uses for factual visual information during wartime, and in a 1946 *New York Times Magazine* article, Iris Barry retrospectively grabbed as much credit as she could for winning the war.

There is no doubt that the motion picture was a vital weapon of war. We know now that it taught our soldiers—millions of them—not only how to fight better but to know better what they were fighting for and against. Films trained men more quickly and more efficiently than they had ever been trained before, whether to load and file a tommy gun, improvise a bridge, deliver a baby, compute altitude, butcher meat or overcome malaria, fire and fear.[55]

This seemingly uncritical faith in films as educational tools extended to historical newsreels as well. Echoing Boleslas Matuszewski's claims from almost fifty years earlier, Barry and Richard Griffith described films as *"living* documents, for in the fact film and newsreel we see historic events from the viewpoint of contemporaries, and 'history' suddenly becomes 'news' again."[56]

The Film Library's public cheerleading and acknowledged blind faith in the factual nature of film both smoothed the circulation of American film propaganda and masked a much subtler understanding of propaganda's complex workings. Barry, Griffith, and the other members of the Film Library's staff didn't naively accept their own positivist rhetoric. If they promoted films as facts publicly, behind the scenes they worked at the forefront of media effects analysis to determine the value and importance of individual films and filmmaking techniques. And the staff confidentially accepted a second wartime mission under the same government contracts that made the Film Library a producer, translator, and distributor of films: to evaluate the propaganda effects and potential of films.

THE THEORY OF PROPAGANDA: THE ROCKEFELLER CONNECTION

From its inception, the Film Library was primed to become the nucleus of the U.S. film propaganda machine. It had been created at the crossroads of modern corporate public relations techniques and a growing theory of film sociology. Both were subfields of the emerging discipline of communication studies being developed in the United States under the auspices of the Film Library's greatest patron, the Rockefeller Foundation. John Hay Whitney may have funded the initial market survey that demonstrated the desirability of a film department, but the Rockefeller Foundation provided the principal support for the Film Library with grants of $338,730 between 1935 and 1954. This funding was given in addition to the many Rockefeller Foundation fellowships to individual filmmakers and scholars at MoMA, including Jay Leyda and British docu-

mentary filmmaker-critic Paul Rotha. The Film Library would most likely never have existed if it had not fit into a much larger Rockefeller
Foundation-supported search for an empirical understanding of visual
communication and a system of institutions to implement its theoretical
findings.

The Film Library was only one of many film institutions the Rockefeller
Foundation and the Rockefeller family's General Education Board established in the 1930s. Others included the Association of School Film
Libraries, the American Film Center at Columbia University, and a collaborative project of the Progressive Education Association and the MPPDA,
Hollywood's public relations organization. As a recent Rockefeller
Foundation report shows, the General Education Board rejected an early
plan for a centralized American Film Institute in order to set up smaller, distinct organizations that corresponded to the stages of production, distribution, and exhibition studied separately by the Rockefeller Foundation's communication theorists. In this way, the foundation could exert precise
influence at each stage in the circuit of mass communication.[57]

The Rockefeller Foundation's institutional patronage, in other words,
can only be understood in conjunction with its theoretical arm. The
Rockefeller Foundation employed and supported numerous communication theorists during the 1930s, 1940s, and 1950s, but its wartime activity revolved around the work of its Communication Seminar (alternately called
the Communication Group). The Communication Seminar included
Harold Laswell and Paul Lazarsfeld, both experts in radio and film propaganda, the American Film Center's director Donald Slesinger, sociologist
Robert Lynd, and linguist I. A. Richards. The group met for only ten
months but produced thirty working papers that they hoped would both
aid in the creation of an empirical method for calculating the effects of
mass media and, at the same time, pave the way for a "genuinely democratic propaganda."[58]

The work of the Communication Seminar resulted from a long and
complicated history of intersecting developments in the study of mass culture and politics. After World War I, scholars had difficulty finding funding
for empirical research on the effects of propaganda; the subject had become
too politicized. If propaganda analysis moved to the back burner, the basis
for the sociological study of film was galvanized by a series of studies on the
effects of film on children funded by the Payne Study and Experiment
Fund between 1929 and 1932. The Payne Fund's studies used a series of laboratory tests to demonstrate film's deleterious effects on children. The results were presented as science, but they fed a massive campaign to reform

and censor sex and violence in American film. The campaign culminated in the formation of the MPPDA's Production Code Administration in 1934. The Payne Fund's studies drove the establishment of the Film Library in several ways. Rockefeller Foundation researchers and Hollywood producers were united in a search for alternatives to film censorship, and the Film Library helped achieve this goal by promoting alternative models of film sociology, connoisseurship, and history. As we have already seen, the creation of the Film Library was a brilliant public relations move for MoMA, improving its American profile. But the Film Library could not have come into being without the support of Hollywood producers as well. Both the Rockefeller family and John Hay Whitney were heavily invested in the film industry in the 1930s, and they knew, as MoMA's (second) film curator Richard Griffith later put it, that "it well suited the public relations of the motion picture industry in 1935 to aid in the setting up of the Film Library."[59] The Film Library didn't combat censorship by defining film as art, though of course it did some of that too. The primary strategy of the Film Library's staff, as we have already seen, was to celebrate the historical and sociological importance of American film.

Most newspapers, for example, responded appropriately to the public relations campaign for the very first film MoMA revived, Thomas Edison's 1896 The May Irwin–John Rice Kiss. The Kiss is a relatively short close-up of the two portly actors, May Irwin and John Rice, re-creating a chaste Victorian kiss from their popular play, The Widow Jones. When MoMA opened its first series of films with The Kiss, every newspaper repeated MoMA's tale that a Film Library employee had found this piece of history in a trash bin in the Bronx. Most shocking was not the fact that the film had almost been lost forever or that MoMA's employees were reduced to searching through garbage cans. With the Production Code in full force in 1935, reporters were most shocked by the claim that the MPPDA's Production Code Administration might not have passed this tame piece of film history, which was an unlikely but effective allegation. The New York Evening Journal's headline milked the story with a tantalizing headline, "Film Library Embalms Hot 'Gay '90s' Kiss." Even the New York Times picked up the story and borrowed the suggested headline from MoMA's press release: "Museum Acquires 50-Foot Film Kiss," referring to the length of the filmstrip.[60] For once, MoMA's public relations department engineered the event perfectly, and as a result the head of the MPPDA, Will Hays, continued to be MoMA's greatest advocate in Hollywood, negotiating the Film Library's first contract with the studios and later with the CIAA.

The Payne Fund's studies also provoked a response from officials at the Rockefeller Foundation, who wanted to combat the dangerous effects of films with education rather than censorship. Foundation officials looked for projects that would either create more educational films or educate viewers about the psychological functioning of films.[61] Donald Slesinger of Columbia University's American Film Center was not the only Rockefeller theorist who saw his role as cultivating "more democratic and intelligent citizens in the face of widespread propaganda."[62] John Marshall, the ex-Harvard medievalist who oversaw communication research at the Rockefeller Foundation, assembled the Communication Seminar in September 1939 to provide a theoretical basis for the foundation's funding of communication-related projects. The plans changed drastically when Hitler invaded Poland the same month. The seminar's members turned exclusively to the study of propaganda and looked for ways the U.S. government could counter propaganda being produced by communist and fascist countries.[63]

Several participants in the Communication Seminar had already experimented with empirical, theoretical, and ethnographic methods of gauging the effects of the media and interpreting propaganda codes. The Rockefeller Foundation first turned to the opinion-making medium of radio, which had been used so effectively by the Roosevelt administration and the Nazis. Significantly, most of the foundation's film projects grew out of radio research. As late as 1948, Paul Lazarsfeld saw radio and film as two prongs of the same attack on public opinion, though he speculated that television could soon shift the balance.[64] Several Communication Seminar scholars adapted technologies developed for radio research to film. The simple yet effective Lazarsfeld-Stanton Program Analyzer, for instance, placed red and green buttons in front of audience members, who could then push the green button when they approved of what they were watching and push the red button when they disapproved.[65] Another member of the Communication Seminar, Harold Laswell, continued to experiment with methods of "content analysis" he had developed while writing his doctoral dissertation, published as *Propaganda Technique in the World War* (1927). Laswell refined models for categorizing and quantifying the content of propaganda and its effects on group psychology. The Rockefeller Foundation established an institute for Laswell at the Library of Congress, where he employed a team of analysts who both studied propaganda and trained military personnel. Once they passed through the training, the officers returned to the various military branches as propaganda analysts or producers themselves.

It was in the field of content analysis that the Film Library made its greatest contributions. Throughout the 1930s, the Rockefeller Foundation had encouraged the Film Library to hire and train film experts with varying subfields. As we saw in chapter 2, MoMA transformed the film education program at Columbia to create a community of film experts in the United States and Latin America. If MoMA's experts initially sought alternatives to censorship, they were soon called on to use their expertise to find quick and functional methods of analyzing propaganda content. In search of this new goal, the Film Library undertook two important projects in addition to analyzing documentaries for the CIAA. First, the Film Library, undeterred by anti-Communist redbaiting, sponsored another left-leaning refugee, Siegfried Kracauer, to study Nazi propaganda. And, second, the Film Library employed a team to evaluate all U.S. films for inclusion in a national film collection at the Library of Congress. In the end, these two activities were integrally related.

SIEGFRIED KRACAUER AND THE LIBRARY OF CONGRESS FILM PROJECT

Many scholars have investigated Siegfried Kracauer's research while he was affiliated with MoMA, because he later developed his World War II film analysis into one of the most famous and influential books of film theory, *From Caligari to Hitler* (1947). It is important, however, to recognize how Kracauer's work fits into an intellectual framework beyond personal biography. Brett Gary's research into the Rockefeller Foundation's internal files has begun to place Kracauer's propaganda analysis within the larger context of the Rockefeller Foundation's communication projects. In the current context, we can also see how Kracauer's nascent theory of film formed the basis of an American national film collection, funded by the Rockefeller Foundation, selected by MoMA's staff, and stored at the Library of Congress.[66]

Kracauer's journey from German public intellectual to propaganda analyst for the U.S. government followed a familiar course, in part because he circulated in the same small circles as many other associates of the Film Library. In 1933, Kracauer escaped from Nazi Germany to Paris, and from there he searched for a way to immigrate to the United States. Kracauer corresponded with his friends at the Institute for Social Research (i.e., the Frankfurt School), which had relocated to Columbia University in 1934. The institute commissioned a study of totalitarian propaganda from Kracauer, but Kracauer refused to implement Theodor Adorno's editorial suggestions and the piece was never published. At around the same time, Kracauer befriended Iris Barry at the suggestion of Columbia art history professor Meyer Schapiro, who suggested that Barry might be another patron for him in America. Kracauer successfully won over Barry at first by writing a glowing review of the Film Library's contribution to the 1938 Jeu de Paume show. Barry, in turn, praised Kracauer's study of composer Jacques Offenbach in the *New York Herald Tribune*. Barry and the institute joined forces to commission a book on the history and sociology of German film from Kracauer, but he was unable to secure the appropriate visas to come to America for another three years. With the aid of Varian Fry and a grant from the Rockefeller Foundation, Kracauer finally moved to New York in February 1941. Kracauer worked at MoMA's Film Library under a number of different fellowships, though he was never directly employed by the museum because of his alien status.[67]

John Marshall at the Rockefeller Foundation carefully weighed Kracauer's credentials (and the fact that he spoke little English at the time) and put him in touch with Austrian and German émigrés Ernst Kris and Hans Speier, who were engaged in a study of Nazi radio propaganda. This was another case in which film research grew out of radio research. Kris and Speier directed the Rockefeller Foundation's Totalitarian Communication Project at the New School for Social Research, and they coordinated their work closely with Laswell's team at the Library of Congress. The report Kracauer produced under this fellowship, "Propaganda and the Nazi War Film," corroborated much of the existing Rockefeller Foundation research. The report—initially confidential but later reprinted as a supplement to *From Caligari to Hitler*—contained close analyses of Nazi newsreels and feature films, examining the synchronization of voice-over, sound, and image to create ideological messages. It is difficult to extrapolate a general theory from Kracauer's detailed work, and the attention to data without general theory is largely the point. Kracauer was interested in identifying the functions of enemy propaganda for some of the same reasons that Goebbels studied *Potemkin*: both to decode it and to reapply its methods in the service of a different ideology.

In one section, for example, Kracauer investigated the Nazis' adaptation of leftist documentary techniques. One effective trick he identified for giving propaganda the impression of unmediated reality was the inclusion of bad photography. Imperfect camera work, he concluded, distracted the audience from the fact that the films had been carefully crafted. Another section, "The Swastika World," looked at the opposite technique: the meticulous manufacture of Nazi iconography. Hitler and

Mussolini both employed public relations professionals to help them develop unique gestures and mannerisms, and like the public relations experts who pioneered the field of propaganda, Nazi filmmakers carefully constructed the iconography of the Nazi soldier and the war. In his report, Kracauer noted that the interplay of word and image in Nazi films were much more complicated than either print or broadcast propaganda. Whereas Nazi radio and newspaper reports spoke of the "revolutionary" war against Allied forces, Nazi films presented an image of German soldiers as extremely conventional. According to Kracauer's subtle analysis, the word "revolution" on the sound track, accompanied by timeless images of German soldiers on the screen, connoted a revolutionary return to eternal values rather than a vanguard revolutionary military movement such as the Russian Revolution.[68] Film could be subtler than radio and print propaganda but, at the same time, film grammar was much harder to describe. Instead of ending the report with an overarching conclusion, Kracauer's argument culminated in an even finer method of analyzing the text: a structural analysis of individual scenes. As such, "Propaganda and the Nazi War Film" followed Laswell's model of content analysis, which accumulated data about the mechanical and psychological working of propaganda in order to influence the production of anti-Axis or even pro-democratic propaganda.

Kracauer may have resisted the urge to develop a general theory of film in favor of more immediately functional close analysis, but he had already begun to formulate the theory of film he would articulate after the war in *From Caligari to Hitler*, the theory that an analysis of German films between 1918 and 1933 could reveal the "deep psychological positions" of the Germans during that period and, ultimately, their predisposition toward totalitarianism. When it was published, *From Caligari to Hitler* drew the ritual redbaiting from Seymour Stern in the *New Leader* and ignited a tremendous controversy. As Martin Jay has noted, "[Other reviewers] worried about the possibility of tracing a similar protofascist lineage in non-German cinema, a thought that continued to trouble Adorno as late as the 1960s."[69] If Kracauer's thesis—that national psychology can be read though films—has become a controversial tenet of film theory, critics often fail to note the remaining two parts of Kracauer's formulation: (a) he expected his method to be "extended to studies of current mass behavior in the United States and elsewhere," and (b) he intended for this method to have policy implications in the crusade for global democracy. "Studies of this kind," he suggested, "may help in the planning of films—not to mention other media of communication—which will effectively implement the cultural aims of the United Nations."[70] *From Caligari to Hitler* grew directly out of the Rockefeller Foundation's communication research agenda, and it can be read backwards into MoMA's work for the Rockefeller Foundation.

"The film," Kracauer wrote while still in Germany, "is the mirror of existing society,"[71] and he continued to refine this formulation over the next few decades. He imparted much of what would become the theoretical basis for *From Caligari to Hitler* to Barbara Deming as early as 1942, when she headed MoMA's Library of Congress Film Project. In conversation with Kracauer, Deming and Iris Barry (as well as other members of the Film Library's staff) devised criteria for selecting an American national film collection that would "reflect the period." The selectors grappled both with the complex system of film's signification and with film's mass appeal in order to create a collection to "serve the student of history rather than the student of art." They identified films that either directly reflected the period or indirectly reflected it by capturing "a current mentality."[72] They considered films that were financially or critically successful as well as films they recognized as being representative of a collective, national psychology. The collection, in short, was an attempt to aid and limit future Siegfried Kracauers who might attempt to reconstruct American national psychology through film. After the publication of *From Caligari to Hitler*, Deming herself followed Kracauer's suggestion and wrote a psychological history of the American film—*Running Away from Myself*— based on the Library of Congress collection, although she couldn't find a publisher for it until 1969.[73]

Plans for an American national film collection had been proposed as early as the first Kinetoscope demonstrations. But suggestions form W. K. L. Dickson, Vachel Lindsay, and even Will Hays failed to produce such a collection. Of course, the Library of Congress had a collection of "paper prints," films that had been deposited for copyright purposes starting in 1894. In lieu of a procedure for copyrighting films, the Edison Manufacturing Company began to copyright entire films as individual photographs by printing them on long strips of photographic paper, hence the term *paper prints*. But the paper prints simply sat in a vault until they were rediscovered in the 1940s. The 1912 Townsend Act finally established a copyright procedure for films. After that the Library of Congress was entitled to copies of every film submitted for a copyright, but the LOC's staff returned all the films they received because they lacked a sufficient storage facility.[74] The MoMA–Rockefeller–Library of Congress project turned out to be the first serious attempt to assemble an American national film collection.

During World War II, Librarian of Congress Archibald MacLeish and the Rockefeller Foundation's John Marshall recognized the potential usefulness of collections that would preserve a history of American mass culture during the war. In 1941 the Rockefeller Foundation funded a radio archive at the Library of Congress, which implemented the theories of Kris, Speir, and others in the formation of a national collection. And in 1942 they contacted MoMA's Film Library to view every film produced in the United States and to select films for inclusion in a national film collection based on criteria extrapolated from Kracauer's developing theory of film and devised in direct discussion with him.

Between 1942 and 1945, a committee of seven alternating analysts evaluated 4,398 films; they recommended for inclusion 603 reels of feature films, 108 reels of newsreels, 62 documentaries, and 118 reels of short subjects.[75] The analysts quickly devised the following selection criteria:

A. Films which present literally actual events, people, places.
B. Films which, through art, represent some aspect of reality in a manner which the analyst finds peculiarly accurate.
C. Films which may fall in neither of the above categories but which deal with problems of outstanding topical significance or arouse special comment or controversy.
D. Films which gross unusually large box office receipts or win prizes.
E. A cross section of the year's releases exhibiting characteristic trends, themes, attitudes and types.
F. Films which contain outstanding performances.
G. Films which mark outstanding technical innovations.[76]

The categories were an attempt to preemptively apply Kracauer's theory, judging the historical importance of individual films without the passage of time. It is useful to look at a few examples before we turn to the overarching demands of the task.

The categories may have been distinct and numbered, but even the analysts admitted that the selection process was personal and idiosyncratic. Many films generated significant controversy among the team. The committee could recommend a successful, big-budget war film like *Guadalcanal Diary* (1943) with no reservations. But no film was guaranteed inclusion, and most films generated at least some controversy. In the midst of the world war, for example, Walt Disney's *Bambi* (1942) apparently posed particularly contentious questions about what it meant to be American. Barry wrote to Archibald MacLeish about the deliberations:

We have had a long discussion of the film BAMBI and the reviewers are still strongly of the opinion that they do not recommend it and that it does not fall under your category 'E,' [exhibiting characteristic trends] since it is derivative and by no means a popular imaginative expression.[77]

Other films were recommended for the collection despite the committee's disagreement over the film's particular politics. When analyst Norbert Lusk recommended Alfred Hitchcock's *Lifeboat* (1944) under categories C (topical films) and F (for Tallulah Bankhead's performance), he noted the dissenting opinion of the committee:

Clearly stated is also that [the characters on the film's eponymous lifeboat] are ineffectuals. For when they can not choose their own leader, the Nazi assumes easy command and from then on symbolizes German efficiency and mastery in the opinion of those who consider the film "injudicious" or ask that it be withdrawn and altered.

Even if a film made it through the committee, Iris Barry often wielded her unofficial right to override the analysts at the end of the deliberation process. In this instance, Barry liked *Lifeboat* and insured that the film would be included despite the analysts' reservations. Barry often handwrote comments to MacLeish over the official form. On the *Lifeboat* report Barry explained that "the 'ineffectual democrats' finally triumph over the Nazi + unite to destroy him! So if there be an allegory intended propaganda content [*sic*] then it is pro-Ally . —IB." Barry overturned Lusk in another instance, writing over his fascinating discussion of the adaptation of Ernest Hemmingway's Spanish Civil War novel *For Whom the Bell Tolls* (1943). Lusk argued that the film was a classic case of Hollywood protecting its financial investment by making a political film that allowed for the identification of spectators on all sides of the issue. The film somehow still managed to offend Barry who wrote: "It is incidentally a bad film as well as a dishonest one + I most definitely do not recommend its preservation on any count. —IB." When Barbara Deming recommended Jacques Tourneur's *I Walked with a Zombie* (1943), an unusually smart genre film, because she thought its subtle treatment of race relations "representative of a new urbanity," Barry again summarily dismissed the film, which she "consider[ed] suitable to the Film Library's purpose but not to that of the Library of Congress."[78]

Barry's comment will remain enigmatic, but the film collections of both the Library of Congress and MoMA were clearly different, and the differences seem determined largely by their intended audiences. MoMA's staff selectively curated shows for immediate political purposes and released the programs to schools, museums, and film societies. The Library of Congress's collection was meant to be a time capsule, perfectly representative of its moment. But both were meant to be propaganda. MoMA's shows were designed to persuade audiences of the dominance of American culture; the LOC's collection was meant to control the conclusions of future historians about that culture.

Deming's explication of the Library of Congress Film Project's selection method reveals a subtle and theoretically informed model of evaluation. The analysts balanced personal reaction and larger questions, seeing themselves both inside and outside their moment. She openly acknowledged that the analysts "play[ed] the historian precociously," but she believed that they could overcome the emotional component of selection. "As soon as it is the human experience that is being explored," she wrote, "it takes a degree of honesty on the part of the analyst to recognize the truth." Deming also described how the method of visual analysis served historiographical goals. The evaluators looked at films for the details of everyday life as well as for abstract qualities. "The historian," she declared, "can often trust a fiction film just as well as an actuality film to tell him how people of the period wore their clothes, handled the daily props of life, pronounced their language." At the same time, analysts extrapolated the abstract propositions of a film like *Lifeboat*, "that worries about . . . how Labor and Capital are going to get along together in democracies."[79] The analysts viewed the films as witnesses to history, and although this was a hurried, wartime exercise, they looked to the preservation of American psychological history, not just the wartime ideological uses of the collection.

The selection process was intended to be more science than propaganda, and everyone involved with the Library of Congress Film Project hoped that it would continue after the war. Archibald MacLeish envisioned the Library of Congress assuming the role of a regular diagnostician of national psychology through film. As an example, one LOC press release announced, "Film Reviewers for Library of Congress Find American Taste in Screen Heroes Is Changing." The LOC's public relations office decided to announce that its film analysts had detected American audiences moving toward valuing collective action over individual accomplishment, as evidenced by "a number of war pictures [that] found their heroes, this last year, in groups rather than individuals."[80] The expense of preserving the volatile nitrate film stock in use before 1950, however, made the continuation of the Library of Congress project impossible.

Nevertheless, the search for a national collection continued at the LOC. John Bradley, director of the Library of Congress Film Project after the war, attempted to raise the necessary funds. He even suggested the desperate measure of creating a purely indexical collection, preserving only one still of each important scene in American films. But the film division was closed in 1947, and much of its collection was destroyed in the 1950s. The LOC's film division was finally rejuvenated in 1968 with funds from the American Film Institute, and the collection was renamed the National Film Collection to designate the renewed mission. The following year, however, the name was changed again to the American Film Institute Collection at the Library of Congress to promote the AFI's public image. Nevertheless, the collection's budget dropped incrementally along with the AFI's until it dried up entirely in 1995. Since the creation of the National Film Preservation Board as a result of the National Film Preservation Act of 1988, the Library of Congress has continued to coordinate the National Film Registry, which annually selects and preserves twenty-five films as national treasures. The Library of Congress now contains the largest collection of films in the United States, largely as a result of copyright deposits and the acquisition of various large collections. But its curators no longer collect film with a distinct theoretical or national mission.[81]

CONCLUSION: INTO THE COLD WAR

The Museum of Modern Art did continue to collect, display, and promote art and film as celebrations of American society after its government contracts dried up. Even without explicit contracts, however, MoMA's trustees and staff maintained close ties with the CIA, the State Department, and the United States Information Agency (America's peacetime propaganda agency). The specific relationship between MoMA and the intelligence community after the war is still a contentious subject, but it is clear that MoMA's curators all steered the museum to aid in the continuing battle against the international spread of communism. Moreover, MoMA's blockbuster shows and traveling exhibits enjoyed considerable and direct assistance from the U.S. government during the cold war. Each museum department, however, took on a different task. Several books have been written about the Department of Painting and Sculpture during the cold war, a few articles and book chapters have looked at the Department of Photography during the same period, but the cold war activities of the Film Library are relatively unknown. This section touches on the Film Library's general cold war strategies and part of the next chapter looks more closely at MoMA's treatment of avant-garde film during the early years of the cold war.

The Department of Photography moved into its most overtly political role during the cold war. Edward Steichen, former director of the U.S. Navy's photographic division, took over the Department of Photography after World War II. Steichen replaced Beaumont Newhall, who had devoted his curatorial tenure to consolidating the place of photography as a fine art. Newhall's exhibits highlighted individual photographers and unique prints as works of art. But MoMA's trustees recognized a new use for the photography department when they invited Steichen to guest curate an exhibit, "Road to Victory," during the war. The exhibit couldn't have been further from Newhall's aesthetic method. Steichen and his installation expert Herbert Bayer laid out "Road to Victory," Christopher Phillips has noted, like an oversized *Life* magazine article. Visitors walked through the narrative exhibit, cumulatively experiencing pristine American landscapes, images of American folk culture, and finally an embattled America at war. By the end, it was hoped, visitors were caught up in the fervor to protect the American way of life and defeat the Axis nations. Steichen repeated this technique in "Power in the Pacific" (1945) and in a host of blockbuster shows that circulated internationally during the cold war: "Korea: The Impact of War in Photographs" (1951), "Family of Man" (1955), and "Bitter Years" (1962), which revisited U.S. government wartime photography. These photo essays responded both directly and indirectly to the threat of nuclear war, the Cuban Missile Crisis, and the fate of American culture in the postwar world. Individual photographers and the photographs themselves were subordinated to the direct political statement of the shows.[82]

The Department of Painting and Sculpture assumed an antithetical approach, one that focused on individual artists and the conditions that allowed them to thrive. In a 1952 article, Alfred Barr responded to senate debates on government support of modern art by answering the question: "Is Modern Art Communistic?" His conclusion was that abstract art couldn't be used as effective communist propaganda because its meaning was difficult to control and its style was generally unpopular. This is why, he argued, Stalin and later the allied Communist parties rejected abstract art and adopted social realism as the official party form. Barr categorically denied the inference that abstract art was inherently communistic, but he didn't directly address the question of whether abstract art could be useful as democratic propaganda. He didn't need to. The article made clear, as did others by Barr, that communist governments wouldn't allow the pro-

duction of art that challenged government authority, and the very controversy generated by American avant-garde painting pointed to the strength
of American democracy. MoMA promoted Abstract Expressionist art, in
particular, as the exemplar of free expression, open markets, and
American ingenuity. The State Department, the USIA, and less directly
the CIA served as intermediaries between MoMA and foreign governments, facilitating the international display of postwar American painting
as the triumph of American individualism.[83]

The Film Library aided the other departments, showing films to accompany exhibits of photographs and paintings. But it also assumed a
unique role as weapon of the cultural cold war. The Film Library continued to chronicle the development of documentary film but with less vigor
than it had during the war. As we will see in the next chapter, unlike the
Department of Painting and Sculpture, the Film Library rejected the work
of the postwar American avant-garde. In place of documentaries and
American avant-garde film, the Film Library returned to its initial mission,
which now assumed new importance, to celebrate Hollywood film as *the*
twentieth-century American art form. The Film Library took its cue from
its successful "D. W. Griffith: The Art of the Motion Picture" program of
1940, which was the only Film Library program until after the war to use
"art" in its title. Barry and the Film Library's staff shied away from discussing art and aesthetics in the 1930s and 1940s, but they devoted all their
resources after the war to recognizing the art of commercial cinema in the
United States and, occasionally, Europe. More specifically, they celebrated the freedom of the creative artist in Hollywood, a position that gave the
Film Library increased currency because of the simultaneous rise of auteurist criticism.[84]

Rather than a retreat into aesthetics, art remained a politically loaded
term. Between 1945 and 1953, the Film Library distributed and continually updated a program called "The Art of Film," an ambitious celebration
of its collection, which was by that point three quarters American film.[85]
Between new incarnations of "The Art of Film," the Film Library circulated programs devoted to individual film artists. John Ford, Charlie
Chaplin, and Marlene Dietrich all earned individual programs in the
1950s. Dietrich could be included because by that point she was considered to be a Hollywood actress, and the Chaplin program carefully avoided controversy—Chaplin was already living in exile—by displaying only
examples of his early career, the "pre-political" Chaplin as it were. Other
programs painted Hollywood as the epitome of the marriage of commerce
and art. "A Producer's Work: Samuel Goldwyn" (1956) demonstrated that

even an independent businessman could be an artist in the film industry. "United Artists, 1919–1954" (1954) honored the studio that spoke most to the American dream of the independent commercial artist; it had been founded by successful film artists Charlie Chaplin, D. W. Griffith, Mary Pickford, and Douglas Fairbanks to give filmmakers greater control over the distribution of their films. Still other programs, such as "Recent Acquisitions and Loans" (1953) or "Masterworks from the Film Library Collection" (1955), solidified the impression that the Film Library now trafficked in film art rather than politics or sociology.

In addition to reinventing itself as the champion of the individual artist in Hollywood, the Film Library engaged in some revisionist historiography, overturning its past sociological veneer. For instance, "50 Years of Italian Film" (1955) reassembled the museum's collection of Italian cinema to display its development as a national art rather than a revelation of national identity. And in 1954, the Film Library symbolically closed the door on its sociological ambitions when it gave Leni Reifenstahl's *Olympia* (1938) a solo show, divorced from any connection to Nazi propaganda or German film.

To be sure, this was a dramatic shift from sociology, history, and mass psychology to film (mainly Hollywood) art and artists. But the transformation was also, in many ways, a continuation of both the Film Library's earlier work and of MoMA's continued nationalistic mission. The Film Library found in Hollywood something akin to the American individualism MoMA's painting curators and the State Department found in Abstract Expressionism. Like the other departments, the Film Library's circulating programs remained invaluable both to American art's infiltration of global financial markets and to the general vision of America abroad. This was, of course, far from the Film Library's earlier sociological interest in Hollywood as an expression of American identity. The continuity of the Film Library from the New Deal to the cold war was not its methodology, but rather its ongoing undertaking to unite Hollywood and America in the arena of world public opinion. The elasticity of the Museum of Modern Art's curatorial methods in pursuit of a larger goal is perhaps the secret to its success, especially when so many earlier institutions had failed to define American film.

6

THE POLITICS OF PATRONAGE
HOW THE NEA (ACCIDENTALLY) CREATED AMERICAN AVANT-GARDE FILM

> Probably nobody will ever know the extent of help [Jerome Hill] has given
> to independent film-makers; because of his humility, practically all help
> was given anonymously. . . . The whole movement of the American avant-
> garde film of the '60s would have taken a completely different turn, much
> slower and thinner, without the help of Jerome. I am not writing a history
> of the American avant-garde film; I am writing a last tribute to Jerome. So
> I am talking in very general terms, and I am skipping details and names
> and figures. But when such a history is written, that history will be dedicat-
> ed to Jerome Hill.
> —Jonas Mekas, "A Poet Is Dead (In Memory of Jerome Hill)," *Film Culture* (1972)

WITH THE HELP of the Museum of Modern Art, Hollywood film became an American national art form. This chapter turns to what
is in some ways the coda to that history: the fate of American
avant-garde film after Hollywood film became museum art. MoMA and
other major institutions of American culture, we will see, rejected avant-
garde film from the 1940s though the late 1960s. In turn, a movement of
avant-garde filmmakers created an alternate system of institutions in an attempt to usurp Hollywood's role as American national film. This history
reveals much about the political and aesthetic decisions that brought
Hollywood to the center of museums and government agencies during the
cold war. And it explains some of the lasting impressions of Hollywood as
somehow inherently American. In order to understand this history, we
need to look at a relationship that is generally suppressed: the avant-garde
and money.

Avant-garde films, as a rule, don't make money, and avant-garde filmmakers rarely survive on the profits from film rentals. Some avant-garde

filmmakers have supported themselves with day jobs as painters and sculptors, as university professors, or as contract workers for commercial film companies. The high points of avant-garde film production, however, have been the result of private or state patronage. During the 1920s, Dada and Surrealist filmmakers found wealthy sponsors in the French aristocrat Compte Etienne de Beaumont and the American financier Arthur Wheeler. Meanwhile, French impressionist and German abstract filmmakers managed to attract financial support from large production companies—Pathé and Ufa, respectively—eager to exploit the aesthetic innovations of the avant-garde. Most fertile periods of avant-garde film production, to be sure, have been enabled by a combination of government arts policy and state subsidies. The clearest examples are the Soviet avant-garde film movement of the 1920s and 1930s, the African and Latin American avant-garde film movements of the 1960s, and the British avant-garde film and video movements of the 1970s and 1980s.[1]

The post–World War II American avant-garde, the most sustained period of avant-garde film production to date, adhered to this same model of government policy and patronage, yet the conditions that allowed it to flourish have been the least understood. These conditions are more politically complicated than those of other avant-garde film movements, and some of them have remained relatively secret. The postwar American avant-garde resulted, this chapter argues, from the dual forces of state support for the arts (the politically complicated part) and private patronage (the secret part). To be more specific, museums and foundations from the late 1930s on and the National Endowment for the Arts (NEA) after 1965 created a model for the full-time avant-garde artist in America, however paradoxical that formulation may seem. Yet these institutions continually frustrated avant-garde filmmakers by excluding them from new avenues of funding. While the NEA, MoMA, the Rockefeller Foundation, and other institutions devoted themselves to funding avant-garde art in every other medium, they supported Hollywood film.

In response, avant-garde filmmakers banded together to campaign for government support, at first, and then, as a last-ditch effort, to strike out on their own. Among other experiments, avant-garde filmmakers tried auctioning off limited numbers of film prints, as one might auction a lithograph; they set up international traveling programs; and they established dozens of organizations. Ultimately, these experiments were insufficiently profitable, and in the end a single, anonymous patron underwrote the movement almost entirely.

That patron was Jerome Hill, grandson of railroad magnate James J.

Hill and a talented filmmaker in his own right. Hill's financial contributions to avant-garde film are not entirely unknown; he has frequently been
designated an "angel" of the postwar avant-garde, bailing out filmmakers
and institutions when they needed money. But this image entirely revers-
es the structure of the American avant-garde, and it all but nullifies the
role of patronage. Jerome Hill didn't fuel an organic movement with occasional financial support. Rather, his patronage provided the underlying
force that shaped the avant-garde. The system of institutions—journals,
foundations, distribution centers, a museum—that funded and distributed
avant-garde film for decades served largely to mask the underpinning system of private patronage. This system replicated romantic, modernist, and
bureaucratic precedents to produce a shifting admixture of money, film,
and definitions of the American artist. Hill maintained his relative
anonymity at first by working through lawyers and his de facto adviser
Jonas Mekas. Later, starting around 1966, Hill revealed himself to a small
circle of filmmakers and critics, and together they established an epistolary community that self-consciously struggled to define its system of financial and aesthetic exchange. Finally, shortly before Hill's death, the patronage system became solidified in the form of a film museum,
Anthology Film Archives. With Hill's support, a community of avant-garde
filmmakers challenged Hollywood's hold on American arts institutions for
a quarter century. And they challenged institutions' power to determine
the definition of American art and artists.

The letters between patron, advisers, and filmmakers provide the extant
proof of this community and, as a result, this chapter is based largely on a
reading of Hill's private correspondence, cancelled checks, and other files,
which have been previously unavailable. These documents offer a unique
picture of an avant-garde movement from the perspective of its patron. It is
a view that reopens a history that has consistently been reopened by filmmakers and scholars. The historiography of the American avant-garde is
now a palimpsest of phenomenological criticism, psychoanalytic-semiotic
feminist criticism, historicist criticism, and Marxist-political criticism. It is
a history that bears retelling and rethinking with this new evidence because
the considerations of patronage, policy, and institutions goes right to the
heart of what makes the avant-garde avant-garde. Conversely, these considerations go to the heart of what makes a museum a museum.

Following Peter Bürger, Andreas Huyssen, and T. J. Clark, avant-garde
art and literature has increasingly been defined as anti-institution art and
explained by its antithetical relationship to artwork stored in museums and
supported by arts institutions.[2] The same formula has been imposed on

the history of avant-garde film, with the commercial film industry standing in for museums. J. Hoberman, for example, defines avant-garde film
as "opposed to commercial cinema, in terms of distribution, production,
and articulation."[3] As we have seen in the previous chapters, for all intents
and purposes Hollywood film had become "museum film" by the end of
World War II. Clearly, avant-garde art, including film, responds negative-
ly to the canons and traditions of institutionally sanctioned standards.
When we look at the development of postwar American avant-garde film,
however, we find that the institutions and the avant-garde are much more
closely intertwined than the current model would allow. Government arts
policy and museums have been both active and accidental participants—
even collaborators—in the creation of some aspects of the avant-garde,
which is to say much more than institutions provide a model to react
against. Moreover, the postwar American film avant-garde throws into relief two strains of the avant-garde: an institutional avant-garde (e.g., Soviet
constructivism or Abstract Expressionism) that either willingly or grudgingly coincided with national politics and gained official acceptance, and
a second, anti-institution avant-garde that was either denied entrance into
cultural institutions or, to see it another way, more successfully opposed
traditions and resisted co-optation.

It is often thought that all avant-garde movements aspire to maintain
their anti-institution status and disintegrate once they establish their own
doctrines or institutions. The dean of the Dada movement, Tristan Tsara,
for example, liked to declare that "Dada is nothing" and that anyone who
thought it formalized enough to resign from misunderstood the meaning
of *nothing*.[4] American avant-garde filmmakers, however, sought to become an institutional avant-garde while consistently having to work outside and against arts institutions. Their striving to become an institutional
avant-garde and usurp Hollywood's role as *the* American national cinema
was so carefully disguised by the rhetoric of artistic freedom and individuality that it has rarely been acknowledged by either the participants or the
historians of the movement. Yet it is this struggle for admission into the
museums, the foundations, and, most surprisingly, the NEA that ultimately defined a rich and otherwise successful period of avant-garde film
production. To investigate the role of museums, foundations, and the government in the creation of American avant-garde film, this chapter returns
to the two framing moments of the postwar American avant-garde film
movement: the reception of Maya Deren and Alexander Hammid's film
Meshes of the Afternoon (1943) and the founding of Anthology Film
Archives (1970). The former historical moment marks the initial rejection

of American avant-garde film from museum, state, and foundation support. The latter moment marks the avant-garde's creation of its own museum and begs the question: Can the avant-garde have a museum at all? Or do museums necessarily rob art of its avant-garde status?

HOW THE U.S. GOVERNMENT LEARNED TO IGNORE AVANT-GARDE FILM

The rise of a community of avant-garde filmmakers in the United States is intertwined with two transformations in government support for artists in America. As we saw in the previous chapter, the first occurred during the decade and a half after World War II, when government support for the arts was limited to covert funding for and manipulation of private museums and foundations. Most ambitiously, officials at the State Department and the newly formed Central Intelligence Agency helped the Museum of Modern Art, the Ford Foundation, and the Rockefeller Foundation circulate avant-garde art as a celebration of American creative freedom and individual expression. In the widely debated case of Abstract Expressionist painting, it is clear that the government's use of the artwork conflicted with both the politics of the artists and the reception of the work abroad; the CIA funded exhibitions of Abstract Expressionist paintings even while the Federal Bureau of Investigation looked into the alleged communist activities of the artists.[5]

Nevertheless, this collaboration between government officials and select private institutions during the early cold war led to the creation of a new class of arts administrators who moved fluidly between the different organizations. Most of MoMA's board of directors in the 1950s, for instance, had worked for intelligence organizations during and after the war. In the same decade, the CIA simultaneously employed many members of the Ford Foundation's staff. In 1953, CIA officer Allen Dulles faced a dilemma indicative of the increasingly fluid boundaries between arts and intelligence administration when he weighed two job offers: the presidency of the Ford Foundation and directorship of the CIA. Dulles decided to stay with the CIA while former assistant secretary of war and committed cold warrior John McCloy took the position at the Ford Foundation.[6]

This new class of arts administrators stepped out from behind the curtain in the 1960s. Led by Nelson Rockefeller in the Republican Party and by John F. Kennedy in the Democratic Party, state and federal government agencies moved poetry, modern dance, and avant-garde painting to the fore of public policy. Furthermore, they installed arts administrators in prominent government positions. Rockefeller had been enmeshed in government arts policy since the 1940s, serving at different times as head of the Office of the Coordinator of Inter-American Affairs (CIAA) and as president of MoMA's board of trustees. Like few others, he knew the propaganda power of art in the sphere of world politics, and in 1960, as governor of the state of New York, Rockefeller initiated the first State Arts Council to disseminate art and, later, to fund arts institutions. Rockefeller framed this move as the official unveiling of his bid for national office, describing the Arts Council as a first step in leading the nation, "towards fulfillment of its high cultural aspirations."[7]

During his tenure as a U.S. senator, John F. Kennedy showed little interest in legislation designed to lend federal assistance to the arts. But beginning with his inauguration ceremony in 1961, Kennedy made art a visible component of his administration. Reading at the inauguration, Robert Frost predicted "a golden age of poetry and power, of which this noonday's the beginning hour."[8] Kennedy's subsequent invitations to well-known artists to perform at the White House were widely publicized. At the policy level, Kennedy tested the waters for public federal support of artists and arts institutions, being careful not to commit any funds right away. Kennedy appointed August Heckscher, former chairman of MoMA's International Program and chief editorial writer for the *New York Herald Tribune*, as a consultant to investigate the role government could play in the world of the arts. After much debate, Kennedy finally developed a prominent though powerless arts advisory council.

Kennedy's overtures to the arts were guarded, but when seen as part of the longer history of government arts support, they cannot be considered trivial. The government's foray into artist relief during the Great Depression—Federal Project Number One of the Works Progress Administration (WPA)—had ended with widespread mistrust of artists and entertainers that intensified during the McCarthy era in the 1950s. In August 1938 the controversial theater productions and murals funded by the WPA became the subject of a formal investigation by the House Committee on Un-American Activities (or HUAC). Committee chairman Martin Dies headed the inquiry into communist influences on artists in the WPA programs; the outcome, four years later, was the abolition of all federal support for art not directly related to the war effort. In the following years, the State Department and intelligence agencies' covert support for the arts was consistently at odds with a vociferous faction in congress, headed by Michigan Republican George Dondero, who persistently branded modern art the result of a communist conspiracy. In 1949, Dondero's lobby proved so powerful that they were able to block the State Department from circulating an exhibit of modern art, titled "Advancing Modern Art," through Europe and Latin America. Dondero and HUAC went after modern art with the same vigor they reserved for Hollywood, but by the late 1950s cracks in this particular anticommunist front began to appear. A new breed of cold warriors, like Rockefeller and Kennedy, who recognized that modern art had become American art, were able to take over. Their new tactics in the cultural cold war may have been tentative, but they laid the groundwork for a second phase of government funding of artists and institutions, a phase that began with the formation of the National Endowment for the Arts in 1965, after Kennedy's assassination.[9]

Both cinema and avant-garde art were central concerns of administrators at the foundations and museums starting in the 1940s and at the NEA after 1965. But, significantly, the two terms—*cinema* and *avant-garde*— never intersected. After World War II, Abstract Expressionist painting became synecdochical for American avant-gardism, brazenly marking America's usurpation of Europe as the beacon of artistic culture. It was through the celebration of Abstract Expressionist painting that, as Serge Guillbaut put it, "New York stole the idea of modern art" from Paris. Nelson Rockefeller shrewdly summarized this imbrication of art, politics, and commerce when he labeled Abstract Expressionism "free enterprise painting."[10] On the other hand, for the agencies, the foundations, and MoMA, cinema meant government-produced documentaries and Hollywood film exclusively. The Rockefeller Foundation's extensive evaluation of American filmmaking was focused almost entirely on educational, documentary films and their potential use in advancing democratic societies. The Rockefeller Foundation worked in conjunction with the State Department and various intelligence agencies as they were renamed and consolidated. The Office of War Information took the most active role in the production and distribution of film; the OWI's Domestic Branch commissioned documentary films during the war, and its Oversees Branch coordinated the export of documentaries and Hollywood films to foreign markets. When the OWI collaborated with the commercial film industry to start the Motion Picture Export Association, it was known tellingly as the "Little State Department."

Beginning in 1967, the NEA looked after the government's interests in Hollywood. Indeed, one of the NEA's largest undertakings was the formation of an American Film Institute. The AFI was so central to the NEA that it was one of the few objectives Lyndon Johnson chose to mention when he signed the NEA legislation into law in a Rose Garden cer-

emony. For quite a while, the AFI was one of the most generously funded of all NEA activities, and it acquired matching funds from the Ford
Foundation and the Motion Picture Association of America (formerly,
the Motion Picture Producers and Distributors of America), uniting government, art institutions, and Hollywood under one roof.[11] The AFI's initial mission was to preserve films stored in American vaults, but it soon
took on the additional role of funding inexpensive (under $400,000)
films. Filmmakers hoped that the AFI's support would extend to them.[12]
But despite small AFI grants to avant-garde filmmakers Storm de Hirsch
and Paul Sharits, avant-garde filmmakers quickly realized that the administrators at the AFI were simply in the business of finding new talent
for Hollywood studios. The AFI's filmmaker grants did something far
more insidious than ignoring the avant-garde; they were developed in
part to enervate the avant-garde just as Andy Warhol's *Chelsea Girls*
(1966) and other films were gaining wider notoriety. As Abstract
Expressionist painting symbolized the creative possibilities of the individual under American democracy, Hollywood came to symbolize the triumph of the American free market. Avant-garde film only challenged this
neat formulation.

Yet this same period, from the mid-1940s through the mid-1970s, also
saw the establishment of the avant-garde filmmaker as a viable occupa-
tion and identity in America. At odds with the government's apparent
separation of film and art, avant-garde filmmaking didn't fit smoothly
into the new channels of support. Nevertheless, the increase in foundation and government support for avant-garde painters and performers, on
the one hand, and for Hollywood, on the other, also made possible the
rise of an avant-garde film movement. Avant-garde film, we will see, was
excluded from government funding out of hand, for ideological reasons:
it was stridently anticapitalist and appeared, to the relevant arts administrators anyway, to be un-American. Of course, the same arguments were
aimed against Abstract Expressionism, but painting didn't have an ac-
ceptable mainstream counterpart as avant-garde film had Hollywood.
Despite the competition from Hollywood, however, the increased desire
for government subsidy and encouragement consistently propelled
avant-garde filmmakers. The perpetually stifled dream of a state-
subsidized avant-garde filmmaker eventually led to an alternate system
of funding and support—one based on private patronage (from Jerome
Hill) and an institutional structure that both mirrored the bureaucra-
tized NEA and, at the same time, harkened back to earlier models of
patron-artist interdependence.

THE BIRTH OF THE AMERICAN AVANT-GARDE FILMMAKER

Filmmaker Maya Deren and the Museum of Modern Art's film curator Iris Barry worked from opposite sides of the artist-administrator dialectic to create the ideal of the avant-garde filmmaker in America. This ideal filmmaker is by now a familiar type: he or she worked independently of Hollywood and made exceedingly personal films, usually performing all the labor of production and reception. The avant-garde filmmaker frequently served as writer, director, and actor as well as exhibitor and principal exegete of his or her own work. This autonomous avant-garde filmmaker, however, often relied on a coterie of other artists, filmmakers, and friends to reflect and confirm the value of his or her work. This model of artist and community is comparable, in many ways, to the model forged by modernist writers such as James Joyce, Joseph Conrad, and D. H. Lawrence, who similarly defined their labor, in part, in terms of financial compensation and audience. As Joyce Wexler's examination of the correspondence between modernist authors and their publishers has revealed, many writers classified their work somewhere between the Romantic paragon—the *amateur* who wrote purely for himself or herself—and the commercial *hack* who wrote purely for money.[13] To navigate between these poles, modernist writers sought to earn a living from their work—to be professional artists—but only on condition that the work wasn't too popular, circulating only among initiated readers. Lawrence Rainey's revisionist account of the publication of Joyce's *Ulysses*, to take one example, confirms that authors, publishers, and critics cooperated over years to suggest that only fifteen or so well-known members of the literati actually acquired copies from the initial printing, more or less ignoring the one thousand copies printed in the first run.[14] Similarly, avant-garde filmmakers clearly did much to separate themselves from the commercial film industry. It is less often recognized, however, that despite their invention of neo-Romantic genres (the film diary, the film letter, and the film poem), avant-garde filmmakers also fought hard to make their art into a self-sustaining profession.[15] Here was the dilemma: how to be professional without being commercial. The evidence that artists in every other field were finding the answer in state, museum, and foundation patronage aggravated the filmmakers' dilemma.

The exclusion of avant-garde film from official support is largely responsible for the unusual position of avant-garde filmmakers in the United States. To be more precise, Iris Barry made the avant-garde filmmaker a special case of the American artist as such when she simultaneously blocked Maya Deren from access to the Museum of Modern Art as a film-screening venue and thwarted Deren's applications for foundation funding. When Deren and her husband Alexander Hackenschmied (changed to Hammid in 1947) made the film that was to launch the postwar avant-garde film movement in America, *Meshes of the Afternoon*, MoMA seemed the appropriate place for its debut. MoMA had actively collected and exhibited avant-garde films of the 1920s, and Hammid knew Barry personally from their mutual affiliation with the OWI during World War II (Barry oversaw the OWI's film projects for MoMA, and Hammid made documentary films for the OWI). If Barry had initially bought a print of *Meshes* for the museum (which she did in 1955 to appease protesting filmmakers), or if she had screened *Meshes* in the museum's auditorium (which MoMA's dance curator George Amberg did just a few years later in 1946), the film might have appeared to be nothing more than a new contribution to the canonical and, by that point, museum-approved body of avant-garde films.

To be sure, many critics have seen *Meshes*'s aesthetic debts to the impressionist films of Germaine Dulac and the Surrealist films of Jean Cocteau, Luis Buñuel and Salvador Dali. Despite Deren's quarrel with the psychoanalytic positions of the Surrealists, *Meshes*'s dreamlike iconography and use of doubles placed it firmly in the Surrealist tradition. There is also plenty of biographical evidence to suggest *Meshes*'s debts to the 1920s avant-garde. Deren had been exposed to earlier avant-garde films in classes at Syracuse University (though it is unclear exactly which films she had seen at that point), and while still living in Prague, Hammid made films in the avant-garde city symphony genre.[16] Barry, however, rejected *Meshes* and, as a result, she helped transform the film from Surrealism's successor into the herald of a new movement of avant-garde film, a movement that wandered for another twenty-five years before finding its own home and museum: the Anthology Film Archives.

Several factors contributed to Barry's rejection of *Meshes*, and to the expulsion of avant-garde film from American art institutions. Some were clearly personal. The businesslike Barry didn't take to the bohemian Deren; "Iris didn't dig *Meshes* or Maya," Hammid recalled.[17] At the time, Barry was also at odds with filmmaker Hans Richter, who had been a leading avant-garde filmmaker and organizer since the end of World War I and was single-handedly trying to resuscitate avant-garde film. For decades, Richter remained one step ahead of other avant-garde filmmakers—from his early abstract films, which had won financial support from the German commercial behemoth Ufa, to the fusion of avant-garde and documentary styles he achieved in essay films in the 1930s. Newly immigrated to New York in 1940, Richter worked on two fronts to build a contemporary avant-garde film movement. He tried both to initiate film projects for his old Dada and Surrealist friends and to mentor a new generation of avant-garde filmmakers in his classes at the City College of New York's Institute of Film Techniques. (Richter's disciples at CCNY would include leaders of the American avant-garde Jonas Mekas and Shirley Clarke.)

Unlike Barry, Richter approved of Deren and her films immediately. In 1944, Richter planned to include *Meshes* in a compilation of Surrealist films he was assembling. The project, to be called "The Movies Take a Holiday," would have included masterpieces of Surrealism by René Clair, Marcel Duchamp, and Man Ray in addition to Deren, symbolically marking the transatlantic migration and continuation of the avant-garde. But, struggling for money, Richter abandoned his compilation idea and applied to the Solomon R. Guggenheim Foundation for funds to work on a new film. Richter had been unusually successful at finding patronage in the past, but all three of his applications for Guggenheim fellowships were turned down, even the proposals cowritten with luminary artists Fernand Léger and Marcel Duchamp.[18] With no real source of support, Richter poured his modest academic salary and small contributions from Peggy Guggenheim and British filmmaker-critic Kenneth MacPherson into a collaborative film, *Dreams That Money Can Buy* (1944–1947). This retro-Surrealist effort with commercial aspirations took over three years to make and it failed both artistically and at the box office.

In spite of these rejections, the Guggenheim Foundation is the one institution that offered any support to filmmakers during the 1940s, although grants went only to animation projects by artists who had achieved success working in other media. Painter Oskar Fischinger and the composer-painter brothers James and John Whitney were all given fellowships to make animated films in the 1940s. In this instance, the funding of a few film projects is the exception rather than the rule. It is an institutional policy that is corroborated, we will see, by Deren's own applications for Guggenheim funding.[19]

In another personal attack, Richard Griffith, assistant film curator at MoMA, insulted Deren and categorically dismissed avant-garde film at a party at the home of publicity agent Arthur Mayer. Griffith apparently criticized Deren even before seeing *Meshes*, and his condemnation was so severe that he avoided screenings of her films for years in fear that she would lash out at him in public. Griffith finally atoned in 1946, publishing a lukewarm review of Deren's work and sending a personal letter of apology. Griffith's review, grudgingly written after Deren had already achieved undeniable success, points to some of the underlying reasons for the MoMA staff's antipathy toward the possibility of a new avant-garde film movement. The review opens with a reiteration of the position Iris Barry had pushed for years, "that the advance-guard had played its role, and that its chief importance had been that of suggesting new ideas to commercial directors, as well as adding to their ranks the important talents of René Clair, Jean Renoir, and Alberto Cavalcanti." Griffith admitted that Deren's "self-created audiences" necessitated that this position be "disavowed." Yet he was careful to differentiate Deren's apolitical, self-exploration through film from the politically engaged avant-garde films of the 1920s. "[Deren] is not interested in shocking the bourgeois, as many of her predecessors," he insisted. "She is in earnest—the films and her voluminous writings about them prove that." Deren, in other words, was lost in the formal properties of what was forged as a politically symbolic vocabulary. As late as 1956, Griffith continued to diminish the achievements of Deren and her colleagues, dismissing their work as derivative of the European avant-garde, the equivalent of "expert copies of old masters painted in the Louvre or the Uffizi." It is best, he cautioned, "to wait for the passing of this period of prentice work."[20]

For Griffith, documentary film had become the true successor to the political avant-garde of the 1920s, and Deren's films only complicated this picture. If Griffith was unwilling to see Deren as the heir to the European and Soviet political avant-garde, he was equally unwilling to see her as a creative individual in the mode of the American artist à la the Abstract Expressionists. Against this claim, Griffith defended Hollywood and political documentaries as the true wellsprings of America's creative spirit: "It is an odd fact that the best and most poetically subjective films have come not from the experimentalist but from the commercial and propaganda fields."[21] The label *propaganda* had a growing currency among both government-sponsored and radical socialist documentary filmmakers in the 1940s. Signaled by Soviet and German films, as we saw in the previous chapter, the term *propaganda* denoted politically influential films rather than an insufficiently truthful genre, as the very same films would later be seen. Griffith's defense of commercial and propaganda films against the avant-garde was perfectly in line with the current government and foundation policies he worked to implement in his various affiliations with MoMA, documentary film collectives, the Office of War Information, and film evaluation boards. Griffith's position vis-à-vis the avant-garde suggests that more than personal squabbles were at stake in all of these attempts to differentiate Deren from earlier avant-garde work and to prevent a new wave of avant-garde film from taking off in the United States.

Barry's rejection of *Meshes* was also the result of a new aesthetic-ideological position that came with her institutional affiliations. In the 1920s, Barry had campaigned to popularize French, German, and Soviet avant-garde film in Britain. She celebrated avant-garde film as an alternative to the Hollywood films flooding the British market along with other American products. In that context, Barry saw the avant-garde as (positively) anti-American. As curator of MoMA's Film Library, Barry created the largest repository for the canonical avant-garde films she had endorsed in the 1920s, and in the Film Library's first year it sponsored a talk by Fernand Léger on "Painting and the Advance Guard Film." But by the 1940s, Barry's utilitarian view of avant-garde film as a potential source of non-Hollywood style had been replaced with a commitment to American democracy and an almost fanatical zeal for social realist documentaries (i.e., "films of fact") and Hollywood film as the only true democratic forms. By the time Deren and Hammid appeared at Barry's office, Barry had come to view the avant-garde as antithetical to commercial and documentary work she thought crucial to the fight against communism and fascism.

More than just banishing Deren's first film from MoMA, Barry also attempted to block Deren from making new films. Barry rejected Deren's application for a Rockefeller Foundation grant in 1945 and thus solidified the exclusion of American avant-garde film from the growing system of private and state-funded support for the arts. In the rejection letter, John Marshall of the Rockefeller Foundation told Deren,

> I know it appears to you that what you need is a chance to make more films; but after a good deal of thought and some further discussion, Miss Barry and I both feel that this would not actually be so advantageous as it seems. Rather, rightly or wrongly, it is our feeling that you can better develop your talent for film-making in finding some way in which it can be utilized in film-making of various types.[22]

An understandably indignant and confused Deren responded: "it is unclear to me what you might have in mind in the way of 'filmmaking of various types' as a substitute for my making more films like the ones (in the same direction, that is) which have apparently impressed you."[23] Deren is obviously right to point to the evasiveness of Marshall's letter, but at the time Barry, Marshall, and the Rockefeller Foundation were in the business of sponsoring documentary films exclusively; it seems a reasonable assumption then that what they had in mind by "film-making of various types" was documentary film, or what they called "films of fact."

Cut off from museum and foundation support, Deren spent several years traveling to colleges and film societies with *Meshes* and her other films. Then, in 1946, Deren "four-walled" a program of the three films she had made at the Provincetown Playhouse on MacDougal Street in Greenwich Village, New York. (*Four-walling*—when a theater is privately rented for the exhibition of a single film or film program—became popular among small independent companies in the 1970s but was an unusual practice in the 1940s.)[24] Deren's one-woman show became the prototype for exhibiting avant-garde films, whereby the individual filmmaker presents his or her work to an initiated audience. The exaggerated exertion of authorship that surrounded the event elided the collaborative nature of all of Deren's films: she made *Meshes* with Hammid, *At Land* (1944) with Hammid and friend Hella Hamon, and *A Study in Choreography for the Camera* (1945) with choreographer Tally Beatty. Yet the reviews and the program notes, which included Deren's statement of artistic purpose, all suggested that the films were the work of a single artist. As an advertisement in *View* magazine read: "The newest in avant-garde film. Three films by MAYA DEREN based on the concept of cinema as an independent art form."[25] The advertisement suggested that Deren's films were not on display as much as a new model of the filmmaker as artist. She not only made the films her own, she also discovered the method for presenting the avant-garde filmmaker as a lone artist. Deren, in other words, encapsulated the same myth of the freewheeling American artist as Jackson Pollock—only without Pollock's backing from the CIA, the Museum of Modern Art, and Peggy Guggenheim.

Just a month before the Provincetown Playhouse screenings, Deren wrote to French critic René Renne, "I find myself in complete isolation in my concept of film as an independent art form."[26] When she wrote the letter, Deren knew that her audience was growing, and campus rentals increased steadily. What surprised everyone, including Deren, however, is the size of the latent audience for avant-garde film that she tapped into with the screenings at Provincetown Playhouse. Many people, including film critic Manny Farber, were turned away from the screenings, and the projectionists' union, after somehow hearing about the size of the crowd outside the theater, insisted that a union member run the projector. The audience drew from different segments of New York's arts communities. Anaïs Nin and other experimental writers attended, as did members of the dance world who knew of Deren from her employment as Catherine Dunham's assistant. Film fans and many future filmmakers, including Richter's CCNY students, also attended the screenings. Two young film lovers, Amos and Marcia Vogel, most clearly saw the potential revealed by the event. Shortly after Deren's screenings, they rented out the Provincetown Playhouse again and began what became American's largest film society, Cinema 16. Cinema 16 boasted 2,500 members at its height and operated successfully until 1963. If it is an oft-repeated myth of the avant-garde that a few screenings launched a movement, it is also a myth that reveals some truth. Deren didn't invent the American avant-garde, but the success of her screenings proved to a dispersed, disenfranchised avant-garde that momentum and excitement existed for poetic, non-Hollywood films.[27]

Deren billed her screenings as "Three Abandoned Films," and the poster reprinted a quote from Paul Valéry: "A work is never completed, but merely abandoned."[28] These were films, however, that had also been abandoned by the institutions that supported art and noncommercial film in the United States. Deren felt scorned by those institutions, and after the success of the Provincetown Playhouse screenings, she wrote to her old professor and mentor at Syracuse University, Sawyer Falk, that now she could "shove this in the face of the Guggenheim (for which I have reapplied) and a few such other institutions who should have helped before."[29] As Deren predicted, the institutions were forced to take notice. In April, Deren won a $3,000 Guggenheim fellowship. Later in the year, MoMA screened *Meshes* under the auspices of its dance department, Richard Griffith sent his apology, and the San Francisco Museum of Art screened Deren's films in its "Art in Cinema" program.

When Deren won the Guggenheim fellowship, she thought she had weathered the brief official rejection of avant-garde film and a new era of foundation films was on the horizon. But the grant turned out to be a lone gesture, and Deren spent the rest of her life trying to create a system of support for avant-garde filmmakers. In 1953 she founded the Film Artists Society (later renamed Independent Filmmakers Association), a group of filmmakers who met regularly until 1956 trying to organize the scattered avant-garde. The following year, in 1954, Deren founded another organization, the Creative Filmmakers Foundation, which futilely worked to secure grants for independent filmmakers. From 1956 until Deren's untimely death in 1961, however, the foundation had to be content to give out Creative Cinema Awards at Cinema 16. We will never know if Deren realized that even though she continually lost the battle to win the support of foundations and museums, she had, perhaps inadvertently, started a

FIGURE 6.1   Maya Deren, *Meshes of the Afternoon* (1943).
(Courtesy of Jonas Mekas and Anthology Film Archives)

grassroots movement of avant-garde film supported by thousands of cine-philes at Cinema 16 and other societies.

MIRRORING THE STATE: AN ALTERNATIVE HISTORY OF THE NEW AMERICAN CINEMA

Even organizations that grow out of the avant-garde produce dissenters, and Cinema 16 eventually became its own form of establishment, creating divisions within the avant-garde community. Amos Vogel regularly reject-ed avant-garde pioneer Marie Menken's films from inclusion in Cinema 16 programs and, in response, Menken and her circle of friends formed a filmmaking collective called the Gryphon Group. Vogel also refused to screen Stan Brakhage's epochal exploration of vision and subjectivity, *Anticipation of the Night* (1958) at Cinema 16,[30] a decision that both sig-naled Vogel's drift away from the avant-garde and toward more commer-cial interests and led to the creation of an alternative distribution agency, the Film-Makers' Cinémathèque. In 1963, Vogel put an end to Cinema

16's screenings and took a job directing the New York Film Festival; four years later he sold Cinema 16's collection to Grove Press. (The collection eventually became the foundation of the Harvard Film Archive.) In both instances, Vogel rejected overtures from a growing faction within the American avant-garde—the co-op movement—which wanted the successful Cinema 16 to join its effort to make avant-garde cinema the American national cinema. The leaders of the co-op movement, we will see, picked up the search for foundation and museum support where Deren had left off, and spurred on by the promise of public support for the arts, they sought the endorsement of the government as well.

The campaign for a new American national cinema found an unlikely leader in the Lithuanian immigrant Jonas Mekas. In 1958 two events in Mekas's life proved decisive in the formation of the co-op movement and in the transformation of the American avant-garde film world. The first event was the chance meeting of Mekas and Jerome Hill shortly after Hill's documentary about Albert Schweitzer won an Academy Award (we will return to this shortly). The second event occurred when Mekas attended the screening of the first version of John Cassavetes' *Shadows* at the Paris Theater in New York. Mekas immediately anticipated that *Shadows* could carry avant-garde film out of obscurity, and he subsequently engineered a new stage in the development of American avant-garde film out of *Shadows'* success. Mekas and Gideon Brachman arranged a second screening of *Shadows* at Manhattan's 92nd Street Y, and the following January, Mekas awarded the journal *Film Culture's* first Independent Film Award to *Shadows*. A few months later, Mekas published "A Call for a New Generation of Film Makers." This manifesto predicted that *Shadows* would lead a new populist and popular independent cinema movement to overtake both the commercial film industry and the existing American avant-garde film movement, which, Mekas feared, had already "become sterile and has frozen into a genre." In a collective statement that challenged its readers to take a position inside or outside the budding faction, the manifesto declared: "We think such a movement is about to begin."[31] When the second version of *Shadows* premiered at Cinema 16 the following year on a double bill with Robert Frank and Alfred Lesilie's 30-minute Beat film *Pull My Daisy*, Mekas declared it overly conventional.[32] But the popularity of this second version gave Mekas the momentum he needed to turn his call for a new generation of filmmakers into an organized movement.

This is the official story. What has fallen out of the narrative, however, is that Mekas, like Deren, initially hoped to gain government and foundation support for filmmakers. In the early 1960s, Kennedy's and Rockefeller's policy initiatives and public rhetoric offered plenty of encouragement. As early as 1961, Mekas participated in discussions with leaders of film institutions to start "an American Film Institute," which bore little resemblance to its later namesake.[33] In the *Third Report of the New American Cinema Group* (1963), Mekas explained to filmmakers weary of co-optation that government sponsorship was a major goal of organization.

> There are people around Washington D.C. today who are trying to persuade the Government to subsidize film-making. It is Hollywood that wants all the money. We don't see why our films shouldn't be subsidized by the government if any of us want it. Only when we have all independent filmmakers behind us, can we pressure Washington, or the Foundations—which are still ignoring cinema—and other such groups or institutions to assist us. . . . These then are a few reasons for maintaining our loose organization.[34]

Mekas wrote this statement just one month after President Kennedy appointed August Heckscher as his Special Consultant on the Arts and just a few days after Sen. Hubert Humphrey introduced legislation to "establish a National Council on the Arts and a National Arts Foundation."[35] It was also two years before the founding of the NEA and four years before the founding of the AFI. As we know already, Hollywood won the battle for government, museum, and foundation film support in the 1960s as it had won a similar battle in the 1940s with the help of Iris Barry, the Museum of Modern Art, and the Rockefeller Foundation. Before the results were in, however, Mekas and other organizers worked to win official favor by remaking the avant-garde to resemble other institutionally supported arts movements. Some of these similarities occurred at an aesthetic level (such as the use of Abstract Expressionist painting techniques in film production). But the most direct mimicking of other successful art movements occurred at the organizational level. The distinctly national ambitions of this restructuring are clearest in the name they chose for the new movement: the New American Cinema.

On the heels of *Shadows'* success, Mekas rallied other filmmakers and established the New American Cinema Group, an organization that took up the task of uniting avant-garde filmmakers where Deren had left off. The New American Cinema Group held its first meeting on November 28, 1960; it became a legal body on May 29, 1961; and it finally gained nonprofit status in 1964.[36] The New American Cinema Group, along with another organization, the Film Culture Non-Profit Corporation (incorporated April 22, 1963; tax exempt status July 15, 1965), together became the two parent organizations of dozens of smaller ventures begun in 1960s: the Film-Makers' Cooperative, the Film-Makers' Distribution Center, and the Film-Makers' Cinémathèque, to name a few. These institutions added up to an elaborate infrastructure ready-made for the government and the foundations to provide funding. While the New American Cinema await-ed the official knock on its door, it appeared to be sustained by the mod-est commercial success of a few filmmakers and the generous support of donors who made up the Friends of New Cinema and the Circle of Angels. In 1964, Jerome Hill decided to jump-start the era of foundation funding, setting aside funds for the Avon Foundation, which gave grants to avant-garde filmmakers. The best way to achieve recognition and support, Mekas and Hill both thought, was to appear to have it already.

The organization and institutionalization of American avant-garde film has generated decades of debate. From early on, Mekas had to defend his organizations against the criticism that, like MoMA or Cinema 16, they made the avant-garde into its own establishment. In now famous name-calling battles, Amos Vogel described Mekas as "a Machiavellian maneu-verer, a history rewriter, an attempted pope." Filmmaker Jack Smith nick-named Mekas "Uncle Fishhook," because of his penchant for hooking unsuspecting filmmakers into his political campaigns.[37] In his defense, Mekas portrayed the Film-Makers' Cooperative as an un-institutional in-stitution, a "chaotic," "anarchic," "irresponsible," "experimental," "amor-phous" organization that conducted business in an "un-businesslike way," an institution born out of "spontaneous happenings." "Who cares about the logic of it anyway?" he protested.[38] Mekas's evasions could neither hold off criticism from filmmakers in the 1950s and 1960s nor the subse-quent barrage of criticism from scholars, who have all found the organi-zations inherently antithetical to the anti-institution position of many avant-garde artists and theorists of the avant-garde.

Despite his protestations, Mekas's organizing was methodical and log-ical. But that does not exclude the New American Cinema from avant-garde status. Critics of the postwar American avant-garde's intuitions have been armed with a lack of information. Investigating both the real and po-tential sources of patronage offers a much clearer definition of the rela-tionship between American avant-garde film and the institutions of film and American culture. In truth, all of these organizations, not just the Avon Foundation, concealed the fact that Jerome Hill was the principal source of funding. When we read Hill's correspondence and files, the complex infrastructure is reduced to a simple communication between

Mekas and Hill, between adviser and patron, between imaginary institutional superstructure and real economic base. Mekas wrote three, four, even five letters a day on behalf of the Film-Makers' Cooperative, the Film Culture Non-Profit Corporation, All Film-Makers, and a half dozen other collective labels. When filmmakers received these letters, it must have appeared that they were part of a growing community that was both gaining recognition and attracting financial support. Both assumptions are true, but not exactly as they appeared. When we examine Hill's copies of those letters, they look like nothing more than widely distributed bills. In one letter written January 31, 1966, for example, Mekas appealed to the Friends of New Cinema on behalf of a few filmmakers who needed money to complete projects: Leroy McLucas needed $159 to cover lab costs, George Kuchar needed $200 for film stock, and Bruce Baillie needed $500 because his hopes of winning a Rockefeller Foundation grant had all but disappeared. Hill received the public letter and, recognizing it as an invoice, he scribbled a balance sheet in the margin of his copy: nothing to McLucas, $150 to Kuchar, and the full $500 to Baillie.[39] The patron gave selectively but generously. It is more than coincidental, we can surmise, that successful African-American photographer McLucas is the only one of the three filmmakers mentioned in the letter who did not go on to have a productive filmmaking career.

By 1966 it was already becoming clear that government, foundation, and museum support would not be forthcoming, and the same day that Mekas wrote publicly on behalf of the filmmakers, he also wrote privately to Hill and Hill's lawyer Allan Masur asking for funds to support the New American Cinema's institutions. *Film Culture* magazine, the Film-Makers' Cinémathèque, and the Film-Makers' Distribution Center had accumulated tens of thousands of dollars in debt during the previous year. Successful filmmakers Lionel Rogosin and Shirley Clarke each pledged $4,000 to the Distribution Center, but Mekas appealed to Hill for the rest. Again, Hill scribbled a balance sheet in the margin, planning to pay a portion—roughly half—of most expenses and the entire pressing $3,000 debt owed by the Film-Makers' Cinémathèque.[40] This letter begins to represent the unraveling of the institutional structure. While Mekas closed the letter with an appeal to the Friends of New Cinema, he addressed it only to Hill and Masur. Hill had been unsuccessful in his attempts to enlist other Friends of New Cinema, and the fiction of a larger circle of support had begun to vanish. Hill's role would only become fully institutionally inscribed, however, after his death in 1972 when the Avon Foundation was renamed the Jerome Foundation.

Many forces made 1966 the beginning of the end of the avant-garde's campaign for outside institutional support. The previous year, Lyndon Johnson had definitively made clear that government support for film would go to Hollywood, and that plans for the AFI were already in place. But the New York Film Festival's decision to include a new program, "The Independent Cinema," pointed to the final fate of avant-garde film in American arts institutions. Worse than being ignored or dismissed, the avant-garde would be warehoused. The first New York Film Festival had been held in September 1963, and it brought together all the gatekeepers of institutional film support. MoMA and Lincoln Center, then under the directorship of John D. Rockefeller III, cosponsored the event. Richard Griffith, by this time the chief curator of MoMA's Film Library, teamed up with the London Film Festival's Richard Roud and Amos Vogel (whose Cinema 16 had fallen into the red) to make the programming decisions. A sponsoring committee seemed to include every power player in Hollywood: John Ford, Samuel Goldwyn, Elia Kazan, Arthur Mayer, Otto Preminger, David O. Selznick, Jack Warner, and Daryl Zanuck. Lincoln Center named Kennedy's former arts adviser August Heckscher as president of the film committee .[41] Mekas sat back cautiously for the first few years of the festival, taking notes as the new class of film tastemakers celebrated European auteurs and passed over the avant-garde. During the summer of 1965, Mekas used his *Village Voice* column to warn the committee that his patience was wearing thin: "Lincoln Center cannot excuse itself [from including avant-garde films] this year for not having 16mm. projection facilities; that excuse was already used for two consecutive years. There should be a better excuse this year, or we are going to topple Lincoln Center down."[42] When the NYFF overlooked the avant-garde again in September, Mekas hostilely branded "The New York Film Festival as an Enemy of the New Cinema."[43]

The following year, the NYFF responded to Mekas's criticism and invited "independent" filmmakers to submit their work for inclusion in a special program. The terms of the invitation, however, caused a controversy among avant-garde filmmakers, which the Film-Makers' Cooperative publicized in an exchange of "open letters." Filmmaker Stan Brakhage voiced the severest criticism. In short, Brakhage argued that the NYFF offered modest recognition without financial compensation. The inclusive term "independent," he complained, would lump avant-garde artists with wannabe Hollywood hacks, and the festival's refusal to pay full rental fees insulted the avant-garde's audience base, which had struggled for years to exhibit avant-garde films. "After all, John," Brakhage closed his letter to program coordinator John Brockman, "what on earth do you think Lincoln Center can possibly offer me *except* money?"[44] Filmmaker Ed Emshwiller tried to control the damage with another "open letter" accusing Brakhage of being "penny wise and pound foolish" and encouraging other filmmakers to grab the little recognition they could get.[45]

On the whole, filmmakers sided with Brakhage, and the New York Film Festival came to represent the epitome of the bourgeois culture the avant-garde opposed. Avant-garde filmmakers increasingly identified with other artists who were either ignored by the institutions of the art world or resisted what they saw as the co-optation of the avant-garde by museums, foundations, and the government. Escalating protests against the war in Vietnam contributed both to the culture of activism and to the artists' desire to participate in real-world politics instead of the staid culture of museums. Things came to a head in the spring of 1968. In March of that year a group of artists and critics protested the opening of MoMA's Dada art show, claiming, as one picket sign read, that "MOMA KILLS DADA." A few months later, a group of artists—including Gary Smith, founder of the Millennium film cooperative—formed their own cooperative exhibition venue, "Museum, a Project of Living Artists."[46] That summer, the art world's protest culture turned its sites toward Lincoln Center and the New York Film Festival. Mekas gave over his *Village Voice* column to the "Down with Lincoln Center" movement and reprinted excerpts from several of the movement's competing manifestoes. The manifestoes linked Lincoln Center with official culture, calling it "the Pentagon of cultural oppression," and they offered a Marxist critique of its role in pacifying resistance to American commercial culture.

> Although much more sophisticated than popular culture and addressed to a narrow constituency—the educated middle- and upper-middle class which is not fully deceived or adequately satisfied by the mass—Lincoln Center for the Performing Arts also functions to maintain the false consciousness which bourgeois culture must induce to prevent a critical spirit, understanding, disaffiliation, and consequent revolt. Like other cultural institutions of the society, like the mass media, its function is coping with rebellion.
>
> The structure of Lincoln Center adequately defines its reactionary role, and its occasional exhibition of radical cinema or theater is a part of that structure itself, not a deviation, since Lincoln Center's presentation of radical art, by plucking it out of social context which could give it life and meaning, effectively nullifies whatever explosive content it might have had. Like any other bourgeois institution, Lincoln Center—in its own sophisticated manner—continually functions to maintain the anti-human capitalist social system.[47]

Borrowing concepts of class critique from Herbert Marcuse's generation-defining *One-Dimensional Man* (1964), these manifestoes reclaimed the avant-garde's position as anti-institution art, which follows the entrenched avant-garde logic that defines museums and cultural institutions as vitiating mortuaries of art and pits them against the organic, political world of artistic production.

Yet there were two competing models of the avant-garde artist in the 1960s. While some avant-gardists stood outside MoMA with picket signs, a clear line of avant-garde artists from Marcel Duchamp through Jackson Pollock and Andy Warhol were represented inside the museum. It wasn't always easy to distinguish between the institutional avant-garde whose work had been adopted by museums, foundations, and the NEA to participate in national politics and the anti-institution avant-garde that defined iftself in opposition to established conventions. In a moment that seemed to blur the line entirely, Marcel Duchamp briefly came out from the opening of MoMA's Dada show where he was being celebrated to condone the protests as long as they were nonviolent.[48]

It would be narrow to conclude that in this instance the museum had successfully depoliticized both Dada's and neo-Dada's radical critiques by embracing them and to conclude more generally with Marcuse and the entire Frankfurt School tradition of theory that once art enters the museum its avant-gardeness withers or is co-opted.[49] Avant-garde art exists both inside and outside museums and institutions. In the case of avant-garde film, movements have consistently intersected with national and official interests. The litany of successful film avant-gardes at the beginning of this chapter—Soviet, German, African, Latin American, British—have all had national ambitions and been supported by official institutions. Postwar American avant-garde film shifted between its organizers' desire to become an institutional avant-garde—a New American Cinema—and its chronic position outside official institutions. The leaders of the avant-garde, we will see, slowly accepted their rejection from official institutions, but never let go of the dream that avant-garde film might have its own institution.

We might even be able to trace Mekas's personal disillusion with existing government, museum, and foundation funding to a single day: May 18, 1966. After confronting the avant-garde's lack of representation at the 1966 Pesaro film festival in Italy, Mekas distributed two open letters in which he offered a new definition of the avant-garde filmmaker as artist. "On the subject of money," Mekas wrote, the position of an artist, of the true avant-garde artist always remains that of a lonely pioneer. Let's not fool ourselves. Let's not be misled away from what we really have to do. We shouldn't let our hearts be muddled by false emotions. There is nobody, no sugar daddy who wants to (or SHOULD) give us money. There is no Foundation that wants to give us money (one or two small grants do not change that).[50]

He continued in the second May 18th letter:

The new film-maker (and that goes for all countries) can not trust any commercial (or State; or one that is based on commercial tradition) for film financing, film production, film distribution, film exhibition or film promotion set-ups and organizations. WE HAVE TO START EVERYTHING FROM SCRATCH, FROM THE BEGINNING. NO COMPROMISES, HOWEVER SMALL.[51]

In the face of perpetual rejection, Mekas moved from actively courting institutional support to reaffirming and embracing the position of the alienated avant-garde artist. Ironically, this could only have been achieved with his "sugar daddy" Jerome Hill.

But money wasn't the only thing at stake. Mekas also rethought the artist's relationship to the state. The assemblage of a traveling library, for example, had been a key element in the campaign to make avant-garde film institutions resemble officially supported arts. Like MoMA's traveling programs of films, sculptures, and paintings—many supported by the CIA and State Department[52]—the Film-Makers' Cinémathèque organized exhibitions of avant-garde films to tour Europe and Latin America. When a disenchanted Mekas began to dismantle the resemblance he had built up between the avant-garde and established institutions, he put an end to the traveling library, fearing any resemblance to the nationalist work of the CIA and State Department.

With the United States using all kinds of "power" to influence other countries, good power and bad power, for good reasons and bad reasons—even the Avantgarde Film Library could be misinterpreted—by some very good people—as America's long fingers to manipulate the film avantgardes of other countries. The less we impose on others, these days—even with good things—the better, I consider. Therefore—home we go, even with art. We know, the armies won't follow our example—but they may.[53]

In addition to redefining the avant-garde artist as an unaffiliated outcast, Mekas replaced the national politics of the New American Cinema, which had aimed to transform institutions of high culture and networks of commercial culture, with a new politics dedicated to transforming everyday life, starting with the unit of the individual artist. In his *Village Voice* column of June 22, 1967, Mekas reformulated avant-garde film as a hippie "political movement" dedicated to "the destruction of phony privacy" by exposing every corner of society until everything seemed equally beautiful.[54]

This is the portrait of the American avant-garde filmmaker—the alienated outcast—that has become familiar if not mythic. Deren articulated it in defense of the institutional rejection of her work, and Mekas rediscovered it after less than a decade of frustrated campaigning for institutional support. By the 1970s, Peter Wollen could speak of "two avant-gardes." One avant-garde consisted of the political films of European filmmakers Jean-Luc Godard, Jean-Marie Straub, and Danièle Huillet, who were the inheritors of the national politics of Soviet avant-garde film. Opposed to this political avant-garde, Wollen described (denounced, really) what he saw as the apolitical American co-op movement, overly bound up in personal exploration and the modernist pursuit of aesthetic innovation and reflexivity.[55]

Today, it is the first Mekas, the crusader at the official gates, who surprises us. The formulation of the alienated artist disengaged from national politics or engaged purely in a politics of everyday life is entirely in line with the zeitgeist of the 1960s and of *one* tradition of the avant-garde. Yet it should also have been an impossibly idealistic stance for artists working in the most obscure corner of the expensive medium of film, especially in the institutionally controlled art world of the 1960s. Statements from the artists and critics of the 1960s contain countless appeals to the new status of the avant-garde artist as amateur. Less expensive means of production, they claim, allowed filmmakers to work in the mode of the hobbyist. But true amateurs pursue filmmaking as an avocation; avant-garde filmmakers pursued their art full time. Only when we ask where the money came from do we realize that the change in the self-definition of the filmmaker as artist is predicated on a structural change in the relationship between patron, advisers, and filmmakers.[56]

JEROME HILL'S CIRCLE

Around 1966 or 1967, Mekas drew up two charts for Jerome Hill, outlining the New American Cinema's institutional structure. One chart presented a bottom-up configuration with the New American Cinema Group and the Film Culture Non-Profit Corporation as the bedrocks on top of which all the other institutions were stacked. Mekas called this the "Underground Cinema Tree," an image of an organic movement that might continue to grow and proliferate. The second chart inverts the first, rearranging the organizations so they appear to hang from the few managing institutions and, eventually, from a single point. This chart looks more like a hanging mobile with all the institutions dangling precariously from Jerome Hill's name. By now we know that Hill was clearly the hidden presence supporting avant-garde filmmakers and institutions.[57] Mekas had worked to create a self-sustaining infrastructure of institutions that would continue to grow if nourished by government and foundation money. But when no external funding came through, Hill was left to single-handedly hold the New American Cinema together, and the top-down model accurately represented the institutional structure of the avant-garde.

Mekas seems to have agreed with this assessment. In September 1967, Mekas and the leading avant-garde film exegete P. Adams Sitney, then president of the Film Culture Non-Profit Corporation, addressed the problems of the avant-garde's institutional structure in an "emergency grant" application to the Avon Foundation. Avant-garde filmmakers doomed themselves, Mekas and Sitney concluded, by creating the false impression that they were "too successful." The infrastructure of the avant-garde seemed to grow without help and, as a result, "All of our applications for Foundation grants during the past three years have been rejected." Without institutional support, it fell back to the American avant-garde filmmaker "to establish a distribution network enabling his work to reach universities, museums, and galleries; to send large expositions of his work to foreign museums and art centers; . . . plus innumerable other service activities." Thus, as they saw it, the "lonely plight" of the alienated American avant-garde filmmaker was reborn, produced again by the indifference of cultural institutions.

In a final plea for institutional patronage, Sitney and Mekas reiterated the claim, slightly qualified this time, that avant-garde film deserved some importance in American national life: "We feel that we are part of American Culture, part of its national and international prestige and that we deserve some assistance."[58] Their grant application represented a last stab at defining the co-op movement in terms of American national culture. But at the same time, the application marked a retreat from the campaign for national subsistence into a private sphere of individual patronage. As Sitney and Mekas both knew, the Avon Foundation was merely a disguise for Jerome Hill, who now played the parts of patron, filmmaker, and in a letter written in support of the grant, referee as well.

Susan Sontag, Elia Kazan, and a number of other filmmakers and intellectuals cosigned Hill's letter supporting the grant. They seconded the claim that the American avant-garde filmmaker "finds absolutely no opportunity to pursue his film-making as a full time operation."[59] When Mekas and his circle abandoned their bid for a place in the institutions of national culture, however, the dream of the full-time avant-garde filmmaker was not transferred intact. The hope that the NEA, foundations, and museums would together create a class of professional avant-garde filmmakers was replaced with a new romantic vision of the filmmaker as a full-time *amateur*. Statements abound elaborating avant-garde filmmakers' adoption of English Romantic and American Transcendental poets as precedents for their amateur mode of production. These statements can be found in the writings of Maya Deren, Hans Richter, Jonas Mekas, and dozens of other filmmakers as well as in the subsequent work of critics, theorists, and historians.[60] Reading Jerome Hill's correspondence, however, we can see that the shift from (unrequited) institutional patronage to private patronage produced the model of the artist as amateur.

Jerome Hill crafted a particularly forceful manifesto of the filmmaker as amateur in an unpublished letter to the editor of the *New York Times*. In the letter, Hill defended the "amateur" or "handmade" quality of his films in response to a Sunday *Times* article by film critic Bosley Crowther. Crowther criticized Hill as an example of an amateur in professional's clothing, indicative of the ruse of avant-garde film.[61] In his statement, Hill attempted to bridge the national and the quotidian political positions of the New American Cinema. He argued that the exploration of "individual expression" in film offered the key to transcending the distinction between professional, commercial entertainment on the one hand and amateur, noncommercial art on the other. In other words, only by retreating to a cinema of personal expression could the avant-garde find affinities with both Hollywood and the American ideal of the sovereign artist: "Have you ever heard of a professional poet?" Hill asked.[62]

The model of the filmmaker as amateur was bound up both with Hill's personal history and with the general contract between patron and artists. The independently wealthy Hill had always pursued filmmaking as a diversion, just as he experimented with painting, music, poetry, photography, and architecture. In interviews and in his Proustian autobiographical film memoir, *Film Portrait* (1971), Hill offered a portrait of the filmmaker as a dilettante. Hill's personal life had been subjected to film from his early childhood, and the ideal movie for him was the home movie. Long before small formats made home moviemaking common, the wealthy Hill family had hired Pathé cameramen to come to their estate and take movies of the children. Hill began to experiment with films of his own in the late 1920s, employing a friend as a cameraman on his short film *The Magic Umbrella* (1927). After buying an early 16mm Kodak camera, Hill picked up the camera himself to make another short film, *Fortune Teller* (1932). At the time, home moviemaking was still the province of the wealthy; a new camera could cost almost as much as a new car. These early experiments were made for family and friends and never released publicly. Hill then turned to more commercial genres. He made a short documentary about skiing released by Warner Bros.; he joined the film division of the army during World War II; and in the 1950s he produced a string of documentary biographies.

When Hill met Mekas in 1958 they embarked on their campaign to make avant-garde film part of American official culture. That crusade seems to have been largely Mekas's. Hill participated from the outside, using lawyers as intermediaries and only intervening via check. Hill also contributed two Jungian feature films to the New American Cinema movement: *The Sand Castle* (1961) and *Open the Door and See All the People* (1964). His personal investment in the movement was largely as a filmmaker who wanted to build a community of colleagues.

In 1966—the same year that Mekas called off his campaign for government and foundation support—Hill's relationship to avant-garde film changed both as a filmmaker and a patron. His father's death left him the bulk of his inheritance and, equally important, the collection of Hill home movies and photographs. Hill dedicated the remainder of his life to assembling this footage into his own autobiographical *Film Portrait* and making short lyrical, animated films. When in an interview Mekas asked about the change in Hill's filmography after 1966, Hill cited, in addition to his personal experience, the successful formation of community of avant-garde filmmakers and an audience for personal filmmaking:

> I would say, that this was very important, having met [filmmakers] Stan Brakhage, and you [Mekas], and Peter Kubelka, and seeing a group of people who were working the way I'd always wanted to work. This was very much a shot in the arm for me. There was also a feeling that there was a public for this kind of film.[63]

At the same time that Hill was discovering autobiographical film, the co-op movement's mission to gain institutional support and the organizational structure of the movement began to crumble. Hill assumed a more active role in the creation of a new avant-garde film community out of the existing co-op movement. He continued to work through his lawyers, foundations, and organizations, but he also revealed his role as patron to a small circle of filmmakers and critics. Still operating from a distance, Hill developed a coterie primarily through an exchange of letters with filmmakers in New York, Colorado, and San Francisco. He wrote from his suite at the Algonquin Hotel in New York or from his villa in Cassis, France, which had previously been owned by Napoleon.

The letter became the circle's preferred genre of communication for structural as well as geographical reasons. The personal tone and individual address of the private letter corresponded closely with the Romantic form of communicating individual subjectivity that characterized both the circle's filmmaking and its idea of artistic identity. The private letter has always had a public dimension, and so did the letters of the avant-garde. Philosopher Jürgen Habermas's *The Structural Transformation of the Public Sphere* vividly, even floridly, excavates the development of the letter as a genre in which "the individual unfolded himself in his subjectivity."[64] For Habermas, letters have a strong historicity: the public sphere was invented in the eighteenth century and died with the spread of mass media. "The eighteenth century became the century of the letter" as epistolary novels, letter-writing handbooks, letters to the editor, and exchanges of letters written explicitly for publication all contributed to the letter's emergence as the ideal form of public-

FIGURE 6.2 Jerome Hill in the opening of his *Film Portrait* (1972).
(Courtesy of Anthology Film Archives)

oriented individuality. "Subjectivity, as the innermost core of the private," Habermas explains, "was always already oriented towards an audience," and letters participated in the development of what he has called the bourgeois public sphere, a forum in which public consensus emerged from the rational debate of individuals. The personal letter defined this particular conception of public-oriented subjectivity as much as it served as the vehicle for individual expression, and Hill's circle adopted the letter to recapture a lost model of the public individual.[65]

The importance of the letter to American avant-garde filmmakers, we have seen, predates the 1966 structural changes. The debate over the New York Film Festival's "Independent Cinema" program is only one example of the Film-Makers' Cooperative's early adoption of the letter as its preferred form of publication. Mekas and Brakhage seem to have been born obsessive letter writers, choosing to place many of their important theoretical contributions in letters. The journals and other publications of the American avant-garde frequently reprinted excerpts from filmmakers' correspondence and occasionally solicited letters to be written for publication. Some filmmakers experimented with a form of epistolary film. Hill's circle used the letter in new ways to remake the avant-garde and restrict the publicness of its sphere. The public letters in which Mekas, for instance, wrote to All Film-Makers on behalf of the Film-Makers' Cooperative were replaced with private letters from one individual to another, though significantly the letters were still written to be circulated more widely. The co-op movement used letters as a form of publication out of financial necessity, a need for immediate communication, and the appearance of informality. Hill's circle distributed letters as a public form of individuation.

In addition to his letter writing, Mekas's filmmaking underwent a dramatic change at exactly the moment the avant-garde shifted from an infrastructure designed to win public patronage to one supported by private patronage outright. Mekas had entertained hopes of becoming a mainstream filmmaker since he was a young man in western European displaced-person camps after World War II. After moving to the United States, Mekas and his brother Adolfas sent unsolicited scripts to Hollywood studios in hopes of breaking into the film industry. In the early 1960s, Mekas's films *The Brig* and *Guns of the Trees* (both 1964) proved to be two of the strongest contributions to the New American Cinema's crusade to reinvent the popular feature film. But after 1966, Mekas too began to make more personal films. First, he released *Cassis* (1966), about a trip to his patron's French villa; years later he turned some of this footage into an elegy for Hill, *Notes for Jerome* (1981). Throughout the second half of the 1960s, Mekas transformed the private film diaries he had kept since immigrating to the United States into a diary film, *Walden: Diaries, Notes, and Sketches* (1970), meant to be seen by the avant-garde film community if not a larger audience. After *Walden's* release Mekas devoted himself exclusively to diary filmmaking. This transformation in style encapsulated the change in the structure of the circle of patronage, the return to a Romantic model of the artist, and the adoption of the letter as the ideal form of communication. The diary, Habermas reminds us, is just a special form of the letter: "The diary became a letter addressed to the sender, and the first-person narrative became a conversation with one's self addressed to another person."[66]

The form of the letter also entailed a personal tone that disguised the power relations of the patron-artist relationship. Filmmakers wrote to Hill as if they were colleagues, as one artist to another. They exchanged thoughts on aesthetics, reactions to each other's work, and details about their personal lives. Money and dependence were effaced in this discourse but always sat just below the surface. A letter to Hill from filmmaker Robert Downey (father of actor Robert Downey Jr.) highlights some of the confusion in seeing Hill as both patron and fellow filmmaker. In the letter—really a thank-you note—Downey tried to distinguish Hill from the funding institutions: "Thank *you*," Downey wrote to Hill, "and thanks to ~~your~~ 'Friends of the New Cinema'—you've made it possible for me to get the lab off my back." After catching himself conflating Hill and the source of the financial assistance, Downey adopted a collegial voice, thanking Hill for expressing admiration for some for his recent work. Downey went on to try to put a finer point on the distinction between patron and friend: "Mr. Masur is A Fine Representative FOR YOUR Films and also 'Friends of the New Cinema'—I can tell that he enjoys seeing people like you and I at work."[67] In the end, then, Downey settled on a formula that pairs the two as filmmakers with a shared institutional affiliation, carefully distinguishing between Hill qua artist and Hill qua Friends of New Cinema/patron. But then why, we might ask, did Downey feel obligated to write Hill a thank-you note in the first place? And why did the familiar, handwritten note have to be relayed to Hill through his lawyer and fund distributor Masur?

The transformations of the patron-filmmaker relationship are clearest in Hill's dealings with Stan Brakhage, whom Mekas, Sitney, and Hill all thought to be the true genius of the movement. Sitney recalled in an interview that Hill felt indebted to Mekas for introducing him to Brakhage, and described meeting Brakhage as "like meeting Picasso."[68] Brakhage's first contacts with Hill, however, were anonymous. Masur sent Brakhage donations on behalf of Friends of New Cinema; Brakhage, in turn, wrote to Masur acknowledging the generosity of the donations; and Masur then passed on the correspondence to Hill. Consider an excerpt from what seems to be Brakhage's first thank-you note to Hill via Masur:

> I have never received as respectful, "no strings-attached", and simply-given, gift before that contained within the envelope you sent and quali-fied with your few well-chosen words. It was the most altogether accept-able donation ever made to my work.
>
> I hope you and Friends of New Cinema, Inc. will enjoy the enclosed strip of my newest film MOTHLIGHT.
>
> Thank you.
>
> > Sincerely,
> > Stan Brakhage[69]

In this interesting note, Brakhage remarked upon the freedom of the gift, but by including a strip of film, he also recognized that an exchange had taken place. The reciprocity is also evident at a formal level: Brakhage, whose letters are rarely shorter than three or four pages, responded in terse prose, echoing the businesslike lawyer's. Brakhage and Masur both framed the act of patronage as a simple transaction, but even when the patron's gift has "no strings" the artist hopes for and works to ensure the bequest of future gifts. Brakhage, who died in 2003, based his life and work on break-ing through the culturally imposed codes of polite silence, and he grew to despise the hypocrisy of the patron-artist relationship.

It's not clear when Brakhage and Hill developed a personal relation-ship, but by the mid-1960s they were writing directly to each other and exchanging work and ideas. Hill even traveled to Brakhage's home in rural Colorado several times. Brakhage's letters to Hill have an unchar-acteristic toadying quality. Brakhage opened one letter to Hill, for exam-ple, by explaining that he was putting down thoughts that came from the "sheer pleasure of a letter to a friend," although there was surely no need to qualify the function of the letter in their relationship. In that letter, Brakhage confessed to being haunted by one of Hill's paintings, and he requested a reproduction of it.[70] The very next day Brakhage wrote a sec-ond letter to Hill containing a long theoretical analysis of Hill's painting technique.[71] Brakhage's attention may have been entirely sincere, but his excessive flattery also played to Hill's insecurities. Throughout his life,

FIGURE 6.3   Stan Brakhage, *Mothlight* (1963).   *(Cortesy of Anthology Film Archives)*

Hill feared that his wealth impeded his receiving untainted criticism and recognition. Brakhage often repeated a story, for example, in which a young Hill had several paintings accepted by a gallery in Paris only to have the paintings withdrawn after the gallery owners discovered Hill's lineage. The owner feared that the public would think Hill had bought his way into the show. In a letter written a few years later, Brakhage reminded Hill of the incident and confessed that "when you told the story *I* felt uncomfortable, almost blushed, because it occurred to me that *I* had never said anything against you: and thus the story troubled me for several days, made me question our whole relationship, as I often do in suspicion of myself."[72]

All of Brakhage's interactions with Hill were fraught with the fear that money would come to the surface. Brakhage frequently told another revealing story about driving Hill to the airport in Colorado. According to the confessional, which is worthy of Augustine or Rousseau, Brakhage forgot to take money with him when he left the house and didn't realize his mistake until he had already pulled into a gas station and filled up the tank. In a panic, he turned to Hill and said, "Jerome, you're going to have to pay for this, because I don't have any cash."

Suddenly, we were in the middle of one of those most terrible moments. First, a look of shock came over Jerome's face, then horror, fear, embarrassment—and then complete confusion as he started searching through his pockets. His initial shock came from his thought that I was hitting him for money, as often happened to him with other artists. His next reaction was of horror at himself for having thought that of me; and then the instant he realized that it was a flat, honest need for cash at the moment, he panicked for fear that he didn't have any on him, either. It was such a terrible moment that, after I had analyzed what had happened—which took a little time—I said to him, "Look, I'll never ask you for money again."[73]

Brakhage knew that any friendship the two enjoyed couldn't escape the unequal financial situation that defined them as patron and artist. Brakhage wanted to believe that he was the one filmmaker with whom Hill had an unadulterated friendship, and their relationship was clearly special. But Brakhage knew that that could happen only when financial dependence no longer structured their interaction.

Brakhage finally pierced the silence of the patron-artist exchange in a long letter to Hill written in September 1969. "There'll be no final honesties between you and me, Jerome," Brakhage confessed, "until I unburden myself completely on this ticklish subject: the whole subject of 'gift giving.'" The letter occasioned the notice that the museum of avant-garde film, Anthology Film Archives, would pay only a nominal fee for films purchased from filmmakers, as the New York Film Festival had done a few years earlier. Brakhage's first response was to offer his films "freely." But in a moment of recognition, he acknowledged the "hypocrisy" of that gesture and saw the gift of films as,

> part of a traditional 'con-game' played between artist and patron: the artist 'gives' to the institute . . . and is, in turn, supposed to receive support, honorariums, etc. indirectly . . . this doesn't even constitute honest begging: and the artist is, anyway, too busy to make himself a good beggar on *any* level (only those who play at art and devote themselves primarily to begging ever succeed very well in this syndrome): NO!—I reject that whole mode of behavior with all my heart . . . it is one of the traditions that has most cruelly divided the artist from any reasonable daily living.

Brakhage had recognized the tacit exchange between patron and artist in his first thank-you note to Masur, but here he finally articulated the concrete transaction of gift giving by both patron and artist. Even more than a concern with hypocrisy, Brakhage feared that patronage ultimately destroyed the possibility for the full-time, professional avant-garde artist. "I think I will not live long enough to see anything like the artist's daily salary . . . ," he wrote in the same letter, "but that dream is intact."[74]

Throughout his career, Brakhage unsuccessfully hatched schemes to free himself from the bonds of patronage. He hoped that through the sale of film prints he would be able to make a living from his films. Brakhage helped found the Film-Makers' Cooperative and other distribution outlets for avant-garde films. In 1967 he revived the dream of starting a market of film collectors. Film theorist and teacher Victor Oscar Freeburg had dreamed of the common private film collections as early as 1915, and the Film-Makers' Cooperative had unsuccessfully staged an auction of avant-garde films in 1963.[75] In the mid-1960s, Brakhage distributed 8mm and 16mm films through his home in Colorado, but his attempt to stimulate a collecting market failed, and he had to resign himself to selling prints for small fees and giving them away to friends and to Jerome Hill.[76] Brakhage hoped for the freedom and openness of the collectors' market. Within the patronage economy, he felt constrained, deceitful, and alienated from his own motivations. "I am not independent enough," he wrote to Hill, "for me to *know* whether I really managed to give you the *Songs* [a series of short 8mm films] or not."[77]

For Hill, on the other hand, the relationship was clear. Brakhage's brief 8mm *Songs* provided the perfect apotheosis of the personal, poetic form he envisioned for the avant-garde. And the gift to a friend or patron was the ideal method of circulation. In a short article comparing Brakhage's *Songs* to Rainer Maria Rilke's *Duino Elegies*, Hill offered a rare glimpse into the viewing habits of the patron:

> Let me first point out that they [Brakhage's songs and Rilke's elegies] are essentially lyric in character. Lyric, as opposed to epic or dramatic poetry, is to be read in intimacy, if possible aloud; to be read often; to be learned by heart. The *Songs*, to me who am used to viewing them in small rooms in the presence of limited gatherings, are not public statements. They address the viewer personally.[78]

This image of the personal film as a free exchange between individuals recaptured a form of art exchange and reception that preceded mass culture, and it couldn't have been further from Mekas's original ambition to make the New American Cinema a national art form with government, foundation, and museum backing. Yet even this far away from their initial dream, members of Hill's circle continued to search for an institutional paradigm for their avant-garde films. They found it in December 1970 when they opened their own film museum, the Anthology Film Archives (Anthology), in the basement of Joseph Papp's Public Theater on Lafayette Street in Greenwich Village.

AN AVANT-GARDE FILM MUSEUM

From its inception, Anthology has been considered the end of the avant-garde film movement that Maya Deren and Alexander Hammid launched with *Meshes of the Afternoon*. One group of filmmakers, for example, responded to Anthology by starting an alternative exhibition venue called the Collective for *Living* Cinema (emphasis added), implying that Anthology had effectively interred avant-garde film. In an important early critique of the power relations of film scholarship and canon formation, Constance Penley and Janet Bergstrom, writing as members of the feminist collective *Camera Obscura*, described Anthology as the last step in a campaign to enshrine an outmoded, phenomenological approach to film interpretation. David James, in his extensive reconsideration of the politics of American avant-garde film, *Allegories of Cinema*, dismissed Anthology as an aberration that misguidedly reproduced the rationalizing, monadic ideology of Hollywood the avant-garde sought to break with in the first place. Even many of Anthology's defenders have seen it as safely housing autonomous, modernist art and forsaking any experimentalism or political relevance the films initially contained. At one point during Anthology's creation, Brakhage wrote to Hill of the need for " 'an academy' for the young to rebel against," suggesting that at least one of Anthology's founders intended it to mark the avant-garde's passage into academic art.[79] The criticism that Anthology effected the death of the co-op movement has been repeated so often that it has rarely been investigated. But in the light of the history of public and private patronage that drove American avant-garde film in the 1940s, 1950s, and 1960s, we can see that Anthology sought to preserve the political and aesthetic power of American avant-garde film at a precarious time in film history. Anthology extended the avant-garde film movement by virtually inscribing the relation of the private patron to film and, at the same time, critiquing the institutions that had been unreceptive to American avant-garde film since the 1940s.

    Several factors led Hill's circle to attempt to create yet another institution of avant-garde film. At least one was internal: Hill was diagnosed with cancer in the late 1960s, and he began spending long periods in the hospital. It became clear that his tenure as patron would soon come to an end, and a contingency plan needed to be in place. Hill's circle, however, was responding largely to the changing state of American film. Some museums and commercial venues had begun to take note of the avant-garde. The New York Film Festival debacle indicated just one of the unwanted directions museum and commercial success might take, and Hill's circle decided to take control of the institutionalization of avant-garde film before Hollywood or museums could completely assimilate it.

The runaway success of Andy Warhol's *Chelsea Girls* held out the possibility that avant-garde film might find a commercial audience. *Chelsea Girls* was so successful that the Film-Makers' Cooperative moved into new upscale headquarters on Lexington Avenue and hired a large staff based entirely on its sales. In the end, however, *Chelsea Girls* proved to be a false portent, and avant-garde films never found a commercial market.[80] While Warhol used his breakthrough to move into more popular sexploitation filmmaking, other avant-garde filmmakers began to gain some recognition from museums and galleries. After fighting off the avant-garde for decades, MoMA capitulated in 1969 and began to invite individual avant-garde filmmakers to appear with their films in its Cineprobe series. In other words, MoMA finally adopted the artist-as-exegete model of avant-garde exhibition that its curator Iris Barry had unwittingly helped to create a quarter century earlier by rejecting *Meshes of the Afternoon*. Hill's circle didn't entirely turn its back on the acceptance of avant-garde filmmakers it had wished for; Hill considered it a triumph when he was asked to appear as a speaker at MoMA's Cineprobe series in 1972, after Anthology's founding. But they did want to control avant-garde film's move into the museums and foundations.

If the promise of new commercial and museum audiences for avant-garde film led Hill's circle to take control of its institutionalization through the establishment of its own museum, an equally important factor was the diminishing of the avant-garde's already limited audience as a result of changes in censorship. Of course one segment of the avant-garde's constituency was interested in aesthetic innovations and radical politics; another segment, however, attended screenings to see nudity, drug use, and other cinematic transgressions that Hollywood filmmakers or art film importers could never get past the review boards. Mekas frequently used the risqué content of avant-garde films to gain attention for individual films or to vie for a foothold in national politics. In the best-known case, Mekas took to the Supreme Court an obscenity charge launched against Jack Smith's orgiastic *Flaming Creatures* (1963). The justices decided not to hear the case, but only after *Flaming Creatures* became a cause célèbre of Susan Sontag and other intellectuals. Jerome Hill funded Mekas's court battle over *Flaming Creatures* because Hill, who was gay himself, saw the film's exuberant, celebratory mishmash of transvestites and androgyny as an important image to champion in the battle for gay rights. Other avant-garde filmmakers, including Jack Smith himself, accused Mekas of manufacturing the scandal, and they objected to the overt use of films for political purposes. Brakhage resigned from the Film-Maker's Cooperative as a result of the *Flaming Creatures* affair. New York intellectual Dwight Macdonald attended a screening of *Flaming Creatures* and unwittingly came out agreeing with Smith and Brakhage's anti-Mekas stance. "The moviemakers of the New American Cinema," he concluded, "are moralists rather than artists."[81]

Only a few years later, *Flaming Creatures* seemed tame, and avant-garde films were forced to compete with soft-core pornographic films both at the art houses and at mainstream theaters. A crucial blow came in 1968 when the Motion Picture Association of America replaced the monolithic Production Code with its variegated rating system (that eventually became G, PG, R, X), allowing for greater audience divisions and, ultimately, for adults-only films. Films produced as a result of the new rating system, including *Midnight Cowboy, M*A*S*H, Goodbye Columbus,* and *Bob and Carol and Ted and Alice,* poached from the avant-garde's audience, and Mekas, for one, noticed the filmgoers fleeing quickly. "Two years ago," he wrote to Sitney in June 1968, "both, the film lovers and the sensation seekers used to come to the Tek [Film-Makers' Cinémathèque], and we did well. Now, we lost all the sensation seekers."[82]

In order to stave off the dispersal of filmmakers and audience members to the museums, the multiplexes, and the porn theaters, Hill's circle innovated new avant-garde institutional practices at the level of exhibiting and collecting. Filmmaker Peter Kubelka's design for Anthology's theater, called the Invisible Cinema, is one of the great experiments of movie theater architecture. He designed his "machine for viewing" to minimize distractions and thus create the most individualized experience possible within the presence of an audience. Kubelka had the entire theater draped in black so that viewers had "no sense of the presence of walls or the size of the auditorium. He should have only the white screen, isolated in darkness as his guide to scale and distance."[83] As its name suggested, the blackened theater receded into the background and became invisible. Kubelka's design further enhanced viewers' absorption in the film through the device of

placing large black hoods on each seat to reduce the awareness of other audience members; other members of the audience then, like the theater itself, receded. Anthology's manifesto claimed that the Invisible Cinema created an experience "at once communal and extremely concentrated," but
there was surely nothing communal about the black, hooded seats. The
manifesto's justification—that "the communal spirit is strongest and most
effective in the absence of disturbance from one's neighbor"—is uncon-
vincing if not oxymoronic. One visitor at Anthology's opening remarked:
"the complete isolation amounts to a kind of alienation."[84]

Clearly, the authors of the manifesto had something unusual in mind by
the phrase "communal spirit." Whatever their intention, the enforced pri-
vateness of Anthology's viewing conditions reproduced the intimate conditions under which Jerome Hill, as patron, viewed avant-garde films.
Anthology's viewer consumed the films like Hill: "not as public statements"
but "addressed to the viewer personally." Indeed, the "communal spirit" of
the Invisible Theater might be characterized as an architectural manifestation of the community of public-oriented individuals that Hill's circle had
created through its filmmaking styles and exchange of letters. In Anthology's
theater, every viewer became a patron as indeed, Thomas Crow points out,
public art venues have often provided forums for crowds to "rehearse before
works of art the kinds of pleasure and discrimination that once had been the
exclusive prerogative of the patron and his intimates."[85]

In addition to asking viewers to assume the patron's viewing posture,
Anthology reinforced the equation of patron and viewer through its unusual collecting policies. The films in the collection were selected by a committee of Hill's personal advisers: Mekas, Brakhage, and Sitney with the addition of critic Ken Kelman and filmmaker James Broughton, who treated
their duties with a comical degree of gravity. They insisted that aesthetic
decisions could only be made when a complete separation from worldly
concerns was achieved, and in the name of art, several members of the
committee demanded more comfortable hotel rooms to facilitate their aesthetic judgment. Each work in the canon was chosen based on Kantian
aesthetic criteria: wholeness, unity, and individual expression. "We felt
there were certain artists on whom one had to agree a priori," Mekas later
explained.[86] With the help of Jerome Hill, Anthology intended to honor
the intention of the filmmakers by purchasing pristine copies of every film
and showing them in their original language without subtitles. The committee debated each film for hours and sometimes days before it could be
admitted to the canon, and they recorded every minute of their lengthy discussions for posterity. Some debates turned into fistfights, and every mem-

FIGURE 6.4 Anthology Film Archives's Invisible Theater (1970).
(Courtesy of Anthology Film Archives)

FIGURE 6.5 Anthology Film Archives's Invisible Theater (1970).
(Courtesy of Anthology Film Archives)

ber resigned at least once; Sitney resigned six or seven times. Brakhage resigned only two or three times, but the final resignation proved decisive. It led Brakhage to write the letter to Hill (discussed above) in which he finally articulated the restrictive terms of the patron-artist exchange. In order to reclaim his freedom, Brakhage left Anthology's selection committee.[87]

It is easy to side with Anthology's critics. Anthology seems to have both reproduced the most supercilious aspects of museum canonization and, through its theater design, to have surpassed Hollywood's voyeuristic model of spectatorship. But Anthology's design must be seen in context. First, we can now see that Anthology's enforced one-to-one filmmaker-viewer communication allowed audience members to play the role of the patron and thus assured the intended viewing position. But Anthology's design and policies also critically responded to the larger context of museum exhibition and commercial cinema as much of avant-garde film critiqued both institutional art and commercial film.

"The historical approach to cinema in all the museums and cinémathèques," Mekas further explained, "has been so overdone that the exaggerated stance that we are taking for the art of cinema is correct."[88] Specifically, Anthology's methods of collecting and exhibiting directly countered those of avant-garde film's old nemesis, MoMA. Anthology's manifesto threw down a direct challenge to MoMA's Film Library, calling Anthology "the first film museum exclusively devoted to *film as an art*," a claim MoMA had made thirty-five years earlier.[89] Where MoMA's film programs took its viewers through stages of cinema's development or introduced them to national cinemas, genres, and director's careers, Anthology displayed a synchronic collection detached from both history and geography. The films were shown in the Invisible Theater in a continuously looping sequence ordered alphabetically by the filmmaker's last name. Where other museums continually repackaged their films in new ways, Anthology displayed a repertory of films, offering repeated exposure to what it called "the essential cinema." The repeated viewing returned spectatorship to a model Deren had pioneered and Hill insisted upon. This model of spectatorship rejected both the commercial practice of one-time theatrical exhibition and the series format of museum film exhibition. Even before the plans for Anthology were concrete, Brakhage worried that the New American Cinema was growing closer to commercial film by "backing the theatrical (one-time showing) experience of films" and that avant-garde films would become lost, like other artworks had been, by placement in museums. Brakhage warned: "Masses of people whisking past paintings in museums, listening to their Hi-Fi's while talking on the telephone, and thumbing though poetry books produce the semblance of culture while effacing its destruction in themselves and as a concept, even, in the nation."[90]

Anthology's design also served as a critique of commercial film exhibition and consumption. The 1960s saw movie palaces that held 2,000 to 5,000 viewers before one screen replaced by multiplexes with multiple theaters equipped on average with fewer than 200 seats. Large palaces were divided into two or three smaller theaters, as were art cinemas. To compete with television, multiplexes increased audience choice and transformed film as a commodity. "If a shopping mall . . . offered a vast array of merchandise in its stores," Douglas Gomery explains, "Cineplex Odeon [the largest theater chain in the 1960s and 1970s] presented the customer with many more than the usual number of choices for its movie shows. . . . If mallgoers loved to browse and make 'impulse' purchases for items from shoes to records, why shouldn't they be able to do the same thing for movies?"[91] The film spectator, as Anne Friedberg noted, was transformed into a "spectator-shopper."[92]

As popular culture seemed to be driven more and more by multiplying consumers' ability to exercise choice (by no means making them freer), Anthology, on the contrary, dictated its film selection from above, as it were. One went to Anthology not to see a particular film but to experience the avant-garde as a continuously revolving loop. The seemingly timeless canon and systematic program completely disregarded the audience. As a result, Anthology's authoritarian structure finally insulated avant-garde film from both the demands of the marketplace and the needs of a wider community. It institutionalized both the coterie and system of patronage that had always structured and driven American avant-garde film. Now the audience was simply invited to look over the shoulder of the patron, turning Anthology into both *an avant-garde film museum* and *a museum of avant-garde film*.

CONCLUSION: "THE AGE OF THE FOUNDATION FILM"

Anthology only subtly acknowledged the contributions of its patron. Hill insisted that the Film Art Fund, an organization he established in 1967, be listed as the source of funding in all press announcements. "Money," Vincent Canby noted in the *New York Times*, "is something that no one connected with Anthology Film Archives cares to talk much about."[93] On a trip to New York in 1973, Australian filmmaker Abbie Thomas perspicaciously noted that where other institutions are named for their donors or bear plaques with the names of contributors, "Anthology's cinema merely suggests its donor in two paintings hanging discretely in its foyer. They are by the late Jerome Hill."[94] Anthology could veil its patron, but the museum lived and died with him.

Hill died in 1972 without making adequate provisions for Anthology in his will. The Avon Foundation (later the Jerome Foundation) continued to fund avant-garde filmmakers and artists, but Anthology, which still exists today, functioned in an increasing state of decay. The year after Hill's death, Joseph Papp dismantled the Indivisible Theater and forced Anthology to move to a new location. By 1975, Mekas had to divulge publicly that Anthology's "present and political conditions do not permit us to screen the Essential Cinema Repertory as it was initially presented. Our projection is still far from perfect, and 3 programs a day is a far dream."[95]

The death of the patron and Anthology's own deterioration coincided with the final and wholesale incorporation of avant-garde film into the world of museum, foundation, and government subsidy. Starting in 1973, the year after Hill's death, the NEA took an active interest in avant-garde film. The agency commissioned a report on the state of avant-garde film to be written by Sheldon Renan, then director of the Pacific Film Archive in Berkeley.[96] That same year, MoMA cosponsored a conference on the now disorganized Independent Film Community in the United States, and a report based on their findings was produced with the financial assistance of the Rockefeller Foundation and the NEA. In 1976 the NEA funded a film series at MoMA on the history of avant-garde film. After viewing two programs of American avant-garde films in the series, critic Andrew Sarris was moved to declare (correctly, I think), that "the age of the foundation film is upon us."[97]

But what did the belated dawn of the foundation film mean? The incorporation of American avant-garde film into American arts institutions did not mark its acceptance but rather a celebration of the end of the New American Cinema. Tributes to Anthology by MoMA and the AFI (both 1977) and by the Academy of Motion Pictures Arts and Science (1982) all magnanimously acknowledged Anthology's enfeebled position. Where Anthology had been designed to preserve the structure of the avant-garde indefinitely (and vilified for it), its demise signaled the triumph of the institutions and the defeat of the struggle to create a New American Cinema outside of Hollywood.

CONCLUSION
THE TRANSFORMATION OF THE STUDIO SYSTEM

COLLABORATIONS BETWEEN Hollywood and cultural institutions belong to the golden era of the studio system. Like the other constituent elements of that period, such collaborations were transformed during the transition from the studio system to what has been called the New Hollywood, in the 1950s, 1960s, and 1970s. The Supreme Court's decision that studios should divest themselves of movie theater chains, as well as the popularity of television and the increasing importance of international ticket sales, among many other factors, forced the American film industry to undergo significant restructuring. The studios continued to exist but the system changed. The New Hollywood entailed both a fragmentation of the moviegoing public and the creation of a more complex, blockbuster-driven, global film industry. Film studios continued to work with universities, museums, and the government in the New Hollywood, but the collaborative projects assumed less ambitious and less monolithic goals. Like all periodizing concepts, the labels *studio system* and *New Hollywood* are fraught with contradictions and oversimplifications. But even as rough guides they help to explain both the function of the collaborations discussed in this book and the reasons it became less advantageous for Hollywood to seek the help of cultural institutions.

We can now identify several reasons why Hollywood collaborated with cultural institutions. The first and primary reason film producers and leaders of universities, museums, and government art and information agencies found common ground was their mutual desire to speak to and include a national audience. Later, they built on these relationships to sell a particular ideal of America to an international audience. Hollywood was able to address a national audience, as much as that is possible, through the standardization of its art and industry. Many factors worked to standardize Hollywood filmmaking and filmgoing in the 1910s and 1920s. Studios were vertically integrated—controlling production, distribution, and exhibition—so they could keep foreign and independent competition out of movie theaters. Film studios became factory-like behemoths, controlling every stage and task of film production. Filmmaking technology, storytelling methods, and visual style were all standardized across the major studios, forging the grammar of classical Hollywood cinema. In the 1930s, the Production Code set limits on the political and moral implications of films. Clearly, not every filmgoer felt included in the mass audience Hollywood created through this standardization, but the film industry was successful enough that studio heads didn't need to worry about those on the margins.[1]

Cultural institutions proved to be a crucial force in the process of making Hollywood into a monolithic industry of national culture. Columbia University and the producers who would soon form Paramount designed a film curriculum that helped draw the middle class into movie theaters while it created a place at Columbia for the children of working-class immigrants. At the same time, Columbia's film program supported the professionalization and regulation of the new art of screenwriting. Significantly, Columbia's film program was founded in 1915, just as the Hollywood studios began to coalesce. A decade later, Harvard's Fogg Art Museum provided a forum for moguls to craft what became the Academy of Motion Pictures Arts and Sciences, which fixed labor practices in the studios and put a singular public face on Hollywood. During World War II and the cold war, the Museum of Modern Art and various government agencies worked to push the Americanizing messages of Hollywood films abroad. In the United States, MoMA worked with the National Endowment for the Arts, the American Film Institute, and private arts foundations to preserve the impression that Hollywood was the sole source of American film art, actively discouraging alternatives.

By the mid-1960s, however, things had changed. The Supreme Court's 1948 *Paramount* decision led studios to sell off their movie theaters over the next decade, transforming if not quite dissolving Hollywood's hegemony. As producer-distributors (and no longer theater owners), the studios began making fewer but more lucrative films, and they worried less about filling theaters all year long. Foreign films and independent films filled in the gaps and found large audiences. Their success gradually showed Hollywood that it could no longer treat American moviegoers as a single entity. The studios had ignored the expanding youth culture and a new audience for films with mature content. By the time *Easy Rider* proved the full box-office potential of the trend in 1969, the studios had already begun to respond. The Motion Picture Association of America replaced the Production Code with a rating system that allowed for variegated films that appealed to smaller segments of the American public. Studios began to produce films that met the tastes and needs of a variety of different audiences, and they increasingly distributed films made by independent production companies. As Hollywood ceased to address moviegoers as a single homogeneous national audience, the usefulness of the kinds of university and museum projects that were part of the studio era became less apparent. Hollywood supported projects like Columbia University's film program and MoMA's Film Library in part to teach Americans how to watch film. Columbia reached out to the middle class while MoMA taught audiences to appreciate old films. In the New Hollywood, film producers found new ways to respond to their audience, and they stopped trying to transform Americans into film spectators.[2]

The transition to the New Hollywood was also precipitated by the rise in global ticket sales in the 1950s and subsequent changes in studio ownership. As we saw in Iris Barry's writings, Hollywood achieved global distribution as early as the 1920s. With the aid of the State Department, the Department of Commerce, and the United States Information Agency, as well as the Motion Picture Export Association, Hollywood significantly expanded its global presence after World War II. During and after both world wars, government agencies supported Hollywood film because they saw it as effective American propaganda. By the mid-1950s, however, Hollywood no longer needed the government's helping hand. A string of internationally successful films, led by 20th Century-Fox's *The Robe* (1953), showed Hollywood that it had already built a successful distribution network and achieved the popularity necessary to produce global blockbusters that could earn four or five times as much as previous hits. Throughout the 1950s and 1960s, approximately half of Hollywood's box-office revenue came from overseas ticket sales, a ratio that has risen and fallen in subsequent decades. The Hollywood studios became global businesses, supporting international coproductions and investing heavily in national film industries on every continent. In 1967, Paramount, the company Lasky and Zukor built, was the first studio to become part of a diversified, multinational conglomerate (Gulf + Western), with interests in real estate, fertilizer, and many other unrelated industries.[3] All the other studios were soon acquired by, or themselves acquired, global corporations. Hollywood studios became part of the largest conglomerates in the world. They no longer needed the support of the institutions that had helped them achieve worldwide success. On the contrary, media conglomerates have continued to fight for less government intervention, except where regulations help break down barriers to distribution set up by other countries or international trade agreements (e.g., NAFTA, GATT, etc.).[4]

Perhaps more importantly, studios found that promoting exclusively pro-American films didn't help sell films on a global scale. The rise of the blockbuster aimed at a global audience has grown in inverse proportion to the desire to address a national audience. With the integration of global film markets it has become less advantageous for Hollywood film to appear principally American. The government's attempt to renew its relationship with Hollywood after the September 11, 2001, attacks on the World Trade Center and the Pentagon proved this point. Shortly after the attacks, President George W. Bush's administration announced its plans to create a new collaboration with Hollywood, one reminiscent, its spokespeople said, of the Office of War Information's World War II collaboration (as discussed in chapter 5). Senior presidential adviser Karl Rove traveled to Hollywood to meet with top producers, who had formed the 9–11 Committee. Motion Picture Association of America president Jack Valenti chaired the meeting as Will Hays had brokered earlier collaborations. It all seemed to conjure the image of Nelson Rockefeller and the CIAA's first reception in Hollywood. But this time, producers refused to agree to make strictly pro-American films. Hollywood did produce at least one public service announcement, an institute of creative professionals at the University of Southern California ran terrorist scenarios, and several producers accepted access to military bases in order to make their films more realistic. But Hollywood's leaders refused to make government propaganda. "That's just not what we do," explained Rob Friedman, vice chairman and CEO of Paramount and also a member of the 9–11 Committee. "Our jobs," he continued, "are to make $60 million movies and make a profit."[5] Of course, when Adolph Zukor ran Paramount, his job was to turn a profit too. But Zukor led the campaign to use universities and museums, and he put his studio at the service of the war effort. At the time, Zukor saw the relationship with American cultural institutions as a way to expand the film audience to include the entire American public and to gain footholds around the world. In the New Hollywood, film producers faced a new problem: how to reach and maintain a global audience.

Another reason Hollywood moguls sought the help of cultural institutions—in addition to creating a national audience—was to give value to films that had lost their commercial appeal. With the introduction of television, cable TV, and VCRs, studios found a way to turn a profit from their film libraries, and cultural institutions lost their monopoly on the traffic in old films. Movie entrepreneurs since Edison had dreamed of television and broadcast technology as a means of cutting out distributors and reaching directly into viewers' homes, thus building an endless second-run market. Adolph Zukor, for example, hedged his bets in 1927 by simultaneously investing in a plan for a broadcasting division of Paramount and pushing for the Harvard film library. But it wasn't until the mid-1950s that studios began to realize the financial potential of their film libraries. At first, heads of the major studios were put off by the low fees that networks could pay for films, and the film talent guilds cut into television profits even further by negotiating for residual fees on films made after 1947. The studios experimented with subscription television, pay-per-view movies, and theatrical television before the television networks could afford the high price of film rentals. In 1955 the major studios began to sell their pre-1948 "backlogs" of films to television for a fraction of their value. RKO sold its library for $15 million, and Paramount sold its backlog to MCA for $50 million. A year and a half after the sale, RKO's backlog had grossed an estimated $150 million; just a few years later, individual films rented to television for more than $1 million. Television profits became such a windfall by the 1960s that talent agent–mogul Lew Wasserman, who had taken over film production at Universal, couldn't see any reason to make good films when every film turned a profit once it reached television. This was a long way from the fear that led Joseph Kennedy to seek Harvard's help in 1927: the fear that a film's value decreased with each showing.[6]

Museum curators and university professors have shared film producers' television dream since Victor Oscar Freeburg prophesized home movie libraries. But museums and universities weren't allowed to share in the realization of that dream. Hollywood's assertion of its copyrights and the expense of film technology have continually thwarted the use of films by museums and universities. In the 1930s and 1940s, MoMA's Film Library successfully negotiated to show Hollywood films because it agreed to exhibit only films two or more years old, films that were thought to be at the end of their profit-earning lives. MoMA's curators' first problem was overcoming audiences' penchant for laughing at films just a few years old. But once a market for those films was created and they gained in financial value, Hollywood studio heads immediately cast aside museums and universities. MoMA's film curator Richard Griffith lamented television's crippling effect on the museum's Film Library:

> [A] severe curtailment of the Film Library's circulating program has arisen out of the sale, *en bloc*, of studio "backlogs" — a term used to indicate all the films produced by a given company before 1948 — to television agencies. Several of the companies have required the Film Library to withdraw films from circulation at least until such time as these sales have been successfully negotiated. . . . This and parallel developments have worked hardship on the Film Library's national program.[7]

Cut off from Hollywood, MoMA's Film Library turned instead to art films and the avant-garde films its curators had initially rebuffed. Today, even the most basic tenet of Vachel Lindsay's prophecy — that museums and universities might contain film departments — seems financially beyond the reach of all but a few institutions.

Hollywood has continued to work with the American Film Institute, the Library of Congress, and a few other film archives to promote the establishment of a canon of Hollywood classics. But the archives have remained relatively impoverished and powerless. When the American Film Institute was founded in 1967, it promised the preservation of Hollywood history through collaboration between the government, the studios, and arts foundations. The AFI received an initial grant of more than a million dollars from Hollywood's Motion Picture Association of American in addition to funding from the Ford Foundation and the National Endowment for the Arts. The AFI, in turn, awarded annual film preservation grants totaling over $350,000. But the AFI's preservation budget continued to shrink, and when the NEA's budget was cut dramatically in 1995, the AFI's grant programs were cancelled. (The NEA has continued to fund archives directly on a smaller scale.)

The AFI has remained in the public eye, but its role in the preservation of film history has been diminished. One of the AFI's most prominent projects since the dissolution of its relationship with the NEA has been the annual publication of lists of great films, starting in 1998 with the "100 Greatest American Movies of All Time," and then continuing with narrower themes (e.g., "100 Funniest American Movies," "100 Heroes & Villains," etc.). A similar task is performed by the Library of Congress's National Film Registry, which annually selects twenty-five films to be preserved as national treasures. These projects frequently make news, but they don't have the scope or impact of, say, Hollywood's own canon-building Academy Awards ceremony, which is seen by over forty million viewers around the world. The moguls' decision in the 1920s to move the Academy Awards from Harvard to the Academy of Motion Picture Arts and Sciences foreshadowed things to come. In the New Hollywood, canon formation and the market for the studios' film libraries is managed by Hollywood with minimal help from museums, universities, or the government.[8]

If Hollywood has ceased to use cultural institutions to build its audience or confer value on its history, a third and final reason for the initial relationship between studios and cultural institutions (universities in particular) has remained strong and productive. Universities have continued to perform the task set out by Columbia in the 1910s and the University of Southern California in the 1920s: to find potential talented filmmakers, educate and train them, and professionalize the many fields of filmmaking. Columbia continues to have a strong screenwriting program, and USC remains an important film school. In addition, New York University, the University of California, Los Angeles, and the AFI's Center for Advanced Film Study in Los Angeles all train screenwriters, actors, directors, cinematographers, and producers. The importance of film schools has actually increased in the New Hollywood. The explosion of the youth-oriented blockbusters in the New Hollywood, for instance, was fed in the 1960s and 1970s by a generation of film school graduates including Francis Ford Coppola (UCLA), Martin Scorsese (NYU), and George Lucas (USC). They brought the aesthetic appeal and maturity of European art films into the commercial machines of the studios. Hollywood's transition from a factory-like studio system that incorporated every element of production—including training filmmakers and movie stars—to being a distribution center for studio-, foreign-, and independently produced films necessitated that a new source of filmmakers be found. Film schools filled the need and began to place talented filmmakers and new films into the film festival circuit, which could then be mined by the studios.[9]

Collaborations between film studios and cultural institutions became victims of their own success. They made Hollywood into an American industry and art form with nationwide appeal, international distribution, and a canon of classics. But like other elements of the studio era,

Hollywood's relationship with universities, museums, and the government were transformed in the New Hollywood, though they did not disappear entirely. Many of these relationships became less advantageous as Hollywood responded to transformations in American culture, the introduction of new technologies, and the rise of a global audience for Hollywood film. If cultural institutions helped to make Hollywood American, they were relegated to the background when Hollywood needed to develop a more complex relationship with its American audience and to become a truly global industry.

NOTES

INTRODUCTION: HOW FILM BECAME ART

1. See, for example: Robert Sklar, *Movie-Made America: A Cultural History of America*, rev. and updated (New York: Vintage, 1994); William Uricchio and Roberta Pearson, *Reframing Culture: The Case of Vitagraph Quality Films* (Princeton: Princeton University Press, 1993); Lary May, *Screening Out the Past: The Birth of Mass Culture and the Motion Picture Industry* (Chicago: University of Chicago Press, 1980); Eileen Bowser, *The Transformation of Cinema, 1907–1915* (Berkeley: University of California Press, 1990).

2. For some interesting contributions to the political interpretation of Hollywood films, see Peter Biskind, *Seeing Is Believing: How Hollywood Taught Us to Stop Worrying and Love the Fifties* (New York: Pantheon, 1983), and Michael Ryan and Douglas Kellner, *Camera Politica: The Politics and Ideology of Contemporary Film* (Bloomington: Indiana University Press, 1988).

3. See esp. Richard Maltby, "Censorship and Self-Regulation," in Geoffrey Nowell-Smith, ed., *The Oxford History of World Cinema* (New York: Oxford University Press, 1996); Jon Lewis, *Hollywood v. Hardcore* (New York: New

York University Press, 2000); and the essays in Matthew Bernstein, ed., *Controlling Hollywood: Censorship and Regulation in the Studio Era* (New Brunswick: Rutgers University Press, 1999).

4. For an account of Hollywood financing in the 1920s and 1930s, see Sklar, *Movie-Made America*, chs. 9 and 10.

5. Vachel Lindsay, *The Art of the Moving Picture* (1922; New York: Liveright, 1970).

6. *Academy Awards* and *Oscar* are registered trademarks of the Academy of Motion Picture Arts and Sciences.

7. Brecht, quoted in Peter Wollen, *Raiding the Icebox: Reflections of Twentieth-Century Culture* (Bloomington: Indiana University Press, 1993), 52. See also Bertolt Brecht, "Emphasis on Sport" in John Willett, ed. and trans., *Brecht on Theatre* (New York: Methuen, 1964), 6–9.

1. VACHEL LINDSAY AND THE UNIVERSAL FILM MUSEUM

1. W. K. L. Dickson and Antonia Dickson, *History of the Kinetograph, Kinetoscope, and the Kinetophonograph* (Salem, N.H.: Ayer, 1894), 51–52.

2. Tom Gunning, *D. W. Griffith and the Origins of American Narrative Film* (Urbana: University of Illinois Press, 1991), 1–3; Kemp Niver, *Early Motion Pictures: The Paper Print Collection in the Library of Congress*, ed. Bebe Bergstrom (Washington, D.C.: Library of Congress, 1985); Doug Herrick, "Towards a National Film Collection: Motion Pictures at the Library of Congress," *Film Library Quarterly* 13.1 (1980); Anthony Slide, *Nitrate Won't Wait: Film Preservation in the United States* (Jefferson, N.C.: McFarland, 1992), 36; and Charles "Bucky" Grimm, "A Paper Print Pre-History," *Film History* 11 (1999): 204–16.

3. Boleslas Matuszewski, "Une nouvelle source de l'historique: Création d'un dépôt de cinématographie historique," *Le Figaro* (March 25, 1898); rpt., "A New Source of History," trans. Laura U. Marks and Dianne Koszarski, *Film History* 7.3 (Autumn 1995): 322. It is also available online in a translation by Julia Bloch Frey, *Screening the Past* (1997; *see* www.latrobe.edu.au/screeningthepast/classics/clasjul/mat.html). For discussions of the essay's reception and importance, see William D. Routt's introduction to the *Screening the Past* translation and Penelope Houston, *Keepers of the Frame* (London: BFI, 1994), 10–12.

4. Annette Michelson, "Dr. Crase and Mr. Clair," *October* 11 (1979): 31–53. Tom Gunning has more recently referred to this as film's "gnostic mission"; see his "In Your Face: Physiognomy, Photography, and the Gnostic Mission of Early Film," *Modernism/Modernity* 4.1 (1997): 1–29.

5. Matuszewski, 324, 322 (italics in original).

6. Houston, *Keepers of the Frame*, 12.

7. Abbé Joye is discussed in Houston, *Keepers of the Frame*, 17. Albert Kahn's fascinating archive is examined by Paula Amad in "Cinema's 'Sanctuary': From Pre-documentary to Documentary Film in Albert Kahn's *Archives de*

la Planète (1908–1931)," *Film History* 13 (2001): 138–59, and *"Archiving the Everyday"*: A *Topos in French Film History, 1895–1931* (New York: Columbia University Press, forthcoming). Alison Trope surveys a number of early archives in "Le Cinéma Pour Le Cinéma: Making Museums of the Moving Image," *The Moving Image* 1.1 (Spring 2001): 29–67.

8. Franz Goerke, "Proposal for Establishing an Archive for Moving Pictures," trans. Cecil L. French and Daniel J. Leab, *Historical Journal of Film, Radio, and Television* 16.1 (1996): 9–12; Richard Abel, *French Film Theory and Criticism, 1907–1939*, vol. 1 (Princeton: Princeton University Press, 1988), 11; Slide, *Nitrate Won't Wait*, 26.

9. Nicholas Reeves, *Official British Film Propaganda During the First World War* (London: Croom Helm, 1986), 102–103; Houston, *Keepers of the Frame*, 13–14; Slide, *Nitrate Won't Wait*, 11.

10. See Slide, *Nitrate Won't Wait*, 11.

11. D. W. Griffith, "Five Dollar Movies Prophesied," *The Editor* (April 24, 1915); rpt. as "Some Prophecies: Film and Theatre, Screenwriting, Education," in Harry M. Geduld, ed., *Focus on D. W. Griffith*, (Englewood Cliffs, N.J.: Prentice-Hall, 1971), 35. Miriam Hansen suggests that this passage looks ahead to the naturalized style of the classical Hollywood cinema; see Miriam Hansen, "Universal Language and Democratic Culture: Myths of Origin in Early American Cinema," in Dieter Meindl and Friedrich W. Horlacher with Martin Christadler, eds., *Myth and the Enlightenment in American Literature* (Erlagen, Ger.: University of Erlangen-Nürnberg, 1985).

12. Hansen, "Universal Language and Democratic Culture," 325.

13. Anne Friedberg, " 'A Properly Adjusted Window': Vision and Sanity in D. W. Griffith's 1908–1909 Biograph Films," in Thomas Elsaesser, ed., with Adam Barker, *Early Cinema: Space, Frame, Narrative* (London: British Film Institute, 1990), 326–35.

14. See especially Scott Simon, *The Films of D. W. Griffith* (Cambridge: Cambridge University Press, 1993), 146–57; Friedberg, " 'A Properly Adjusted Window' "; Gunning, *D. W. Griffith*, 162–64; and Lary May, *Screening Out the Past: The Birth of Mass Culture and the Motion Picture Industry* (Chicago: University of Chicago Press, 1980), ch. 4.

15. D. W. Griffith, interview, *New York American* (February 28, 1915), 9; rpt., Geduld, ed., *Focus on Griffith*, 29.

16. Vachel Lindsay, *The Art of the Moving Picture* (1922; rpt., New York: Liveright, 1970), 215. All subsequent references are to this reprinting of the 1922 edition. This revised and expanded edition contains almost the entire original 1915 edition within it, so even when I refer to different versions, I still cite the text and pagination as it appeared in the 1970 reprinting of the 1922 edition.

17. Eric Hobsbawm, "Introduction: Inventing Traditions" and "Mass-Producing Traditions: Europe, 1870–1914," in Hobsbawm and Terence Ranger, eds., *The Invention of Tradition* (Cambridge: Cambridge University Press, 1983), 1, 279–80.

18. This element of *The Art of the Moving Picture* is usually emphasized to the exclusion of the rest of the book. On Lindsay's theory of film as hieroglyphics, see Warren Susman, *Culture as History* (New York: Pantheon, 1984), xvii; Miriam Hansen, *Babel and Babylon* (Cambridge: Harvard University Press, 1991), 77–78; Glenn Joseph Wolfe, *Vachel Lindsay: The Poet as Film Theorist* (New York: Arno Press, 1973), ch. 8; and Antonia Lant, "The Curse of the Pharaoh, or How the Cinema Contracted Egyptomania," *October* 59 (Winter 1992): 87–112.

19. For an unusual recent reading of Lindsay's book and its similarities to the film theory of Giles Deleuze, see William D. Routt, "The Madness of Images and Thinking Cinema," *Postmodern Culture* 8.2 (1998); *see* http://muse.jhu.edu/journals/pmc/v008/8.2routt.html.

20. Tony Bennett suggests that in this context, "Culture's target is always male. The museum, the reading room, the art gallery, the library—it is always changes in the behavior of working-class men that are aimed for when the virtues of these institutions are extolled. Where the working-class woman appears, it is not in her own right but as the potential beneficiary of reformed male conduct." See Tony Bennett "The Multiplication of Culture's Utility," *Critical Inquiry* 21 (Summer 1995): 883. Interpal Grewal argues that middle-class women were also targeted by British museums but as consumers rather than the objects of social reform; see *Home and Harem: Nation, Gender, Empire, and the Cultures of Travel* (Durham: Duke University Press, 1996), 127.

21. Bennett, "Multiplication of Culture's Utility," 882.

22. Tony Bennett, *The Birth of the Museum* (New York: Routledge, 1995), 25–33. The embourgeoisement of the museum subject is eloquently captured in Didier Maleuvre, *Museum Memories* (Stanford: Stanford University Press, 1999), 103–104. Ruskin, quoted in Susan P. Casteras, "The Germ of a Museum, Arranged First for 'Workers in Iron': Ruskin's Museological Theories and the Curating of the Saint George's Museum," in *John Ruskin and the Victorian Eye* (New York: Harry N. Abrams and the Phoenix Art Museum, 1993), 207.

23. On the creation of public spaces in the 1870s, see Burton J. Bledstein, *The Culture of Professionalism: The Middle Class and the Development of Higher Education in America* (New York: Norton, 1978), 57–65. Quasi-public spaces like department stores emerged with similar acculturating functions. For an argument, which will be taken-up in chapter 3, that privileges public spaces in the creation of an elite class, see Paul DiMaggio, "Cultural Entrepreneurship in Nineteenth-Century Boston: The Creating of an Organizational Base for High Culture in America," *Media, Culture, Society* 4 (1982): 33–50, and "Cultural Entrepreneurship in Nineteenth-Century Boston, Part II: The Classification and Framing of American Art," *Media, Culture, Society* 4 (1982): 303–322.

24. Richard F. Bach, *Museums in the Industrial World* (New York: Gilliss Press, 1926), 1.

25. G. Brown Goode, *The Principles of Museum Administration* (York: Coultas and Volans Exchange, 1895), 3 (emphasis added).

26. Roger Chartier, "Libraries Without Walls," *The Order of Books*, trans. Lydia G. Cochrane (Stanford: Stanford University Press, 1994), 62.

27. Michel Foucault suggests that "microcosm" was the most commonly used word in the sixteenth century: *The Order of Things* (1966; New York: Vintage Books, 1973), 31. On the many permutations of the universal collection, see Eilean Hooper-Greenhill, *Museums and the Shaping of Knowledge* (New York: Routledge, 1992); Carol Duncan and Alan Wallach, "The Universal Survey Museum," *Art History* 3.4 (1980): 448–69; Carol Duncan, *Civilizing Rituals* (New York: Routledge, 1995), ch. 2; and Bennett, *Birth of the Museum*, 33–58.

28. Wayne A. Wiegand, *Irrepressible Reformer: A Biography of Melvil Dewey* (Chicago: American Library Association, 1996), 23; James Thompson, *A History of the Principles of Librarianship* (Hamden, Conn.: Linnett, 1977), 152.

29. Janice Radway, *A Feeling for Books: The Book-of-the-Month Club, Literary Taste, and Middle-Class Desire* (Chapel Hill: University of North Carolina Press, 1997), 136–37; Dee Garrison, *Apostles of Culture: The Public Librarian and American Society, 1876–1920* (New York: Free Press, 1979).

30. John Cotton Dana, *A Library Primer*, 2d ed. (Chicago: Library Bureau, 1900), 45. For an account of Dana's career, see Edward P. Alexander, "John Cotton Dana," *Museum Masters: Their Museums and Influence* (Nashville: American Association for State and Local History, 1983), 379–411.

31. Dana, *A Library Primer*, 122.

32. Ibid., 12.

33. As one influential text stated: "The ideal public library of the future will thus not only be a warehouse of books, where the most complete adaptation of the best technical methods for their arrangement, classification, and management shall be employed, but a realization of a people's university" (Lewis H. Steiner, "The Future of the Free Public Library," *Library Journal* 1 [1876]: 74–81, rpt. in, Dianne J. Ellsworth and Norman D. Stevens, eds., *Landmarks of Library Literature, 1876–1976* [Metuchen, N.J.: Scarecrow Press, 1976], 235). See also Robert Ellis Lee, *Continuing Education for Adults Through the American Public Library, 1833–1964* (Chicago: American Library Association, 1966).

34. "Moving Pictures in Library Work," *Wisconsin Library Bulletin* 6 (November 1910): 138–40; Vera Snook, "Motion Pictures in Library Work," *Public Libraries* 26 (1921): 574; William S. Learned, *The American Public Library and the Diffusion of Knowledge* (New York: Harcourt, Brace, 1924), 22–25. See ch. 2 of the present volume for a discussion of the incorporation of films into state university libraries, which generally proceeded public library collections.

35. Dana, *A Library Primer*, 13. See also the discussion of the library in Raymond Calkins, *Substitutes for the Saloon*, rev. ed. (Boston: Houghton Mifflin, 1919), 111–15.

36. Jesse Torrey, *The Intellectual Torch; Developing an Original, Economical and Expeditious Plan for the Universal Dissemination of Knowledge and Virtue;*

By Means of Free Public Libraries. Including Essays on the Use of Distilled Spirits (1817; Woodstock, Vt.: Elm Tree Press, 1912), 27.

37. Roy Rosenzweig, *Eight Hours for What We Will: Workers and Leisure in an Industrial City, 1870–1920* (Cambridge: Cambridge University Press, 1983), ch. 8; Gunning, *D. W. Griffith*, 164; Friedberg, *Window Shopping*, 236.

38. Anne Friedberg explains that "Griffith's quasi-theoretic speculations about the relation of cinema to alcoholism (the concomitant similarities of incorporation, habituation, desire for loss of self, replacement with other) are twisted into a suggestion of cinema as *cure*, an effective substitute for drinking and vice, a potential superintendent of domestic unity" (*Window Shopping*, 236–37). The use of alcohol or drugs as an analogy for film has been common throughout the history of film theory. In chapter 4 we will see that Iris Barry thought of the cinema as a drug. And Soviet filmmaker Dziga Vertov spoke of "cinema-vodka, spiked with the antidote of propagandistic power" (*Kino-Eye: The Writings of Dziga Vertov*, ed. Annette Michelson, trans. Kevin O'Brien [London: Pluto Press, 1984], 48).

39. See William Uricchio and Roberta E. Pearson, *Reframing Culture: The Case of the Vitagraph Quality Films* (Princeton: Princeton University Press, 1993), 35.

40. Adele F. Woodward, "The Motion Picture as Saloon Substitute," in Calkins, *Substitutes*, 359.

41. Perry R. Duis, *The Saloon: Public Drinking in Chicago and Boston, 1880–1920* (Urbana: University of Illinois Press, 1983), 293.

42. Philip Fisher, *Making and Effacing Art: Modern American Art in a Culture of Museums* (New York: Oxford University Press, 1991), 7; see also Bennett, *Birth of the Museum*, 44.

43. André Malraux, *The Voices of Silence*, trans. Stuart Gilbert (1949, 1950; Princeton: Princeton University Press, 1978), 15–16.

44. Quoted in Lawrence W. Levine, *Highbrow/Lowbrow: The Emergence of Cultural Hierarchy in America* (Cambridge: Harvard University Press, 1988), 151.

45. Alan Wallach, "The American Cast Museum: An Episode in the History of the Institutional Definition of Art," *Exhibiting Contradictions* (Amherst: University of Massachusetts Press, 1998), 38–56. On the early history of the Metropolitan Museum of Art, see Duncan, *Civilizing Rituals*, ch. 3. On the aesthetic vs. education debate over the fate of the Boston museum cast collection, see Walter Muir Whitehill, *Museum of Fine Arts Boston: A Centennial History*, vol. 1 (Cambridge: Belknap Press of Harvard University Press, 1970), ch. 6.

46. Anne McCauley, "Invading Industry," in Mark Haworth-Booth and Anne McCauley, *The Museum and the Photograph: Collecting Photography at the Victoria and Albert Museum, 1853–1900* (Williamstown, Mass.: Clark Art Institute, 1998), 23–70; Wallach, "The American Cast Museum," 54–56; Levine, *Highbrow/Lowbrow*, 160–61.

47. Ruskin, quoted in Bennett, "Multiplication of Culture's Utility," 867. On Ruskin's museological theory and limited experience as a museum administrator, see Casteras, "'The Germ of a Museum.'"

48. Duncan, *Civilizing Rituals*, 49.

49. Michael Denning, *Mechanic Accents* (New York: Verso, 1987), 48–49.

50. Benjamin, quoted in Douglas Crimp, *On the Museum's Ruins* (Cambridge: MIT University Press, 1995), 203–204.

51. Andrew Ross, "The Great Un-American Numbers Game," *Real Love* (New York: New York University Press, 1998), 123.

52. Duncan, *Civilizing Rituals*, 49.

53. Daniel J. Sherman offers a particularly lucid and convincing argument that "the internal coherence of the art museum is itself a construction" and scholars have been too ready to conflate bourgeois culture and national ideology in studies of nineteenth-century museums. See his "The Bourgeoisie, Cultural Appropriation, and the Art Museum in Nineteenth-Century France," *Radical History Review* 38 (1987): 38–58. See also Vera Zolberg's analysis of the complex management of the Chicago Art Institute, "Conflicting Visions in American Art Museums," *Theory and Society* 19.1 (January 1981): 103–125.

54. See Pierre Bourdieu and Alain Darbel with Dominique Schnapper, *The Love of Art: European Art Museums and Their Public*, trans. Caroline Beatie and Nick Merriman (Stanford: Stanford University Press, 1990), and Daniel M. Fox, *Engines of Culture: Philanthropy and Art Museums* (1963; New Brunswick: Transaction, 1995).

55. On the style of classical Hollywood cinema, see Noël Burch, *Life to Those Shadows*, trans. and ed. Ben Brewster (Berkeley: University of California Press, 1990), and David Bordwell, Janet Staiger, Kristin Thompson, *The Classical Hollywood Cinema* (New York: Columbia University Press, 1985).

56. Hansen, *Babel and Babylon*, 78.

57. The classic and still the best study of the agrarian myth in American culture is Richard Hofstadter, *The Age of Reform* (New York: Vintage, 1955).

58. It is Lindsay's specific names rather than the naming process that are idiosyncratic. Many institutions declared themselves the "new Athens."

59. Leo Marx, *The Machine in the Garden* (New York: Oxford University Press, 1964), 234.

60. See Lee Rust Brown, "The Emerson Museum," *Representations* 40 (Fall 1992): 63 and passim.

61. Significantly, the two films Lindsay chose for comparison are about characters teetering on the line between madness and sanity. From this example, spectators seem not only to compare norms of representation but psychological norms as well. Rather than norms being imposed by the institution, Lindsay's film museum threw open the definition of the normal for debate.

62. The occasional use of silence in movie theaters during the silent era is discussed in Rick Altman, "The Silence of the Silents, "*Musical Quarterly* 80.4 (1997): 648–718.

63. Eggers, in Lindsay, *The Art of the Moving Picture*, xxiv.

64. Thomas J. Schlereth, *Victorian America* (New York: HarperPerennial, 1991), 255.

65. On Lindsay's "higher vaudeville" and its similarities to Chautauqua, see Ann

Massa, *Vachel Lindsay: Fieldworker for the American Dream* (Bloomington: Indiana University Press, 1970), 232–34. John E. Tapia's *Circuit Chautauqua* (Jefferson, N.C.: Macfarland, 1997) is the most concise and complete history of circuit Chautauqua. And Alan Trachtenberg's description of William James's encounter with Chautauqua captures its symbolic importance for the Gilded Age; see "The Politics of Culture," *The Incorporation of America: Culture and Society in the Gilded Age* (New York: Hill and Wang, 1982), 140–81.

66. Vachel Lindsay, *The Letters of Vachel Lindsay*, ed. Marc Chéntier (New York: Burt Franklin, 1979), 130, 142.

2. OVERLAPPING PUBLICS: HOLLYWOOD AND COLUMBIA UNIVERSITY, 1915

1. Lindsay's film criticism includes "'The Movies," *New Republic* (January 13, 1917): 302–303; "Photoplay Progress," *New Republic* (February 17, 1917): 76–77; "Back Your Train Up to My Pony," *New Republic* (March 10, 1917): 166–67; "Venus in Armor," *New Republic* (March 28. 1917): 380–81; "Queen of My People," *New Republic* (July 7, 1917): 280–81; "A Plea for the Art World," *Moving Picture World* (July 21, 1917): 368; "The Great Douglas Fairbanks," *Ladies Home Journal* (August 1926). His second book of film theory wasn't published in his lifetime, but it was reconstructed by Myron Lounsbury as *Progress and Poetry of the Movies* (Lantham, Md.: Scarecrow Press, 1995).

2. An exhibitor from Sacramento, Edgar Strakosch, coined the word *photoplay* when he won a 1910 contest sponsored by the Essanay Company to find a new name for the "movies." The name quickly caught on and was frequently used to distinguish a "high-class" feature film from a "movie." On the history and significance of the word *photoplay*, see William Paul, "Uncanny Theater: The Twin Inheritances of the Movies," *Paradoxa* 3.3–4 (1997): 322–23, and Anthony Slide, *Early American Cinema*, rev. ed. (Metuchen, N.J.: Scarecrow Press, 1994): 221. Also see W. Stephen Bush, "The Dreadful Word," *Moving Picture World* (October 30, 1915): 760, in which he suggests replacing both the vulgar "movie" and the overlong "photoplay" with the term "film."

3. The *Ben-Hur* case is: *Kalem Co. v. Harper Bros.*, 222 US 55, U.S. Supreme Court, November 13, 1911. See Doug Herrick, "Towards a National Film Collection: Motion Pictures at the Library of Congress," *Film Library Quarterly* 13.1 (1980): 9; Siva Vaidhyanathan, *Copyrights and Copywrongs: The Rise of Intellectual Property and How It Threatens Creativity* (New York: New York University Press, 2001), 93–105; Paul Goldstein, *Copyright's Highway: From Guttenberg to the Celestial Jukebox*, rev. ed. (Stanford: Stanford University Press, 2003), 50–51. The phrase "scenario fever" belongs to Edward Azlant, "The Theory, History, and Practice of Screenwriting, 1897–1920," Ph.D. diss. (University of Wisconsin-Madison, 1980), 124–31. See

also David Bordwell, Janet Staiger, Kristin Thompson, *The Classical Hollywood Cinema* (New York: Columbia University Press, 1985), 137–39; Thomas Ince, "The Undergraduate and the Scenario," *The Bookman* 47 (March-August 1918): 415–18.

4. Sumiko Higashi, *Cecil B. DeMille and American Culture: The Silent Years* (Berkeley: University of California Press, 1994), 17–18.

5. "Lasky Company Offers Scholarship to Columbia Students," *Moving Picture World* (October 3, 1915); "Lasky Scholarship for College Scenario Course," *Moving Picture News* (November 6, 1915); Frances Taylor Patterson, *Cinema Craftsmanship* (New York: Harcourt, Brace, and Howe, 1920), 86, 129, 184, passim; Frances Taylor Patterson, ed., *Motion Picture Continuities* (New York: Columbia University Press, 1929); and Arthur Leads, "Thinks and Things," *Writer's Monthly* 8.5–6 (November-December 1916): 208. Much of my information on the Columbia photoplay composition courses comes from catalogs, syllabi, reports, and other records in the Columbiana Library, Columbia University.

6. Vachel Lindsay, *The Letters of Vachel Lindsay*, ed. Marc Chéntier (New York: Burt Franklin, 1979), doesn't include any of Lindsay and Freeburg's correspondence, but it does include several letters in which Lindsay discusses Freeburg and his work; see pp. 143, 162, and 336.

7. Frances Taylor Patterson, "Signs and Portents," *Exceptional Photoplays* 3.6 (April 1923): 4.

8. "Home-Made Motion Pictures Predicted for Near Future," *New York Times* (April 22, 1917), sec. 8, p. 5; Victor O. Freeburg, *The Art of Photoplay Making* (New York: Macmillan, 1918), 9–10. Freeburg abandoned writing and music analogies in his later book, *Pictorial Beauty on the Screen* (1923; New York: Benjamin Blom, 1972). Stanley Cavell later developed a similar theory of the movie star in *The World Viewed* (New York: Viking, 1971).

9. For more on the studios' preservation practices, see David Pierce, "The Legion of the Condemned—Why American Silent Films Perished," *Film History* 9 (1997): 5–22.

10. Noël Burch, *Life to Those Shadows*, trans. and ed. Ben Brewster (Berkeley: University of California Press, 1990), 47.

11. For early attendance figures that support the thesis that working-class patrons dominated American nickelodeon audiences in the 1900s, see Michael M. Davis, *Exploitation of Pleasure: A Study of Commercial Recreations in New York City* (New York: Russell Sage Foundation, 1911), 21–31. It is clear that early film historians overstated the working-class character of nickelodeons, but recent scholarship has borne out the theory that middle-class attendance in nickelodeons was localized and sporadic before World War I. For the important contributions to the debate, see Russell Merritt, "Nickelodeon Theaters, 1905–1914: Building an Audience for the Movies," in Tino Balio, ed., *The American Film Industry* (Madison: University of Wisconsin Press, 1976); Douglas Gomery, "Movie Audiences, Urban Geography, and the History of American Film," *The Velvet Light Trap* 19 (1982): 23–9; Robert C.

Allen, "Motion Picture Exhibition in Manhattan, 1906–1912," in John Fell, ed., *Film Before Griffith* (Berkeley: University of California Press, 1983); Robert Sklar, "Oh! Althusser: Historiography and the Rise of Cinema Studies," in Robert Sklar and Charles Musser, eds., *Resisting Images: Essays on Cinema and History* (Philadelphia: Temple University Press, 1990); Ben Singer, "Manhattan Nickelodeons: New Data on Audiences and Exhibition," *Cinema Journal* 34.3 (Spring 1995): 5–35; and Robert C. Allen, "Manhattan Myopia; Or, Oh! Iowa!" and Ben Singer, "New York, Just Like I Pictured It . . . " both in *Cinema Journal* 35.3 (1996): 75–103, 104–128, .

12. Burch, *Life to Those Shadows*, 48. See also Tom Gunning, "Weaving a Narrative: Style and Economic Background in Griffith's Biograph Films," in Thomas Elsaesser, ed., with Adam Barker, *Early Cinema: Space, Frame, Narrative* (London: British Film Institute, 1990), 336–47.

13. Accounts of this incident differ significantly. Some, for example, place the number of fatalities as high as 180, but I have taken a conservative figure from Kristin Thompson and David Bordwell, *Film History* (New York: McGraw-Hill, 1994), 15. The attention the fire drew to the cinema actually seems to have increased the numbers of fairground moviegoers, but these new patrons were predominantly from the working class. See Jacques Deslandes and Jacques Richard, *Histoire comparée du cinéma*, vol. 2: 1897–1906 (Paris: Casterman, 1968), 164. For accounts of American film fires and regulations during the nickelodeon and pre-nickelodeon periods, see Charles Musser, *The Emergence of Cinema: The American Screen to 1907* (Berkeley: University of California Press, 1990), 443–44, passim.

14. Yuri Tsivian, *Early Cinema in Russia and Its Cultural Reception*, trans. Alan Bodger, ed. Richard Taylor (Chicago: University of Chicago Press, 1994), 49–52.

15. Terry Ramsaye, *A Million and One Nights* (New York: Simon and Schuster, 1926), 353–57. Ramsaye places the number of deaths at 180.

16. Charles Musser, *Before the Nickelodeon: Edwin S. Porter and the Edison Manufacturing Company* (Berkeley: University of California Press, 1991), 445.

17. "The Alleged Relation Between Films and Fires," *Motography* 13.1 (January 2, 1915): 13–14.

18. "Can Films Be Preserved for Posterity?" *Motography* 8.14 (April 3, 1915): 521.

19. "Film Containers," *Motography* 18.2 (July 14, 1917): 88.

20. "No Export of Damaged Film," *Motography* 18.6 (August 11, 1917): 310. It is true that a Pathé plant was converted into a munitions factory and that the nitrate base of film stock shares chemical properties with guncotton. But despite the retelling of this story in film textbooks, I have found no evidence that U.S. or European governments converted old film prints into explosives.

21. "Lasky Negative Vault," *Motography* (July 4, 1914): 4.

22. George Blaisdell, "Adolf [*sic*] Zukor Talks of Famous Players," *Moving Picture World* 15.2 (January 11, 1913): 136.

23. A photograph of the studio's ruins appears in Richard Koszarski, *An Evening's Entertainment: The Age of the Silent Feature Picture, 1915–1928* (Berkeley: University of California Press, 1990), 19.

24. Quoted in Neal Gabler, *An Empire of Their Own: How the Jews Invented Hollywood* (New York: Doubleday, 1989), 29.

25. The information about the composition of the photoplay courses comes primarily from promotional articles, which at least give a sense of Columbia's *intended* public. See Frances Taylor Patterson, "A New Art in an Old University," *Photoplay Magazine* (January 1920): 65; Elizabeth Clark, "The Rebel Cry," December 24, 1930 (clippings files, Billy Rose Theatre Collection, Lincoln Center Branch, New York Public Library); Mary Kelly, "Columbia's Cinema Class," *New York Times* (December 7, 1930). The one quantitative figure that exists is that 22 students were enrolled in photoplay composition courses through the Home Study (i.e., correspondence) division between 1925–1932; see George Baxter Smith, *Purpose and Conditions Affecting the Nature and Extent of Participation of Adults in Courses in the Home Study Department of Columbia University, 1925–1932* (New York: Teachers College, Columbia University, 1935), 83.

26. Gerald Graff, *Professing Literature* (Chicago: University of Chicago Press, 1987); Lawrence J. Oliver, *Brander Matthews, Theodore Roosevelt, and the Politics of American Literature, 1880–1920* (Knoxville, Tenn.: University of Tennessee Press, 1992); Kermit Vanderbilt, *American Literature and the Academy: The Roots, Growth, and Maturity of a Profession* (Philadelphia: University of Pennsylvania Press, 1986), 133–34; John Angus Burrell, *A History of Adult Education at Columbia University* (New York: Columbia University Press, 1954), 54.

27. Carol S. Gruber, *Mars and Minerva: World War I and the Uses of Higher Learning in America* (Baton Rouge: Louisiana State University Press, 1975), 18. For a concise account of the influence of German universities on the teaching of English literature, see Gerald Graff and Michael Warner, introduction, in Graff and Warner, eds., *The Origins of Literary Studies in America* (New York: Routledge, 1989), 14. For more detailed considerations of the German influence, see Laurence R. Veysey, *The Emergence of the American University* (Chicago: University of Chicago Press, 1965); Roger L. Geiger, *To Advance Knowledge: The Growth of American Research Universities, 1900–1940* (New York: Oxford University Press, 1986); and Gruber, *Mars and Minerva*. For a detailed though confusing history of the transformations in adult education, see George M. Woytanowitz, *University Extension: The Early Years in the United States, 1885–1915* (Iowa City: National University Extension Association/American College Testing Program, 1974).

28. The literature on "the Wisconsin idea" is vast. Two texts which discuss it in terms directly applicable here are Richard Hofstadter, "The Rise of the Expert," *Anti-Intellectualism in American Life* (New York: Knopf, 1963), and Gruber, *Mars and Minerva*, 29–31.

29. Thomas Bender, *New York Intellect* (Baltimore: Johns Hopkins University Press, 1987), 283–84.

30. Thorstein Veblen, *The Higher Learning in America* (1918; New York: Augustus M. Kelly, 1965), 23.

31. A summary of these changes can be found in Daniel Bell, *The Reforming of General Education* (New York: Columbia University Press, 1966). Like most discussions of Columbia during this period, much of Bell's information comes from Lionel Trilling, "The Van Amringe and Keppel Eras," and Justus Buchler, "Reconstruction in the Liberal Arts," both in *A History of Columbia College on Morningside* (New York: Columbia University Press, 1954).

32. Albert Shiels, "The School and the Picture Theater," *Motography* 12.1 (July 4, 1914); W. H. Dudley, "Report of the Committee on Visual Instruction," Third Annual Conference, National University Extension Association, Pittsburgh (1917).

33. Don Carlos Ellis and Laura Thornborough, *Motion Pictures in Education: A Practical Handbook for Users of Visual Aids* (New York: Crowell, 1923), 21.

34. On the use of films in secondary schools, see Stuart Alan Selby, *The Study of Film as an Art Form in American Secondary Schools* (1963; New York: Arno Press, 1978), and William Lewin, *Photoplay Appreciation in American High Schools* (New York: Appleton-Century, 1934). On films in adult education: T[homas]. R[itchie]. Adam, *Motion Pictures in Adult Education* (New York: American Association for Adult Education, 1940), and William Uricchio and Roberta E. Pearson, *Reframing Culture: The Case of the Vitagraph Quality Films* (Princeton: Princeton University Press, 1993), ch. 1. No secondary works directly address the production and exhibition of films by museums and universities during the silent era, but a survey of the *Readers Guide to Periodicals* turns up many examples. See, for example, "Yale's Historical Motion Pictures," *School and Society* 18.460 (October 20, 1923): 464; "Motion Pictures and Museums," *Outlook* 114 (October 25, 1916): 407–408; and Elliott Huger, "The Museum and the Motion Picture," *National Board of Review Magazine* 2.3 (March 1927): 9. Also see Ellis and Thornborough, *Motion Pictures in Education*, and the journals *Educational Screen* and the *Journal of Adult Education*.

35. J. Voorheis, "Columbia Movies," *Motion Picture Magazine* (August 1915): 93–94; Koszarski, *An Evening's Entertainment*, 95–97.

36. The Carmen Committee report of 1946, quoted in Bell, *The Reforming of General Education*, 13.

37. Bender, *New York Intellect*, 286–89.

38. The best source of information on Columbia's adult education programs are the annual reports of the directors in the Columbiana Library and articles in *Columbia University Quarterly*, esp. 23.4 (December 1931) and 24.1 (March 1932). For a general account see Burrell, *A History of Adult Education*.

39. Koszarski, *An Evening's Entertainment*, 97.

40. "Motion Picture Production," University Extension brochure (1923), and letter Nicholas Murray Butler to Will H. Hays (December 29, 1926),

Columbiana Library, Columbia University; Burrell, *A History of Adult Education*.

41. Russell Potter, "The Institute of Arts and Sciences," *Columbia University Quarterly* 23.4 (December 1931): 469. For more on the declining acceptance of Jewish students at Columbia, see Bender, *New York Intellect*, 286–93.

42. Uricchio and Pearson. *Reframing Culture*, 34.

43. Buchler, "Reconstruction in the Liberal Arts," 50–51. Buchler suggests that the emphasis on cultivating reading skills resulted from the influence of John Dewey's pragmatism.

44. Egbert, quoted in Burrell, *A History of Adult Education*, 30.

45. "Motion Picture Production"

46. Patterson, "A New Art," 65.

47. Patterson, *Cinema Craftsmanship*, v, "A New Art," 65, and *Scenario and Screen* (New York: Harcourt, Brace, 1928); Clark, "The Rebel Cry"; Kelly, "Columbia's Cinema Class." It is interesting to note that for all of Patterson's descriptions of herself as a reformer of the disenfranchised, her one screen credit was for an adaptation of a popular Yiddish play, *Broken Hearts* (1926). Unfortunately, Patterson never discussed this experience. See J. Hoberman, *Bridge of Light: Yiddish Film Between Two Worlds* (Philadelphia: Temple University Press, 1991), 108.

48. *Columbia University Extension Catalogue, 1916–1917*, Columbiana Library, Columbia University.

49. Freeburg, *The Art of Photoplay Making*, 7–8.

50. William Morgan Hannon, *The Photodrama: It's Place Among "the Fine Arts"* (New Orleans: Ruskin Press, 1915), 43–45.

51. Joan Shelly Rubin, *The Making of Middlebrow Culture* (Chapel Hill: University of North Carolina Press, 1992), 168, 169. See also Buchler, "Reconstruction in the Liberal Arts," 52–53.

52. Trilling, "The Van Amringe and Keppel Eras," 44.

53. Rubin notes that Erskine's xenophobic comments informed his "Great Books" philosophy:

> Erskine's assertion that immigrants ought to become familiar with "great books" barely concealed his dismay that they and their children comprised a rapidly increasing percentage of undergraduates in the postwar period. He had written to his mother in 1918, "When I see these boys [at Beaune] and realize that of the students at Columbia, many are those selfish immigrants who don't want to do anything for America, I feel as though I should stay here and work for the soldiers." In subsequently urging that "we [not] refuse to assume responsibility for the making of the foreign elements in the United States into a unified nation," lest we suffer the "ignorance, the disease and the discontent which in various ways menace our society," Erskine spoke as a Weehawken Episcopalian trying to keep Union Hill workers within bounds. Thus, he made tradition serve order in one final respect: more urgently and explicitly than Woodberry, but along the lines he laid out, Erskine employed it to dispel the

threat of class conflict and social disarray. "Great books" can be considered a type of "Americanization" program, with all the antidemocratic characteristics associated with the term: the reassertion of white Anglo-Saxon Protestant superiority, the fear that foreigners (and, in the Columbia case particularly Jews) would undermine that superiority, and the insistence that immigrants become acculturated to an existing white middle-class mold. (Rubin, *The Making of Middlebrow Culture*, 176–77; all brackets in Rubin's text)

W. B. Carnochan identifies indirect connections between the Great Books programs and openly nativist, paternalistic, racist, and sexist theories of education including Woodberry's long history of racist writings and Erskine's essentializing analysis of gender differences that span his career; see *The Battleground of the Curriculum* (Stanford: Stanford University Press, 1993), 82–85.

54. John Erskine, foreword to William C. de Mille, *Hollywood Saga* (New York: Dutton, 1939); Rubin, *The Making of Middlebrow Culture*, 184–85; Mortimer Adler, *Philosopher at Large* (New York: Macmillan, 1977), 192–94, and *Art and Prudence: A Study in Practical Philosophy* (New York: Longmans, Green, 1937).

55. Most of the articles about the course simply reiterate the press release. For a sampling of responses that veer slightly from the prepared text, see Irene Thirer, "Columbia University to Offer Film Study Unit," *New York Post*, June 22, 1937; "Film Study at Columbia University," *School and Society* (July 117, 1937); V. K. Richards, "The Drama Desk: Is it Art?" *Toledo Ohio Blade*, September 15, 1937; "The Art of Motion Pictures," *Journal of Adult Education* (October 1937): 474; and "Cinema: Fine Arts Em1-Em2," *Time* 30.15 (October 11, 1937): 36.

56. Russell Potter, "Division of Film Study: Report of the Director for the Academic Year Ending June 30, 1938," 251–52, Columbiana Library, Columbia University.

57. "Motion Picture Parade" brochures are collected in both the Columbiana Library, Columbia Univeristy, as well as the Department of Film Collection, Museum of Modern Art Film Study Center, New York.

58. Iris Barry, lecture delivered March 29, 1938, Department of Film Collection, Museum of Modern Art Study Center, revised and published as "History in the Movies," *National Board of Review* (April 1941): 4–7.

59. Potter, "Division of Film Study," 251.

60. "Cinema: Fine Arts Em1-Em2," 36; Potter, "Division of Film Study," 251.

3. MANDARINS AND MARXISTS: HARVARD AND THE RISE OF FILM EXPERTS

1. This proposed Harvard Film Library has no relation to the current Harvard Film Archive. Two years after the drafting of the Harvard Film Library Agreement, Harvard began to collect educational films when it started the University Film Foundation (later the University Film Service). In 1936

Harvard donated that collection to the Museum of Modern Art Film Library. The Harvard Film Archive that exists today began in 1979 and combined the university's various collections of film; it later acquired the important Cinema 16 Film Society collection from Grove Press.

2. A public announcement and a publicity article in the *Boston Transcript* meticulously reconstruct this concatenation. Both are reprinted in Joseph P. Kennedy, ed., *The Story of the Film* (Chicago: A. W. Shaw, 1927). This was not the first collaboration between the Fogg and the Business School. A course on the "History of the Printed Book" set a precedent in 1910. See George H. Chase, "The Fine Arts, 1874–1929," in Samuel Eliot Morrison, ed., *The Development of Harvard University Since the Inauguration of President Eliot, 1869–1929* (Cambridge: Harvard University Press, 1930), 136.

3. Kennedy, ed., *The Story of the Film*, 27.

4. On the Harvard course see Kennedy, *The Story of the Film*, which describes the course in an introduction and reprints the lectures delivered to the class. On this period in the history of the Harvard Business School, see William Leach, *Land of Desire: Merchants, Power, and the Rise of a New American Culture* (New York: Vintage, 1993), 285–92. On Kennedy's career in the film industry, see Donald Crafton, *The Talkies: American Cinema's Transition to Sound, 1926–1931* (New York: Scribner's, 1997), 136–42; David E. Koskoff, *Joseph P. Kennedy: A Life and Times* (Englewood Cliffs, N.J.: Prentice-Hall, 1974), 27–41; Janet Wasko, *Movies and Money: Financing the Film Industry* (Norwood, N.J.: Ablex, 1982), 77–97; and Giuliana Muscio, *Hollywood's New Deal* (Philadelphia: Temple University Press, 1996), 58–59.

5. Leach, *Land of Desire*, 287.

6. Kennedy, *The Story of the Film*, 23.

7. Ibid., 5–6. The global expansion of Hollywood in the 1920s is discussed in chapter 4.

8. Statement of June 20, 1927, quoted in Robert Osborne, *65 Years of the Oscar* (New York: Abbeville Press, 1994), 9.

9. On the labor movement in Hollywood and the professionalization of movie-making, see Murray Ross, *Stars and Strikes: Unionization of Hollywood* (New York: Columbia University Press, 1941);Tino Balio, "A Mature Oligopoly, 1930–1948," in Tino Balio, ed., *The American Film Industry*, rev. ed. (Madison: University of Wisconsin, 1985), 271–79; Danae Clark, *Negotiating Hollywood: The Cultural Politics of Actors' Labor* (Minneapolis: University of Minnesota, 1995), esp. ch. 3; and Muscio, *Hollywood's New Deal*, ch. 4. Robert Sklar emphasizes Hays's role in managing labor in *Movie-Made America: A Cultural History of the American Movies*, rev. ed. (New York: Vintage, 1994), 83–85. Steven J. Ross chronicles earlier unionization in *Working-Class Hollywood: Silent Film and the Shaping of Class in America* (Princeton: Princeton University Press, 1998), 130–34.

10. For a concise history of the Academy of Motion Pictures Arts and Sciences, see Richard Shale, introduction, *Academy Awards*, 2d ed. (New York: Ungar, 1982), 5–25; on the Academy's educational projects, see Pierre Normand

Sands, A *History of the Academy of Motion Pictures Arts and Sciences,* *1927–1947* (New York Arno Press, 1973), ch. 4. On USC's courses, see "A College Course in the Photoplay," *School and Society* 29 (February 16, 1929): 219. The lectures from USC's first course are reprinted in *Introduction to the Photoplay* (Los Angeles: University of Southern California Press and the Academy of Motion Picture Arts and Sciences, 1929). USC incorporated classes on the business of the film industry in 1938; see "U.S.C.'s Film Business Course Is Away to Brilliant Beginnings," *American Cinematographer* (May 1938): 203.

11. Sands, A *History*, 105–107.

12. Kennedy, *The Story of the Film*, 360–61.

13. Ibid., 360.

14. Ibid., 359.

15. Ibid., 361

16. Ibid.

17. Ibid., 359.

18. The Academy first employed a full-time librarian in 1936. It began to subsidize screenings of MoMA's circulating film programs in 1940 and that began a long-standing collaboration with MoMA. See collection V-239, box 12, "Museum of Modern Art: Film Classics Proposal," Margaret Herrick Library, Academy of Motion Pictures Arts and Sciences, Los Angles; also see Sands, A *History*, 57–59, 115.

19. Other important early art history programs include those at Bryn Mawr, Princeton, Vassar, and Yale. See the essays in Craig Hugh Smyth and Peter M. Lukehart, eds., *Early Years of Art History in the United States: Notes and Essays on Departments, Teaching, and Scholars* (Princeton: Department of Art and Archaeology, Princeton University, 1993).

20. Paul DiMaggio, "Cultural Entrepreneurship in Nineteenth-Century Boston: The Creating of an Organizational Base for High Culture in America," *Media, Culture, Society* 4 (1982): 33–50, and "Cultural Entrepreneurship in Nineteenth-Century Boston, Part II: The Classification and Framing of American Art," *Media, Culture, Society* 4 (1982): 303–322; Neil Harris, "The Gilded Age Revisited: Boston and the Museum Movement," *American Quarterly* 14.4 (Winter 1962): 545–66; and Ronald Story, *Harvard and the Boston Upper Class: The Forging of an Aristocracy, 1800–1870* (Middletown, Conn.: Wesleyan University Press, 1980). Alan Wallach discusses the impact of Boston Brahmin culture on the rise of American art museums after the Civil War in *Exhibiting Contradictions: Essays on the Museum in the United States* (Amherst: University of Massachusetts Press, 1998), ch. 1. An organizational base is, of course, only one factor in the emergence of class distinctions. Chandra Mukerji and Michael Schudson position DiMagio's intervention in relation to other methodologies that analyze the high/popular culture divide as it influences class in the introduction to their volume, *Rethinking Popular Culture: Contemporary Perspectives in Cultural Studies* (Berkeley: University of California, 1991), 1–54.

21. Thomas Crow, *The Intelligence of Art* (Chapel Hill: University of North Carolina, 1999), 9.

22. Erwin Panofsky, "Art History in the United States," *Meaning in the Visual Arts* (Garden City, N.Y.: Doubleday/Anchor, 1955), 324; Priscilla Hiss and Roberta Fansler, *Research in Fine Arts in the Colleges and Universities of the United States* (New York: Carnegie Corporation, 1934), 23; Van Wyck Brooks, *An Autobiography* (New York: Dutton, 1965), 110.

23. Norton, quoted in James Turner, *The Liberal Education of Charles Eliot Norton* (Baltimore: Johns Hopkins University Press, 1999), 202–203. Norton had a fascinating career that seemed to touch every aspect of American Victorian life. On Norton's contribution to art history at Harvard, see Chase, "The Fine Arts, 1874–1929." On Norton's general biography, see T. J. Jackson Lears, *No Place of Grace: Antimodernism and the Transformation of American Culture, 1880–1920* (New York: Pantheon, 1981), 243–47; Kermit Vanderbilt, *Charles Eliot Norton: Apostle of Culture in a Democracy* (Cambridge: Belknap Press, 1959); Turner, *Liberal Education*; and Richard Poirier's iconoclastic review essay, "Humanism and Mediocrity: The Vapor Trail of Charles Eliot Norton," *New Republic* (May 8, 2000): 25–33.

24. On Norton's place in the generalist tradition that linked Thomas Carlyle, John Ruskin, and Matthew Arnold to the American "Great Books" tradition, see Gerald Graff, *Professing Literature* (Chicago: University of Chicago Press, 1987), 82–84.

25. According to Sybil Gordon Kantor's thorough history of Harvard's Department of Fine Arts, Barr only attended sporadically because he had already stopped taking classes. Other attendees included Henry-Russell Hitchcock and Jere Abbott. The following year's course included John Walker and Agnes Mongan, and in 1930–31 Beaumont Newhall was enrolled. See Kantor, "The Beginnings of Art History at Harvard and the 'Fogg Method' " in Smyth and Lukehart, eds., *Early Years of Art History*, 173.

26. E. H. Gombrich, *Aby Warburg* (Chicago: University of Chicago Press, 1986); Nicholas Fox Weber, *Patron Saints: Five Rebels Who Opened America to a New Art, 1928–1943* (1992; New Haven: Yale University Press, 1995), 19–27, passim.

27. Forbes, quoted in Caroline A. Jones, *Modern Art at Harvard* (New York: Abbeville Press, 1985), 25.

28. Agnes Mongan, "Harvard and the Fogg," in Smyth and Lukehart, eds., *Early Years of Art History*, 47–50. Other descriptions of Sachs's course can be found in Karen Cushman, "Museum Studies: The Beginnings, 1900–1926," *Museum Studies Journal* 1.3 (Spring 1984): 8–18; Alice Goldfarb Marquis, *Alfred H. Barr, Jr.: Missionary for the Modern* (Chicago: Contemporary Books, 1989), 37–39; Weber, *Patron Saints*, 24–27; and Lincoln Kirstein, *Mosaic: Memoirs* (New York: Farrar, Straus, and Giroux, 1994), 162–72.

29. Quoted in Marquis, *Alfred H. Barr, Jr.*, 38.

30. Charles G. Loring, "A Trend in Museum Design," *Architectural Forum* 47 (December 1927): 579, quoted in Carol Duncan, *Civilizing Rituals* (New York: Routledge, 1995), 56.

31. See Weber, , *Patron Saints*, ch. 1.

32. Harry Alan Potamkin noted that it is "strange to say a good deal of our movie commentary has since issued from the academic precincts of Harvard University" and listed writings on film by Hugo Münsterberg, Harold Stearns, Kenneth MacGowan, Alfred Kuttner, Gilbert Seldes. See Potamkin, "New York Notes: V," *Close-Up* (October 1930).

33. Kennedy, *The Story of the Film*, 360.

34. Ibid., 354.

35. Ibid., xv.

36. John Cotton Dana, "A School for Museum Workers," *School and Society* (May 16, 1925): 591, quoted in Cushman, "Museum Studies," 14 (emphasis added).

37. John Cotton Dana and Holger Cahill, "The Machine Industry's Need for Art," *Forbes* (August 15, 1929): 30, 32, 34; John Cotton Dana, "The Use of Museums," *The Nation* 115.2988 (October 11, 1922): 374–76.

38. Rémy Saisselin, *The Bourgeois and the Bibelot* (New Brunswick: Rutgers University Press, 1984), 68. For an empirical study of gender and collecting, see Russell W. Belk and Melanie Wallendorf, "Of Mice and Men: Gender and Identity in Collecting," in Susan M. Pearce, ed., *Interpreting Objects and Collections* (New York: Routledge, 1994), 240–53.

39. Sachs, quoted in Edward P. Alexander, "Paul Joseph Sachs Teaches a Pioneering Course in Museum Studies," *The Museum in America: Innovators and Pioneers* (Walnut Creek, Calif.: AltaMira Press, 1997), 214.

40. *Machine Art* (catalog) (New York: Museum of Modern Art, 1934). See also Sidney Lawrence, "Clean Machines at the Modern," *Art in America* (February 1984); Terry Smith, *Making the Modern* (Chicago: University of Chicago Press, 1993), 385–404.

41. Hilton Kramer, "Lincoln Kirstein and the 'Aesthetic' Generation," *The New Criterion* 10.4 (December 1991): 4–7.

42. Thomas Bender, *New York Intellect* (Baltimore: Johns Hopkins University Press, 1987), 324–28.

43. Seldes, quoted in Myron Osborn Lounsbury, *The Origins of American Film Criticism, 1909–1939* (1966; New York: Arno Press, 1973), 172.

44. Richard Abel, *French Cinema: The First Wave* (Princeton: Princeton University Press, 1984), 272–73.

45. Jan-Christopher Horak, "Avant-Garde Film," in Tino Balio, ed., *Grand Design* (Berkeley: University of California Press, 1993), 290.

46. Kirstein, *Mosaic*, 162.

47. Oscar Wilde, "The Critic as Artist," *The Portable Oscar Wilde*, rev. ed., ed. Richard Aldington and Stanley Weintraub (New York: Viking, 1981), 130–31.

48. Lincoln Kirstein, "Films: Experimental Films," *Arts Weekly* 1.3 (March 26, 1932): 52 (emphasis added).

49. On the humanism/Marxism debate, see Leonard Greenbaum, *The Hound and Horn: The History of a Literary Quarterly* (The Hague: Mouton, 1966), 77–95, 189–221; Daniel Aaron, *Writers on the Left* (1961; New York: Columbia

University Press, 1992), 231–68; Warren Susman, "The Culture of the Thirties," *Culture as History* (New York: Pantheon, 1984), 150–83; and James Gilbert, *Writers and Partisans: A History of Literary Radicalism in America* (1968; New York: Columbia University Press, 1992), 97–98.

50. Quoted in Aaron, *Writers on the Left*, 237.

51. Lincoln Kirstein, "Films: *The Road to Life*," *Arts Weekly* 1.1 (March 11, 1932): 14, and "Films: The News Reel," *Arts Weekly* 1.2 (March 18, 1932): 35. Interestingly, *Road to Life* was a film criticized at the time of its release for its "sentimentalism"; see Jay Leyda, *Kino: A History of the Russian and Soviet Film*, 3d ed. (Princeton: Princeton University Press, 1983), 284.

52. Lincoln Kirstein, "Films: *Que Viva Méjico*," *Arts Weekly* (April 10, 1932): 176 (emphasis added). Kirstein's attempt to purchase the film is mentioned in H. A. Bull, "Twelfth Street Razz," *Town and Country* (October 1, 1933). On T. S. Eliot and humanism in the thirties, see Aaron, *Writers on the Left*, 337, 239, 247–50, and Susman, *Culture as History*, 176.

53. For example, see Alfred Barr, "Sergei Michailovitch Eisenstein," *The Arts* 14.6 (December 1928): 316–21, and Jere Abbott, "Eisenstein's New Work," *Hound and Horn* (January-March 1929): 159–62. *Hound and Horn* even published Eisenstein's own important speech, "The Dynamic Square," *Hound and Horn* (April-June 1931): 406–410.

54. Granville Hicks, "Inheritance Tax," *New Republic* (April 20, 1932): 278–79. The debate took place in a series of letters to the editor in the May 25, 1932, and July 14, 1932, issues of the *New Republic*. See also Granville Hicks, *The Great Tradition* (New York: Macmillan, 1933), 283–87, and Greenbaum, *The Hound and Horn*, 198–205. For an example of Kirstein's ambivalent feelings on the politics of ballet, see his "Revolutionary Ballet Forms," *New Theatre and Film* (October 1934), reprinted in Herbert Kline, ed., *New Theater and Film, 1934 to 1937: An Anthology* (New York: Harcourt Brace Jovanovich, 1985), 212–19.

55. These essays are collected in *Hound and Horn: Essays on Cinema* (New York: Arno Press/New York Times, 1972).

56. Kirstein, "Films: Experimental Films," 52.

57. Julien Levy, *Memoir of an Art Gallery* (New York: Putnam's, 1977), 151.

58. Abel, *French Cinema*, 480.

59. Levy, *Memoir of an Art Gallery*, 148.

60. For a list of programs, see Ingrid Schaffner and Lisa Jacobs, eds., *Julien Levy: Portrait of an Art Gallery* (Cambridge: MIT Press, 1998), 34–39.

61. Levy, *Memoir of an Art Gallery*, 153.

62. Ibid., 152

63. Ibid., 154–55.

64. Aaron, *Writers on the Left*, 219–20, 243–47. For a biographical sketch of Potamkin, see Lewis Jacobs, preface, Harry Alan Potamkin, *The Compound Cinema*, ed. Lewis Jacobs (New York: Teachers College Press, 1977), xxv–xlii.

65. The term "radical modernists" belongs to Alan M. Wald, *The New York Intellectuals: The Rise and Decline of the Anti-Stalinist Left from the 1930s to the 1980s* (Chapel Hill: University of North Carolina Press, 1987), ch. 3.

66. Quoted in Jacobs, introduction to Potamkin, *The Compound Cinema*, xxv.

67. Lincoln Kirstein, "In Memory of Harry Alan Potamkin, 1900–1933," *Hound and Horn* (October-December 1933): 3–4; Greenbaum, *The Hound and Horn*, 208–209.

68. Potamkin, *The Compound Cinema*, 220.

69. See Bertolt Brecht, "Emphasis on Sport," in John Willett, ed. and trans., *Brecht on Theatre* (New York: Methuen, 1964), 6–9.

70. Potamkin, *The Compound Cinema*, 216.

71. On Potamkin and "little cinemas," see Peter Decherney, "Cult of Attention: An Introduction to Seymour Stern and Harry Alan Potamkin (Contra Kracauer) on the Ideal Movie Theater," *The Spectator* 18.2 (Spring/Summer 1998): 18–25.

72. Potamkin, *The Compound Cinema*, 219. Subsequent references are cited in the text.

73. Kennedy, *The Story of the Film*, vi.

74. See Brecht, "Emphasis on Sport," 37.

75. Walter Benjamin, "The Work of Art in the Age of Mechanical Reproduction," *Illuminations*, ed. Hannah Arendt, trans. Harry Zohn (New York: Schocken, 1968), 231.

76. Benjamin, "The Work of Art," 244n6.

77. Walter Benjamin, "Eduard Fuchs: Historian and Collector," in Andrew Arato and Eike Gerhardt, eds., *The Essential Frankfurt School Reader* (New York: Urizen, 1978), 233, 234.

78. Benjamin, "Eduard Fuchs," 227.

79. Walter Benjamin, *The Arcades Project*, trans. Howard Eiland and Kevin McLaughlin (Cambridge: Harvard University Press, 1999), 204, 209.

80. See "Cinema Italia" and the other essays collected under the heading "National Traits" in Potamkin, *The Compound Cinema*.

81. William Troy, "An Academy of the Film," *The Nation* (November 22, 1933): 605–606; Russell Campbell, *Cinema Strikes Back: Radical Filmmaking in the United States, 1930–1942* (Ann Arbor: UMI Research Press, 1982), 56–57; William Alexander, *Film on the Left: American Documentary Film from 1931 to 1942* (Princeton: Princeton University Press, 1981).

4. IRIS BARRY, HOLLYWOOD IMPERIALISM, AND THE GENDER OF THE NATION

1. Following Barry's example, the position of librarian became a stepping-stone for curators of future departments. Beaumont Newhall, soon to be the first curator of photography at MoMA, succeeded Barry as librarian.

2. Pound initiated the relationship between himself and Barry after reading a few of her poems in *Poetry and Drama* 8 (December 1914). Following a pattern of mentorship that Pound repeated with other poets, he suggested books for Barry to read, critiqued her writing, and eventually encouraged her to move to London to be near him. Pound secured a flat and a series of jobs for Barry, and he helped her to publish in prominent journals. Barry and Pound

continued a correspondence at least until 1939, and at least once Pound visited Barry at the Museum of Modern Art. Barry had two children with Wyndham Lewis, and she posed for several drawings and paintings of Lewis's including the important *Praxitella*. In 1925 Barry married another member of Lewis's circle, the poet Alan Porter. Many of Pound's letters to Barry are included in Ezra Pound, *The Letters of Ezra Pound, 1907–1941*, ed. D. D. Paige (New York: Harcourt Brace, 1950) . For more information on this period in Barry's life, see Mary Barnard, *Assault on Mount Helicon: A Literary Memoir* (Berkeley: University of California Press, 1984); J. J. Wilhelm, *Ezra Pound in London and Paris, 1908–1925* (University Park: Pennsylvania State University Press, 1990); and Jeffrey Meyers, *The Enemy: A Biography of Wyndham Lewis* (London: Routledge and Kegan Paul, 1980), 92–100.

3. Ivor Montagu mentions that before Barry became a film critic, she made extra money by reporting on trade shows for the film exhibitor Sidney Bernstein, who Barry later brought into the London Film Society. See Ivor Montagu, "Birmingham Sparrow: In Memoriam, Iris Barry, 1896 [*sic*]–1969," *Sight and Sound* (Spring 1970): 106–107.

4. Iris Barry, "American Prestige and British Films," *The Spectator* (July 11, 1925): 51. Barry's notes for an autobiography are collected in the Iris Barry Collection, Film Study Center, Museum of Modern Art, New York (hereafter IBC). For a series of impressionistic portraits of Barry, see Margareta Akermark, ed., *Remembering Iris Barry* (New York: Museum of Modern Art, 1980).

5. Iris Barry, "Progress Is Being Made," *The Spectator* (February 11, 1925): 235 (emphasis added).

6. Tom Ryall, *Alfred Hitchcock and the British Cinema* (London: Croom Helm, 1986), 35.

7. Jules and Edmond Goncourt's *Journal* from the time of the Paris Universal Exhibition of 1867 used the term americanization (l'américanisation), and it was later popularized by Charles Baudelaire. An important early British use is W. T. Stead's *The Americanisation of the World, or the Trend of the Twentieth Century* (London: H. Markley, 1902). For an introduction to recent theories of cultural imperialism, see John Tomlinson, *Cultural Imperialism* (Baltimore: Johns Hopkins University Press, 1991). For a discussion of cultural imperialism and film, see Toby Miller, Nitin Govil, John McMurria, and Richard Mazwell, *Global Hollywood* (London: British Film Institute, 2001).

8. See Dick Hebdige, "Towards a Cartography of Taste, 1935–1962," *Hiding in the Light: On Images and Things* (New York: Routledge, 1988), 45–76, and *Subculture: The Meaning of Style* (London: Methuen, 1979). British theories of Americanization as a response to mass culture are surveyed in Dominic Strinati, *An Introduction to Theories of Mass Culture* (New York: Routledge, 1995), 21–38.

9. The development of a British national cinema has been examined in great detail and from many different perspectives. See Rachel Low, *The History of the British Film, 1918–1929* (London: Allen and Unwin, 1971); Andrew Higson, *Waving the Flag: Constructing a National Cinema in Britain* (Oxford: Clarendon, 1995); Margaret Dickinson and Sarah Street, *Cinema*

and State: The Film Industry and the Government, 1927–1984 (London: British Film Institute, 1985); Sarah Street, British National Cinema (New York: Routledge, 1997); Ryall, Alfred Hitchcock; Charles Barr, ed., All Our Yesterdays (London, BFI, 1986); Simon Hartog, "State Protection of a Beleaguered Industry," in James Curran and Vincent Porter, eds., British Cinema History (Totowa, N.J.: Barnes and Noble, 1983): 59–73; and Andrew Higson and Richard Maltby, eds., "Film Europe" and "Film America": Cinema, Commerce, and Cultural Exchange, 1920–1939 (Devon, Eng.: Exeter University Press, 1999).

10. Iris Barry, Let's Go to the Movies (New York: Payson and Clarke, 1926), 58. Let's Go was published simultaneously and with identical pagination in Britain as Let's Go to the Pictures (London: Chatto and Windus, 1926).

11. Iris Barry, "Hollywood Is Not America," The Sunday Review (March 11, 1934): 8.

12. Iris Barry, "A National or International Cinema?" The Bioscope (January 28, 1924): 29. Vachel Lindsay's The Art of the Moving Picture was reprinted in Britain in 1922. Rachel Low identifies this reprinting as a major event on the development of British film theory, and it certainly influenced Barry. Lindsay's book is one of the few works in the bibliography of Barry's 1925 Let's Go to the Movies, and in that book and other places Barry adopted Lindsay's unique terminology. For example, she dubs Cecil B. DeMille the king of the "film of splendor" (Let's Go, 70).

13. See for example Alfred Barr, "Notes on the Film," Hound and Horn (January–March 1934): 278–83; and Siegfried Kracauer, From Caligari to Hitler: A Psychological History of the German Film (Princeton: Princeton University Press, 1947).

14. Barry, "A National or International Cinema?" 29.

15. Barry, Let's Go, 239.

16. Hays, quoted in Toby Miller, "Hollywood and the World," in John Hill and Pamela Church Gibson, eds., The Oxford Guide to Film Studies (Oxford: Oxford University Press, 1998), 373. Miller also offers a concise summary of the role of film in American cultural and economic imperialism. See also Victoria de Grazia, "Mass Culture and Sovereignty: The American Challenge to European Cinemas, 1920–1960," Journal of Modern History 61.1 (1989): 53–87; Thomas J. Saunders, Hollywood in Berlin: American Cinema and Weimar Germany (Berkeley: University of California Press, 1994); and for a summary of the British situation, see Ryall, Alfred Hitchcock.

17. Hayes, quoted in Mary Ann Doane, "The Economy of Desire: The Commodity Form in/of the Cinema," in John Belton, ed., Movies and Mass Culture (New Brunswick: Rutgers University Press, 1996), 121.

18. C. A. Lejeune, "Britain Versus America" (March 1935), in Anthony Lejeune, ed., The C. A. Lejeune Film Reader (Manchester: Carcanet, 1991), 56–61.

19. Ryall, Alfred Hitchcock, 42.

20. Iris Barry, "The British Film Situation I: Decline and Fall," The Spectator (January 9, 1926): 43. Also see Barry's comments in "Films for Empire," The Spectator (October 30, 1926): 736.

21. Charles Merz, "When the Movies Go Abroad," *Harper's* (January 1926), rpt. as "American Moving Pictures as Foreign Ambassadors," in W. Brooke Graves, ed., *Readings in Public Opinion: Its Formation and Control* (New York: Appleton, 1928), 370–80.

22. Merz, "When the Movies Go Abroad," 380.

23. Low, *The History of the British Film*, 36; On the Paris conference and its place in the larger "Film Europe" movement, see Higson and Maltby, eds., *"Film Europe" and "Film America."*

24. Barry, "American Prestige and British Films," 51; Iris Barry, "Of British Films," *The Spectator* (November 14, 1925): 870–71.

25. Barry, *Let's Go*, 15.

26. Iris Barry, "Lesser Glories," *The Spectator* (March 6, 1926): 415.

27. Barry, "Of British Films," 51.

28. Iris Barry, "Hotel Imperial " *The Spectator* (January 29, 1927): 148. By 1927 Barry started to catalog the stale narrative devices of American genres; see "Gag-Men of the Film," *Daily Mail*, August 19, 1927, 8; "Film Men Who Are Too Clever," *Daily Mail*, August 29, 1927, 8; "Old Fashioned Film Stories," *Daily Mail*, April 2, 1928, 17.

29. Barry, *Let's Go*, 55: "In *The Thief of Baghdad* there was a lot of insistence on Décor, derived at several removes from Reinhardt through a few German films. For fairness I should like to record here that *The Thief of Baghdad* was composed of one-quarter *Sumurun*, a film made by Lubitsch in Germany; of one-quarter *The Niebelungs*, a film made by Lang in Germany; of one-quarter Fairbanks pure and the rest came out of the property room, palaces and all."

30. Barry, *Let's Go*, 15; Barry, "American Prestige and British Films." These remarks were written in response to Edward S. Van Zile's celebratory book on Hollywood and Americanization: *That Marvel—The Movie: A Glance at Its Reckless Past, Its Promising Present, and Its Significant Future* (New York: Putnam's, 1923).

31. Iris Barry, "Sublimity Versus Vulgarity," *The Spectator* (October 11, 1924): 501–502.

32. Iris Barry, "Why They Go to 'The Pictures' " *Daily Mail*, April 10, 1928, 17.

33. Iris Barry, "Warning Shadows," *The Spectator* (November 15, 1924), 35.

34. Barry, "American Prestige and British Films," 52.

35. Paul Hammond, ed., *The Shadow and Its Shadow: Surrealist Writings on Cinema* (London: BFI, 1976); F. R. Leavis, *Mass Civilization and Minority Culture* (Cambridge: Minority Press, 1930); and Theodor Adorno and Max Horkheimer, *The Dialectic of Enlightenment*, trans John Cumming (1944; New York: Seabury Press, 1972).

36. On the readership of the *Daily Mail*, see Harold Perkins, "The Origins of the Popular Press," *The Structured Crowd* (Totowa, N.J.: Barnes and Noble, 1981), 47–56.

37. Pound to Barry, July 1916, reprinted in *The Letters of Ezra Pound*, 86–87.

38. Joan Shelly Rubin identifies these two institutions as exemplary of interwar

middlebrow culture in *The Making of Middlebrow Culture* (Chapel Hill: University of North Carolina Press, 1992).

39. See Anne Friedberg, "Writing About Cinema: *Close-Up*, 1927–1933" (Ph.D. diss., New York University, 1983); James Donald, Anne Friedberg, and Laura Marcus, eds., *Close-Up, 1927–1933: Cinema and Modernism* (Princeton: Princeton University Press, 1998); Alan Burton, "The Emergence of an Alternative Film Culture: Film and the British Consumer Co-operative Movement Before 1920," *Film History* 8 (1996): 446–57; Don MacPherson, ed., *British Cinema: Traditions of Independence* (London: BFI, 1980); Bert Hogenkamp, *Deadly Parallels: Film and the Left in Britain, 1929–1939* (London: Lawrence and Wishart, 1986); Ivan Butler, *"To Encourage the Art of the Film": The Story of the British Film Institute* (London: Robert Hale, 1971); Street, *British National Cinema*; Ryall, *Alfred Hitchcock*; Low, *The History of the British Film*.

40. On French ciné-clubs see Richard Abel, *French Cinema: The First Wave, 1915–1929* (Princeton: Princeton University Press, 1984). On Soviet workers' clubs see Vance Kepley, Jr., "Cinema and Everyday Life," in Robert Sklar and Charles Musser, eds., *Resisting Images: Essays on Cinema and History* (Philadelphia: Temple University Press, 1990). And on American film clubs, see notes in the discussion of "little cinemas" in the preceding chapter.

41. Adrian Brunel, *Nice Work: The Story of Thirty Years of British Film Production* (London: Forbes Robertson, 1949), 113–14.

42. Ivor Montagu, interview, *Screen* 13.3 (Autumn 1972): 72.

43. Huntly Carter, *The New Spirit in the Cinema* (London: Harold Shaylor, 1930), 277.

44. Nigel West, *Venona: The Greatest Secret of the Cold War* (London: HarperCollins, 1999).

45. Jen Samson, "The Film Society, 1925–1939," in Charles Barr, ed., *All Our Yesterdays*, 310. On Montagu's and the Film Society's politics, see the *Screen* interview with Montagu cited above (n. 3), Montagu's *The Political Censorship of Films* (London: Victor Gollancz, 1929), and his autobiography, *The Youngest Son* (London: Lawrence and Wishart, 1970).

46. See, for example, Barry's review of D. W. Griffith's film *Love and Sacrifice*: "A Film of the American War of Independence," *The Spectator* (September 13, 1924): 354. Barry disagreed with censorship for political reasons, but, surprisingly, she supported and even encouraged the Board of Film Censors when it banned films for reasons of decorum and propriety.

47. Samson, "The Film Society," 306; Barry recorded reflections on the London Film Society in a journal that is now part of the Iris Barry Collection, Film Study Center, Museum of Modern Art, New York (hereafter cited as IBC).

48. The London Film Society's papers are located at the British Film Institute, London.

49. Barry's correspondence is collected in the IBC.

50. Dulac's view is put forward in "Avant-Garde Cinema," trans. Robert

Lamberton, in P. Adams Sitney, ed., *The Avant-Garde Film: A Reader of Theory and Criticism* (New York: Anthology Film Archives, 1987), 43–48.

51. Iris Barry, "Necessity for Good Films," *The Spectator* (October 24, 1925): 692.

52. Iris Barry, "Films Made on a Girder," *Daily Mail*, April 23, 1928, 21, and *Let's Go*, 244, 246.

53. Iris Barry, "New Projects of the Cinema," *The Spectator* 135 (September 5, 1925): 362.

54. Barry, "New Projects," 363 (emphasis added).

55. Iris Barry, "British Films, the Quota, and Reciprocity," *The Spectator* (April 24, 1926): 755–56, and "Films for the Empire," *The Spectator* (October 30, 1926), 736–37; on the influence of the London Film Society and avant-garde film on Hitchcock, see Ryall, *Alfred Hitchcock*.

56. The Commission on Educational and Cultural Films, *The Film in National Life* (London: Allen and Unwin, 1932). The development of the British Film Institute (BFI), the National Film Archive, and related projects are discussed in Butler, *"To Encourage the Art of the Film,"* and Low, *History of the British Film*, 35–36.

57. Barry, *Let's Go*, 69.

58. Barry, "Of British Films," 870–71. She also expected the London Film Society to demonstrate the artistic possibilities of film and interest writers in the medium. The organization advertised H. G. Wells and George Bernard Shaw among its members.

59. Barry, *Let's Go*, 59. See also Andreas Huyssen, "Mass Culture as Woman: Modernism's Other," *After the Great Divide* (Bloomington: Indiana University Press, 1986), 44–62, and Patrice Petro, *Joyless Streets: Women and Melodramatic Representation in Weimar Germany* (Princeton: Princeton University Press, 1989).

60. The list of works on women's social mobility at the turn of the twentieth century is very long and contentious. By citing the movie theater as a space for the instrumentalization of social mobility, I am drawing most directly on Anne Friedberg, *Window Shopping: Cinema and the Postmodern* (Berkeley: University of California Press, 1993).

61. Autobiographical notes in IBC. See also "Iris Barry," *The Silent Picture* 16 (Spring 1970): 16.

62. Barry, "The British Film Situation I," 43.

63. For two accounts of the complex ways women responded to modernist literature and "cultures of travel," see, respectively, Rita Felski, *The Gender of Modernity* (Cambridge: Harvard University Press, 1995), and Interpal Grewal, *Home and Harem: Nation, Gender, Empire, and the Cultures of Travel* (Durham: Duke University Press, 1996).

64. Barry, *Let's Go*, 53.

65. Dorothy Richardson, "Continuous Performance XII—The Cinema of Arcady," *Close-Up* 3.1 (July 1928): 55.

66. Barry, *Let's Go*, 65.

67. Iris Barry, "Back to Simplicity," *The Spectator* (July 17, 1926): 88.

68. Barry's first husband Alan Porter wrote candidly about rebuilding a failing marriage in "Unhappy Marriages," *The Spectator* (November 24, 1928).

69. Barry, *Let's Go*, ix.

70. Virginia Woolf, "The Cinema," *The Captain's Death Bed and Other Essays* (New York: Harcourt, Brace, 1950), 180.

71. See especially Miriam Hansen, *Babel and Babylon* (Cambridge: Harvard University Press, 1991), 124–25, passim; Doane, "The Economy of Desire"; and Petro, *Joyless Streets*, ch. 1. For a more general consideration of women as shoppers, see Rachel Bowlby, *Just Looking: Consumer Culture in Dreiser, Gissing, and Zola* (London: Methuen, 1985), ch. 2, and the review essay by Mary Louise Roberts, "Gender, Consumption, and Commodity Culture," *American Historical Review* (June 1998): 817–44.

72. Barry, *Let's Go*, 63. Barry speculated shortly before her death that "I feel sure that it was the earliest of French Productions of *Les Miserables* which, around 1913, really fixed my taste for movies" (*The Silent Picture*, 16).

73. Barry, "Back to Simplicity," 88; "Cinema Notes," *The Spectator* (August 2, 1924): 158.

74. Fatimah Tobing Rony, *The Third Eye: Race, Cinema, and Ethnographic Spectacle* (Durham: Duke University Press, 1996), 80.

75. Iris Barry, *Portrait of Lady Mary Wortley Montagu* (London: Ernest Benn, 1928).

76. Barry, *Let's Go*, 16.

77. Iris Barry, "On Hailing Columbia" (second draft, n.d.), p. 6 (IBC).

78. Barry, "On Hailing Columbia," 8.

5. THE MUSEUM OF MODERN ART AND THE ROOTS OF THE CULTURAL COLD WAR

1. The complete formulation of his argument is worth quoting: "This book deals for the most part with moving pictures made in America. There was a time when this geographical limitation would be quite serious, and there may be such a time again. At the moment, however, production of moving pictures outside the United States seems to me to be divided into two classes: *First*, the pictures made under the direct control of governments for purposes of propaganda, and *Second*, pictures made for competition with American pictures in the world market." Gilbert Seldes, *The Movies Come from America* (New York: Scribner's, 1937).

2. Many of the significant contributions to this debate are collected in Francis Frascina, ed., *Pollock and After: The Critical Debate*, 2d ed. (New York: Routledge, 2000). See also Frances Stonor Saunders, *The Cultural Cold War: The CIA and the World of Arts and Letters* (New York: New Press, 2000).

3. Alfred H. Barr Jr., *Painting and Sculpture in the Museum of Modern Art, 1929–1967* (New York: MoMA, 1977); Russell Lynes, *Good Old Modern: An Intimate Portrait of the Museum of Modern Art* (New York: Atheneum, 1973); Alice Goldfarb Marquis, *Alfred H. Barr, Jr.: Missionary for the Modern* (Chicago: Contemporary Books, 1989).

4. Alfred Barr, "The 1929 Multidepartmental Plan for the Museum of Modern Art: Its Origins, Development, and Partial Realization" (1941), 11 (Department of Film Collection, Film Study Center, Museum of Modern Art, New York; hereafter, DOF). The Film Study Center's staff generously allowed me access to this collection while they were in the process of cataloging it. As a result I cannot give folder and file numbers for documents.

5. John E. Abbott and Iris Barry, "An Outline of a Project for Founding the Film Library of the Museum of Modern Art" (April 17, 1935), reprinted in *Film History* 7 (1995): 325–35; Iris Barry, "The Film Library and How it Grew," *Film Quarterly* 22.4 (Summer 1969): 21.

6. The Museum of Modern Art Film Library, *Work and Progress* (New York: MoMA, January 1937), n.p.

7. George Creel, *How We Advertised America* (1920; New York: Arno Press, 1972).

8. John C. Stauder and Sheldon Rampton, *Toxic Sludge Is Good for You: Lies, Damn Lies, and the Public Relations Industry* (Monroe, Me.: Common Courage Press, 1995), 22; Stuart Ewen, *PR!: A Social History of Spin* (New York: BasicBooks, 1996), 74–81; Edward Bernays, *Propaganda* (New York: Liveright, 1928). The U.S. Government improved on the Creel Committee during World War II, setting up an elaborate propaganda network as part of the intelligence agencies. After the war, government propaganda was divided between the Central Intelligence Agency, which undertook propaganda secretly, and the discreet yet unconcealed peacetime propaganda agency, the United States Information Agency, which continues to oversee the Voice of America's radio broadcasts and the Fulbright scholarship program, among other projects. Since World War II, however, the government has generally relied on private public relations firms to promote America domestically and abroad.

9. Marquis, *Alfred H. Barr, Jr.*, 79.

10. Alfred Barr, *The Public as Artist* (New York: MoMA, July 1932), n.p.

11. Lynes, *Good Old Modern*, 88–91, 142; Terry Smith, *Making the Modern* (Chicago: University of Chicago Press, 1993), ch. 11.

12. "The two most important twentieth century arts are architecture and the movies. While the Museum's work in painting and sculpture will doubtless be its central activity for many years to come, an extremely important service might be achieved by the organization of a film department. The possibilities of expanding the museum's public, increasing support, interesting new members, is obvious. In no other field is intelligent and influential leadership more needed." Alfred Barr, "Notes on the Departmental Expansion of the Museum" (June 24, 1932), 7 (DOF).

13. Barr, "The 1929 Multidepartmental Plan," 6.

14. Alan R. Blackburn Jr,, "Creating Motion Picture Departments in Museums of Art," *National Board of Review Magazine* 8.8 (June 1933): 7, 8.

15. See Walter Kalaidjian, *American Culture Between the Wars: Revisionary Modernism and Postmodern Critique* (New York: Columbia University Press, 1993).

16. See Lynes, *Good Old Modern*, 71, 98–101; Marquis, *Alfred H. Barr, Jr.*, 94–95.

17. John Abbott, "The Film as a Museum Piece," for the American Association of Museums, n.d. (DOF).

18. MoMA Film Library, *Work and Progress*, 4.

19. Reported in Lynes, *Good Old Modern*, 187.

20. Iris Barry, preface to Lewis Jacobs, *The Rise of the American Film* (New York: Harcourt, Brace, 1939), viii.

21. Iris Barry, "Hollywood Is Not America," *The Sunday Review* (March 11, 1934): 8.

22. Iris Barry, "The Museum of Modern Art: Last Year and This," *The Magazine of Art* 30.1 (January 1937): 41.

23. *Chicago Tribune*, January 8, 1936.

24. *Columbus (Ohio) State Journal*, January 8, 1936.

25. Robert Stebbins, "The Movie: 1902–1917," *New Theater and Film* (March 1936); reprinted in Herbert Kline, ed., *New Theater and Film, 1934–1937: An Anthology* (San Diego: Harcourt Brace Jovanovich, 1985), 234.

26. The Museum of Modern Art Film Library, *Film Library Bulletin* (1938–1939): 3.

27. Frank S. Nugent, "Celluloid Pageant: Camera!," in Clippings Scrapbook, vol. 1, 58–59 (Museum of Modern Art Film Study Center).

28. John Abbott, *Report of the Museum of Modern Art Film Library* (November 6, 1936): 5 (DOF).

29. "The New Deal's First Major Movie Effort Packs a Terrific Punch," *Washington Daily News*, May 11, 1936; "Are There Political War Clouds in U.S. Movie of Dust Clouds?" *Washington News*, May 8, 1936; Robert Snyder, *Pare Lorentz and the Documentary Film* (Norman: University of Okalahoma Press, 1968), 39–43.

30. John Abbott, speech at the Mayflower Hotel, May 10, 1936 (box 2, folder 4, Museum of Modern Art–Library of Congress Papers, Film Study Center, Museum of Modern Art, New York; hereafter, MoMA–LOC).

31. John Abbott and Iris Barry, "Soviet/European Diaries 5–16 to 8–21" (DOF); Abbott, *Report* (November 6, 1936) (DOF); Iris Barry, "Hunting Film in Germany," *American German Review* (June 1937): 40–43.

32. Alfred Barr, "Nationalism in German Films," *Hound and Horn* (January 1934); reprinted in Irving Sandler and Amy Newman, eds., *Defining Modern Art: Selected Writings of Alfred H. Barr, Jr.* (New York: Abrams, 1986), 158–62.

33. Iris Barry, diary entries for June 18 through June 27, 1936 (DOF). On German World War II propaganda, see Nicholas Reeves, *The Power of Film Propaganda* (London: Cassell, 1999).

34. Quoted in Klaus Kreimeier, *The Ufa Story: A History of Germany's Greatest Film Company, 1918–1945*, trans. Robert and Rita Kimber (New York: Hill and Wang, 1996), 191–92.

35. Barry, "Hunting Film," 43.

36. Abbott, *Report* (November 6, 1936), 4 (DOF).

37. Seymour Stern, letter to the editor, *New York Times*, January 13, 1935, sec. 9, p. 4.

38. Seymour Stern, "Film Library Notes Build 'CP Liberators' Myth," *New Leader* (March 23, 1940).

39. Ronald S. Magliozzi, "Witnessing the Development of Independent Film Culture in New York: An Interview with Charles Turner," *Film History* 12 (2000): 84, 94*n*29; Charles "Buckey" Grimm, "A Paper Print Pre-History," *Film History* 11 (1999): 206–207; Chuck Kleinhans, "Theodore Huff: Historian and Filmmaker," in Jan-Christopher Horak, ed., *Lovers of Cinema: The First American Film Avant-Garde, 1919–1945* (Madison: University of Wisconsin Press, 1995).

40. Huff to Pickford, October 8, 1940 (Mary Pickford Collection, box 79.f.6, "Museum of Modern Art," Margaret Herrick Library, Academy of Motion Picture Arts and Sciences, Los Angeles; hereafter, AMPAS). Actually, Huff's film suggestion was probably a good one. *Life with Father* was eventually filmed in 1947 with Irene Dunne and William Powell, and it was a top-grossing film that year.

41. Jim Waverly, letter to the editor, *New Leader* (July 27, 1940).

42. Editorial, *New Leader* (August 17, 1940).

43. Iris Barry, "Film Library, 1935–1941," *Bulletin of the Museum of Modern Art* 8 (June-July 1941): 3–16. On the Johnson and Blackburn incident, see Lynes, *Good Old Modern*, 92–93.

44. "Museum's Pact with Coordinator Pends," *Motion Picture Herald* (June 26, 1943).

45. See Helen van Dongen's memories of working under Buñuel at MoMA in Abé Mark Nornes, "Interview with Helen van Dongen," *Documentary Box* 17 (n.d.), <www.city.yamagata.yamagata.jp/yidff/docbox/docbox-e.html>.

46. Jay Leyda to Alfred Barr, September 5, 1939; Iris Barry to Luis Buñuel, September 13, 1939; Iris Barry to Lothar Wolff (of *March of Time*), November 7, 1939; Luis Bunuel to John Abbott, January, 4, 1941 (all in DOF).

47. Luis Buñuel to Iris Barry, letter of resignation, June 30, 1943 (DOF).

48. Iris Barry and Richard Griffith, *The Films of Fact* (New York: Museum of Modern Art Film Library, 1942), 23.

49. Thomas Doherty, *Projections of War: Hollywood, American Culture, and World War II* (New York: Columbia University Press, 1993), ch. 2. The impetus behind the move to films of fact came partly from Film Library employee Richard Griffith, who came to MoMA after attending the first traveling film program at Haverford College (John Abbott's alma matter) and, after leaving the museum, eventually returned to replace Barry as curator after her retirement in 1951. Griffith's involvement with documentary film ranged from production work for the socialist documentary collectives in New York to editing work on Frank Capra's government-sponsored, wartime *Why We Fight* series.

50. See "The Museum and the War," a special issue of the *Bulletin of the Museum of Modern Art* 10 (October-November 1942); Lynes, *Good Old Modern*, 237.

51. *History of the Office of the Coordinator of Inter-American Affairs: Historical Report on War Administration* (Washington, D.C.: U.S. Government

Printing Office, 1947), ch. 6; Cary Reich, *Worlds to Conquer, 1908–1958* (New York: Doubleday, 1996), 214–22.

52. Iris Barry, "Facts about the Museum of Modern Art Film Library" (May 21, 1947), unpublished (Iris Barry Collection, Film Study Center, Museum of Modern Art, New York; hereafter, IBC).

53. Correspondence and contracts between the Film Library and subcontractors are in box 5, folders C, F, G (MoMA–LOC).

54. War Film Library Collection (AMPAS).

55. Iris Barry, "Challenge of the Documentary Film," *New York Times Magazine*, January 6, 1946, 16.

56. Barry and Griffith, *Films of Fact*, 3.

57. William Buxton, "Rockefeller Support for Projects on the Use of Motion Pictures for Educational and Public Purposes, 1935–1954," *Rockefeller Archive Center for Research Reports Online* 1 (April 2001); *see* www.rockefeller.edu/archive.ctr/racrro1b.html.

58. John Marshall, quoted in Brett Gary, *The Nervous Liberals: Propaganda Anxieties from World War I to the Cold War* (New York: Columbia University Press, 1999), 93.

59. Richard Griffith, *A Report on the Film Library, 1941–1956* (New York: MoMA, fall 1956), 9.

60. *New York Evening Journal*, July 11, 1935; "Museum Acquires 50-Foot Film Kiss," *New York Times*, July 11, 1935; "Film Museum," *Time* (July 1, 1935); "Film Museum Shows '96 Kiss, 1935 Fantasy," *New York Herald Tribune*, July 11, 1935; "Ashcan in Bronx Yields Film of 1896 with a 50-Foot Kiss," *New York World-Telegram*, July 11, 1935.

61. Buxton, "Rockefeller Support for Projects on the Use of Motion Pictures," n.p.

62. Slesinger, quoted in Gary, *Nervous Liberals*, 95.

63. Everett Rogers, *A History of Communication Study: A Biographical Approach* (New York: Free Press, 1994), 220.

64. Paul F. Lazarsfeld and Patricia L. Kendall, *Radio Listening in America: The People Look at Radio—Again* (New York: Prentice-Hall, 1948), 5.

65. Leo A. Handel, *Hollywood Looks at Its Audience: A Report of Film Audience Research* (Urbana: University of Illinois Press, 1950), 46–47.

66. See especially Martin Jay, "The Extraterritorial Life of Siegfried Kracauer," *Permanent Exiles: Essays on the Intellectual Migration from Germany to America* (New York: Columbia University Press, 1986); Mark M. Anderson, "Siegfried Kracauer and Meyer Schapiro: A Friendship," *New German Critique* 54 (Fall 1991): 18–29; David Culbert, "The Rockefeller Foundation, The Museum of Modern Art Film Library, and Siegfried Kracauer, 1941," *Historical Journal of Film, Radio and Television* 13.4 (1993): 495–511; and Gary, *Nervous Liberals*. The information in this paragraph and the next are drawn from these sources.

67. Culbert, "The Rockefeller Foundation," 495; Anderson, "Siegfried Kracauer and Meyer Schapiro," 21–22. Barry mentions her review in the notes she compiled for her autobiography (IBC).

68. Siegfred Kracauer, *From Caligari to Hitler: A Psychological History of the German Film* (Princeton: Princeton University Press, 1947), 297, 285.

69. Jay, "Extraterritorial Life," 170.

70. Kracauer, *From Caligari to Hitler*, v.

71. Kracauer, quoted in Jay, "Extraterritorial Life," 169.

72. Barbra Deming, "The Library of Congress Film Project: Exposition of a Method," *Library of Congress Quarterly Journal of Acquisitions* 2.1 (November 1944): 3–4. Kracauer, in turn, refined his position in *From Caligari to Hitler* in response to Deming's article.

73. Barbara Deming, *Running Away from Myself: A Dream Portrait of America Drawn from the Films of the Forties* (New York: Grossman, 1969).

74. Anthony Slide, *Nitrate Won't Wait: Film Preservation in the United States* (Jefferson, N.C.: McFarland, 1992), 36–37; Tom McGreevey and Joanne L. Yeck, *Our Movie Heritage* (New Brunswick: Rutgers University Press, 1997), ch. 3; Doug Herrick, "Towards a National Film Collection: Motion Pictures at the Library of Congress," *Film Library Quarterly* 13.2–3 (1980): 5–25.

75. Deming, "The Library of Congress Film Project," 3–36; Slide, *Nitrate Won't Wait*, 39.

76. MoMA–LOC, box 3, file H.

77. Iris Barry to Archibald MacLeish, May 20, 1943 (MoMA–LOC, box 3, file H).

78. MoMA–LOC, box 3, file H.

79. Deming, "The Library of Congress Film Project," 9, 10, 17.

80. MoMA–LOC, box 3, file H.

81. John G. Bradley, "A National Film Library—The Problem of Selection," *Journal of the Society of Motion Picture Engineers* 47.1 (July 1946): 63–72; McGreevey and Yeck, *Our Movie Heritage*, 31, 66–74; Slide, *Nitrate Won't Wait*, ch. 6; National Film Preservation Board (*see* www.loc.gov/film).

82. Christopher Phillips, "The Judgment Seat of Photography," *October* 22 (Fall 1982): 27–63; Mary Anne Staniszewski, *The Power of Display: A History of Exhibition Installations at the Museum of Modern Art* (Cambridge: MIT Press, 1998), ch. 4.

83. Alfred Barr, "Is Modern Art Communistic?" and "Artistic Freedom," both in Sandler and Newman, eds., *Defining Modern Art*.

84. Two leading auteur critics, Andrew Sarris and Peter Bogdanovich, wrote program catalogs for the Film Library during this period. Sarris offers his own history of the Film Library in "Dreammerchants, Ultrasnobs, Moviemanes, Filmophiles: MoMA and the Movies," *ARTnews* (October 1979): 109–113.

85. Barry, "Facts About the Museum of Modern Art Film Library" (May 21, 1947) (DOF).

6. THE POLITICS OF PATRONAGE: HOW THE NEA (ACCIDENTALLY) CREATED AMERICAN AVANT-GARDE FILM

1. For an introduction to the institutions of these avant-garde movements, see Richard Abel, *French Cinema: The First Wave, 1915–1929* (Princeton:

Princeton University Press, 1984); Roy Armes, *Third World Filmmaking and the West* (Berkeley: University of California Press, 1987); Manthia Diawara, *African Cinema: Politics and Culture* (Bloomington: Indiana University Press, 1992); Michael Chanan, *The Cuban Image* (London: BFI, 1985); and A. L. Rees, *A History of Experimental Film and Video* (London: BFI, 1999).

2. Peter Bürger, *Theory of the Avant-Garde*, trans. Michael Shaw (Minneapolis: University of Minnesota Press, 1984), and "The Institution of 'Art' as a Category of the Sociology of Literature" *Cultural Critique* 2 (Winter 1985–86): 5–33; Andreas Huyssen, "The Hidden Dialectic: Avant-Garde— Technology—Mass Culture," *After the Great Divide: Modernism, Mass Culture, and Postmodernism* (Bloomington: Indiana University Press, 1986), and "The Search for Tradition: Avant-Garde and Postmodernism in the 1970s," *New German Critique* 22 (Winter 1981): 23–40. See also T. J. Clark and Michael Fried's debate in Francis Frascina, ed., *Pollock and After: The Critical Debate*, 2d ed. (New York: Routledge, 2000).

3. J. Hoberman, "After Avant-Garde Film," in Brian Wallis, ed., *Art After Modernism* (New York: Museum of Contemporary Art, 1984): 59.

4. Tristan Tsara, "Lecture on Dada" (1924), in Herschel Chipp, ed., *Theories of Modern Art* (Berkeley: University of California Press, 1968), 385.

5. See David Craven, *Abstract Expressionism as Cultural Critique: Dissent During the McCarthy Period* (Cambridge: Cambridge University Press, 1999).

6. Frascina, ed., *Pollock and After*; Frances Stonor Saunders, *The Cultural Cold War: The CIA and the World of Arts and Letters* (New York: New Press, 2000), 141.

7. Rockefeller, quoted in Alice Goldfarb Marquis, *Art Lessons: Learning from the Rise and Fall of Public Arts Funding* (New York: Basic Book, 1995), 54.

8. Frost, quoted in Michael Brenson, *Visionaries and Outcasts: The NEA, Congress, and the Place of the Visual Artist in America* (New York: New Press, 2001), 14.

9. See Jane de Hart Mathews, "Art and Politics in Cold War America," and the other essays in Frascina, ed., *Pollock and After*. Andrew Ross's "Containing Culture in the Cold War," *No Respect: Intellectuals and Popular Culture* (New York: Routledge, 1989), offers an illuminating reading of the intellectual roots and underlying tropes of these debates, and Saunders, *The Cultural Cold War*, and Brenson, *Visionaries and Outcasts*, contribute more recent revelations about modern art, the U.S. Congress, and the cold war.

10. Saunders, *The Cultural Cold War*, 258.

11. Joseph Wesley Zeigler, *Artists in Crisis: The Endowment for the Arts Versus America* (Chicago: a capella books, 1994), 21. The collaboration between industry, government, and foundations was part of a larger project of the Ford Foundation to create a system of matching grants; see Toby Miller and George Yúdice, *Cultural Policy* (London: Sage, 2002), 47.

12. Jerome Hill, for example, saved the following clippings: Vincent Canby, "New Filmmakers Get an Assist Under American Institute Plan," *New York*

Times, March 19, 1968, and Anna Kisselgoff, "Filmmakers Win Production Grants for Short Movies," n.d. (Jerome Hill Papers, Department of Film, Museum of Modern Art, New York; hereafter JHP). Williard van Dyke, documentary filmmaker and curator of MoMA's Film Library, sat on the advisory board that selected the AFI's grant recipients.

13. Joyce Piell Wexler, *Who Paid for Modernism? Art, Money, and the Fiction of Conrad, Joyce, and Lawrence* (Fayetteville: University of Arkansas Press, 1997).

14. Lawrence Rainey, *Institutions of Modernism: Literary Elites and Public Culture* (New Haven: Yale University Press, 1998), 42–43.

15. The exception is Jan-Christopher Horak, "The First American Avant-Garde, 1919–1945," in Horak, ed., *Lovers of Cinema: The First American Film Avant-Garde, 1919–1945* (Madison: University of Wisconsin Press, 1995).

16. Stan Brakhage considers *Meshes* to be Hammid's film, down to its "European roots" (Stan Brakhage, *Film at Wit's End* [Kingston, N.Y.: McPherson, 1989], 93). For more on Hammid, see Thomas E. Valasek, "Alexander Hammid: A Survey of His Filmmaking Career," *Film Culture* 67–69 (1979): 250–322.

17. Vève Clark, Millicent Hodson, Catrina Neiman, *The Legend of Maya Deren: A Documentary Biography and Collected Works, Volume 1, Part 2: Chambers (1942–1947)* (New York: Anthology Film Archives/Film Culture, 1988).

18. Cecile Starr, "Hans Richter in the U.S.A.," *Film Culture* 79 (Winter 1996): 17–26; Hans Richter, "A History of the Avantgarde," in Frank Stauffacer, ed., *Art in Cinema* (San Francisco: Art in Cinema Society / San Francisco Museum of Art, 1947; rpt., New York: Arno, 1968); Stephen C. Foster, ed., *Hans Richter: Activism, Modernism, and the Avant-Garde* Cambridge: MIT Press, 1998).

19. Fischinger's fellowships are often attributed to personal connections. He charmed Guggenheim curator Hilda Rebay on a trip to New York in 1938, which resulted in his first fellowship a few years later.

20. Richard Griffith, "A Report on the Film Library, 1941–1956," *Museum of Modern Art Bulletin* 24 (Fall 1956): 12.

21. Richard Griffith, "Three Experimental Films," *New Movies* (March 1946): 22–23, reprinted in *The Legend of Maya Deren*, vol. 1, part 2, 385–86.

22. John Marshall to Maya Deren, July 9, 1945, reprinted in *The Legend of Maya Deren*, vol. 1, part 2, 352.

23. Deren to Marshall, July 14, 1945, reprinted in *The Legend of Maya Deren*, vol. 1, part 2, 352–53.

24. Frederick Wasser, "Four Walling Exhibition: Regional Assistance to the Hollywood Film Industry," *Cinema Journal* 34.2 (Winter 1995): 51–65.

25. Ad in *View* magazine (October 1945), reprinted in *The Legend of Maya Deren*, vol. 1, part 2, 361.

26. Deren to René Renne, January 9, 1946, reprinted in *The Legend of Maya Deren*, vol. 1, part 2, 361.

27. Scott MacDonald, "Cinema 16: Documents Toward a History of the Film Society," *Wide Angle* 19.1 (1997): 3–48; Stephen J. Dobi, "Cinema 16," (Ph.D. diss., New York University, 1984).

28. The poster is reproduced in *The Legend of Maya Deren*, vol. 1, part 2, 363.

29. Deren to Sawyer Falk, February 28, 1946, reprinted in *The Legend of Maya Deren*, vol. 1, part 2, 371.

30. David Curtis, *Experimental Cinema* (New York: Dell, 1971).

31. Jonas Mekas, "A Call for a New Generation of Film Makers," *Film Culture* 19 (1959): 1–3. On the production and reception history of *Shadows*, see Stephanie Watson, "Spontaneous Cinema? In the Shadows with John Cassavetes," in Jack Sargent, ed., *The Naked Lens: An Illustrated History of Beat Cinema* (London: Creation Books, 1997), 55–68; and Ray Carney, "No Exit: John Cassavetes' *Shadows*," in Lisa Phillips, ed., *Beat Culture and the New America, 1950–1965* (New York: Whitney Museum of American Art, 1995), 235–41.

32. On Mekas's reactions to the different version of *Shadows*, see Watson, "Spontaneous Cinema?"

33. Colin Young, "An American Film Institute: A Prospect," *Film Quarterly* 14.4 (Summer 1961): 37–50.

34. Jonas Mekas, *The Third Report of the New American Cinema Group* (April 15, 1963) n.p. (JHP).

35. "The National Endowment for the Arts, 1965–2000: A Brief Chronology of Federal Support for the Arts" (*see* www.nea.gov/about/Chronology/NEAChronWeb.pdf).

36. See U.S. Treasury Department, Internal Revenue Service, Form M-4280 (JHP).

37. Amos Vogel, quoted in Calvin Tompkins, "All Pockets Open," *The New Yorker* (January 6, 1973): 37; and Jack Smith, "Uncle Fishhook and the Sacred Baby Poo-poo of Art," *Semiotext(e)* 3.2 (1978): 192–203.

38. All of these words and phrases come from Mekas, *The Third Report of the New American Cinema Group*.

39. Jonas Mekas to Friends of New Cinema, January 31, 1966 (JHP).

40. Jonas Mekas to Jerome Hill and Allan Masur, January 31, 1966 (JHP).

41. Raymond Haberski Jr., *It's Only a Movie!: Films and Critics in American Culture* (Lexington: University of Kentucky Press, 2001), 157–58.

42. Jonas Mekas, "On the Degeneration of Film Festivals," *Village Voice* (July 1, 1965), reprinted in *Movie Journal: The Rise of a New American Cinema, 1959–1971* (New York: Macmillan, 1972), 194–95.

43. Jonas Mekas, "The New York Film Festival as an Enemy of the New Cinema," *Village Voice* (September 16, 1965), reprinted in *Movie Journal*, 203.

44. Stan Brakhage to John Brockman (late June 1966) (JHP). Circulated by Film-Makers' Cooperative with Brakhage's permission.

45. Ed Emshwiller to Stan Brakhage, August 1, 1966 (JHP). Circulated by Film-Makers' Cooperative with Brakhage's permission.

46. Therese Schwartz, "The Politicization of the Avant-Garde," *Art in America* 59.6 (November-December 1971): 100, and "The Politicization of the Avant-Garde II" *Art in America* 60.2 (March-April 1972): 72.

47. Quoted in Jonas Mekas, "Ten Reasons Why the New York Film Festival

Should Be Closed," *Village Voice* (August 29, 1968), reprinted in *Movie Journal*, 317.

48. Schwartz, "Politicization I," 100.

49. Herbert Marcuse, *One-Dimensional Man* (Boston: Beacon Press, 1964); Theodor Adorno, "Valery Proust Museum," *Prisms*, trans. Samuel and Shierry Weber (Cambridge: MIT Press, 1967); Bürger, *Theory of the Avant-Garde.*

50. Jonas Mekas, "A Letter to Film-Makers (More Exactly, to Members of the Film-Makers' Cooperative)," May 18, 1966, 2 (JHP).

51. Jonas Mekas to [the] Pesaro [film festival] and World Film-Makers, May 18, 1966, 2 (JHP).

52. See Saunders, *The Cultural Cold War*, and de Hart Matthews, , "Art and Politics in Cold War America".

53. Jonas Mekas for the Film-Makers' Cinémathèque to the Film-Makers, July 15, 1968, 2 (JHP).

54. Jonas Mekas, "On Private Property" (June 22, 1976), reprinted in *Movie Journal*, 281.

55. Peter Wollen, "The Two Avant-Gardes," *Studio International* (December 1975), reprinted in *Readings and Writings: Semiotic Counter-Strategies* (London: Verso, 1982), 92–104. Wollen later revised this distinction, claiming that he hadn't seen key films of the co-op movement: "I realize now that the very convergence of the two avant-gardes I called for in 1975 had already been achieved in New York in the '60s" (Peter Wollen, "Together," *Sight and Sound* [July 1996]).

56. My argument—that a structural and financial change in the community of avant-garde filmmakers allowed for a new Romantic model of the filmmaker as amateur—compliments P. Adam Sitney's and David James's brilliant analyses of the intellectual and aesthetic reasons for these affinities. See P. Adams Sitney's classic *Visionary Film: The American Avant-Garde, 1943–1978*, 2d ed. (Oxford: Oxford University Press, 1979); and David James, "Film Diary/Diary Film: Practice and Product in *Walden*," in David James, ed., *To Free the Cinema: Jonas Mekas and the New York Underground* (Princeton: Princeton University Press, 1992), and David James, "Stan Brakhage: Filmmaker as Poet," *Allegories of Cinema* (Princeton: Princeton University Press, 1989).

57. Although one chart notes Hill as a drafter, both appear to have been typed on Mekas's typewriter, and some handwritten notes appear to be in Mekas's script. Mekas himself told me that he drew up the charts, although it is not clear whether Hill was involved in the process. The top-down, mobile-like diagram has another name above Hill's, either Paul "Schectman" or "Schecman." According to Mekas, he directed an arts center in Great Neck, New York, where Mekas had programmed films for a brief period in the 1960s. The center apparently gave a few small grants to avant-garde institutions, but the relationship didn't grow beyond that. Telephone conversation with Jonas Mekas (March 25, 2004).

58. P. Adams Sitney and Jonas Mekas to A. A. Heckman, Avon Foundation, September 28, 1967 (JHP).

59. Elia Kazan, Susan Sontag, Shirley Clarke, Arthur Mayer, Brendan Gill, George Plimpton, Willard Van Dyke, Jerome Hill, Judy Freed, Mitch Miller, Stan Vanerbeek to A. A. Heckman, Avon Foundation, September 28, 1967 (JHP).

60. See especially P. Adams Sitney, *Visionary Film*, and James, *Allegories of Cinema*, ch. 2,

61. Bosley Crowther, "Critic Hollers 'Help!' " *New York Times*, April 23, 1967.

62. Hill to Editor of the *New York Times*, April 25, 1967, unpublished (JHP).

63. Jonas Mekas, "An Interview with Jerome Hill, September 5, 1971, New York. Interviewer: Jonas Mekas," *Film Culture* 56–67 (Spring 1973): 12.

64. Jürgen Habermas, *The Structural Transformation of the Public Sphere: An Inquiry into a Category of Bourgeois Society*, trans. Thomas Burger (1969; Cambridge: MIT Press, 1989), 48.

65. Criticism of Habermas's theory and historiography of the public sphere has focused on his inattention to structural factors that excluded women, the working class, and other large segments of society from voicing opinions in the public sphere. Leisure time, financial means, and literacy were among the many qualifications for entrance into the debate. As Habermas described it, the public sphere was an ideal of universal inclusion and parity that never really existed. Certainly Hill's exclusively male coterie of patron-pleasers fell far from the universal ideal. In fact, Hill's elite circle intended to set itself apart from the all-inclusive, hippie ideals of the co-op movement. Habermas, *Transformation of the Public Sphere*, 49.

   Within the vast literature on the public sphere, see Tony Bennett's discussion of the public sphere as it pertains to the history of museums in *The Birth of the Museum* (New York: Routledge, 1995) and Miriam Hansen's discussion of the concept as it is applicable to American silent film in *Babel and Babylon* (Cambridge: Harvard University Press, 1991). Habermas responded to some of the criticism of his theory of the public sphere in "Further Reflections on the Public Sphere," in Craig Calhoun, ed., *Habermas and the Public Sphere* (Cambridge: MIT Press, 1992).

66. Habermas, *Transformation of the Public Sphere*, 49. Keith Kelly's review of *Notes for Jerome* (*Millennium Film Journal* 4–5 [Summer-Fall 1979]: 172–74) discusses the patron-artists relationship in the film. Mekas, Brakhage, and Sitney all wrote celebrations of *Film Portrait*: Jonas Mekas, "A Few Notes on Jerome Hill's *Film Portrait*," in Philip Nobile, ed., *Favorite Movies, Critics' Choice* (New York: Macmillan, 1973), 126–32; Brakhage, *Film at Wit's End*; P. Adams Sitney, "Autobiography in Avant-Garde Film," *Millennium Film Journal* (Winter 1977–78), reprinted in Sitney, ed., *The Avant-Garde Film* (New York: Anthology Film Archives, 1978), 199–246. Sitney's essay, written after Hill's death and after the end of the co-op movement (as I discuss below), was supported by an NEA grant.

67. Robert Downey to Jerome Hill, n.d. (JHP).

68. P. Adams Sitney interviewed by Gretchen Kreuter (February 6, 1984), 19 (JHP).

69. Stan Brakhage to Allan Masur, n.d. (JHP).

70. Stan Brakhage to Jerome Hill, mid-November 1968 (Stan Brakhage Papers, Anthology Film Archives, New York; hereafter, SBP).

71. Stan Brakhage to Jerome Hill, late November 1968 (SBP).

72. Stan Brakhage to Jerome Hill, mid-September 1969, 5 (SBP).

73. Brakhage, *Film at Wit's End*, 23.

74. Stan Brakhage to Jerome Hill, mid-September 1969 (SBP).

75. Mekas, *Third Report of the New American Cinema Group*.

76. Jonas Mekas to "Members of the Co-op," May 10, 1967 (JHP).

77. Stan Brakhage to Jerome Hill, mid-September 1969 (SBP).

78. Jerome Hill, "Brakhage and Rilke," *Film Culture* 37 (Summer 1965): 13. Hill noted that, at the time, Brakhage had made ten songs, like Rilke's ten elegies. Brakhage went on to make a total of thirty songs, and the final song was about Jerome Hill.

79. Constance Penley and Janet Bergstrom, "The Avant-Garde: History and Theories" in Bill Nichols, ed., *Movies and Methods*, vol. 2 (Berkley: University of California Press, 1985), 287–300. Sitney, Penley, and Bergstrom continued the debate in *Screen* 20.3–4 (Winter 1979–80): 149–50; see also James, *Allegories of Cinema*. The Brakhage quote comes from a letter: Stan Brakhage to Jerome Hill, early September 1968 (SBP). For a related critique of the university training of avant-garde filmmakers, see Fred Camper, "The End of Avant-Garde Film," *Millennium Film Journal* 16–17–18 (Fall-Winter 1986–87): 99–124. On the institutionalization of feminist avant-garde film and theory, see Patricia Mellencamp, "Receivable Texts: U.S. Avant-Garde Cinema, 1960–1980," *Wide Angle* 7.1–2 (1985): 74–91.

80. See Jonas Mekas for the Coop to the Members of the Film-Makers' Cooperative, May 10, 1967 (JHP).

81. Sitney discussed Hill's involvement in the *Flaming Creatures* case in the Kreuter interview; Dwight Macdonald, "Hallelujah the Hills [July 1964]," *On Movies* (New York: Da Capo, 1969), 327. On the exhibition and legal history of *Flaming Creatures*, see J. Hoberman and Jonathan Rosenbaum, *Midnight Movies* (New York: Da Capo, 1983), 61; Susan Sontag, "Jack Smith's *Flaming Creatures*," *Against Interpretation* (New York: Dell, 1966); Michael Moon, "Flaming Closets," *A Small Boy and Others: Imitation and Initiation in American Culture from Henry James to Andy Warhol* (Durham: Duke University Press, 1998); Douglas Crimp, "Getting the Warhol We Deserve," *Social Text* 17.2 (Summer 1999): 49–66.

82. Jonas Mekas to P. Adams Sitney, June 16, 1968 (JHP). For a compelling history of the MPAA's rating system, see Lewis, *Hollywood v. Hard Core*, ch. 4.

83. P. Adams Sitney, Anthology Film Archives manifesto, *The Essential Cinema*, ed. P. Adams Sitney (New York: Anthology Film Archives, 1975), vii.

84. Quoted in Howard Thompson, " Silence Says a Lot for Film Archives," *New York Times*, December 4, 1970, 56.

85. Thomas Crow, *Painters and Public Life in Eighteenth-Century Paris* (New Haven: Yale University Press, 1985), 3. For a brief history of crowd versus individual psychology in movie theater architecture, see Peter Decherney, "Cult of Attention: An Introduction to Seymour Stern and Harry Alan Potamkin (Contra Kracauer) on the Ideal Movie Theater," *The Spectator* 18.2 (Spring-Summer 1998): 18–25. Also see Annette Michelson's reading of the design of Anthology's theater: "Gnosis and Iconoclasm: A Case Study of Cinephilia," *October* 83 (Winter 1998): 4–18.

86. Jonas Mekas to Annette Michelson, reprinted in *Artforum* 10.1 (September 1971): 10.

87. Brakhage to Hill, mid-September 1969 (JHP).

88. Mekas to Michelson in *Artforum* 10.

89. Sitney, manifesto, *The Essential Cinema*.

90. Stan Brakhage to Jonas Mekas, late September 1967, reprinted in Robert Haller, ed., *The Brakhage Scrapbook: Collected Writings, 1964–1980* (New Paltz, N.Y.: Documentext, 1982), 131–32.

91. Gomery, quoted in Anne Friedberg, *Window Shopping: Cinema and the Postmodern* (Berkley: University of California Press, 1993), 122.

92. Friedberg, *Window Shopping*, 122.

93. Vincent Canby, "Now You Can See Invisible Cinema," *New York Times*, November 29, 1970.

94. Abbie Thomas, "Anthology Film Archives: 1973," *Polemics for a New Cinema* (Sydney: Wild and Woolley, 1978), 316.

95. Mekas, quoted on Anthology Film Archives Web site (*see* www.anthologyfilmarchives.org).

96. The NEA no longer has a copy of Renan's report, which was submitted February 23, 1973.

97. Andrew Sarris, "Avant-Garde Films Are More Boring Than Ever," *Village Voice* (May 17, 1976), reprinted in William M. Hammel, ed., *The Popular Arts in America: A Reader*, 2d ed. (New York: Harcourt Brace Javanovich, 1977), 167.

CONCLUSION: THE TRANSFORMATION OF THE STUDIO SYSTEM

1. Tino Balio, "Part IV: Retrenchment, Reappraisal, and Reorganization, 1948–," in Balio, ed., *The American Film Industry* (Madison: University of Wisconsin Press, 1976); David Bordwell, Janet Staiger, Kristin Thompson, *The Classical Hollywood Cinema* (New York: Columbia University Press, 1985); Jon Lewis, *Hollywood v. Hardcore* (New York: New York University Press, 2000).

2. Peter Biskind, *Easy Riders, Raging Bulls: How the Sex-Drugs-and-Rock'n'Roll Generation Saved Hollywood* (New York: Simon and Schuster, 1998); Geoff King, *New Hollywood Cinema: An Introduction* (New York: Columbia University Press, 2002).

3. Thomas Schatz, "The New Hollywood," in Jim Collins, Hilary Radner, and Ava Preacher Colli, eds., *Film Theory Goes to the Movies*, (New York: Routledge, 1993), 12; King, *New Hollywood Cinema*, 61; Balio, "Retrenchment," 443.

4. Thomas Guback, "Hollywood's International Market," in Balio, ed., *The American Film Industry*, 473–74; Toby Miller, Nitin Govil, John McMurria, Richard Mazwell, *Global Hollywood* (London: British Film Institute, 2001), 34–41.

5. Nina Teicholz, "Privatizing Propaganda," *Washington Monthly Online* (December 2002; see www.washingtonmontly.com); Rick Lyman, "Hollywood Discusses Role in War Effort," *New York Times*, November 12, 2001, B2; John Lippman, "Hollywood Vows to Support War Effort in Meeting with the White House," *Wall Street Journal*, November 12, 2001, B3; Rene Sanchez, "Hollywood's White House War Council; A Bicoastal Meeting of Minds Is Bipartisan, Too," *Washington Post*, November 12, 2001, C1; Jim Rutenberg, "TV Greetings Produced for Armed Forces," *New York Times*, December 5, 2001, B3; Rick Lyman, "3 Minutes of Patriotism," *New York Times*, December 20, 2001, E1; Jim Rutenberg, "Hollywood Enlists Ali's Help to Explain War to Muslims," *New York Times*, December 23, 2001, A1; "Hollywood's War Effort: A Script Still in Development," *Washington Post*, February 18, 2002, C1; "Hollywood Group Offers First TV Spot on Tolerance Aimed at Arab Youth," *New York Times*, September 5, 2002, A14.

6. Dennis McDougal, *The Last Mogul: Lew Wasserman, MCA, and the Hidden History of Hollywood* (New York: Da Capo, 2001), 346. On the sale of film libraries to television, see William Lafferty, "Feature Films on Prime-Time Television," in Tino Balio, ed., *Hollywood in the Age of Television* (London: Unwin Hyman, 1990), 235–56, and Michel Hilmes, *Hollywood and Broadcasting: From Radio to Cable* (Urbana: University of Illinois Press, 1990).

7. Richard Griffith, *A Report on the Film Library, 1941–1956* (New York: Museum of Modern Art (Fall 1956), 10.

8. Tom McGreevey and Joanne L. Yeck, *Our Movie Heritage* (New Brunswick: Rutgers University Press, 1997), 66–74; Anthony Slide, *Nitrate Won't Wait: Film Preservation in the United States* (Jefferson, N.C.: McFarland, 1992), ch. 6; National Film Preservation Board (see www.loc.gov/film); AFI's lists (see www.afi.com/tvevents/100years/100yearslist.aspx).

9. John Belton, *American Cinema/American Culture* (New York: McGraw-Hill, 1994), 301–304.

INDEX

Note: page numbers in *italics* indicate illustrations.